IFR Flights of "13MIKE"™

for versions 4.0 and 5.0

A Microsoft® Flight Simulator® Action Book

by
Professor Fred J. Calfior
and
Professor Douglas W. Miller

Book Two - Level B

Covering the
Chicago, Los Angeles, San Francisco, Seattle, and New York areas

IFR Flights of "13MIKE"™

© 1994 by CalMil Publishing. All rights reserved.

Printed in the U.S.A.

No part of this publication may be reproduced, stored in a retrieval system, or transmitted, in any form or by any means, electronic, mechanical, photocopying, recording, or otherwise, without the prior written permission of the publisher. For information, contact CalMil Publishing, 2224 Katahn Drive, Prescott, AZ 86301-3976.

First edition, 1994.

International Standard Book Number: 0-9639052-1-X.

Library of Congress Catalog Card Number: 94-94166.

This book is sold as is, without warranty of any kind, either expressed or implied, respecting the contents of this book, including but not limited to implied warranties for the book's quality, performance, merchantability, or fitness for any particular purpose. Neither CalMil Publishing nor its dealers or distributors shall be liable to the purchaser or any other person or entity with respect to any liability, loss, or damage caused or alleged to be caused directly or indirectly by this book.

Microsoft is a registered trademark of Microsoft Corporation.

Flight Simulator is a trademark of Bruce Artwick.

13MIKE and Airienteering are trademarks of CalMil Publishing.

About the Authors

Professor Fred J. Calfior

Fred Calfior is a 1975 graduate from the United States Naval Academy, with a degree in Aerospace Engineering. He has instructed in both the T2C Buckeye (a twin engine jet) and the TA4J Skyhawk (a single engine jet). Upon joining the Embry-Riddle Aeronautical University faculty, Professor Calfior acquired his Masters in Aeronautical Science. He has been involved in all levels of flight instruction, as well as academic instruction, in the areas of Aerodynamics, Flight Performance, and VFR/IFR Navigation.

Professor Douglas W. Miller

Douglas Miller is a Professor at Embry-Riddle Aeronautical University where he teaches Aerodynamics and Electronic Flight Control Systems. Professor Miller has an extensive background in aircraft system design and simulation development. As a consultant to the aerospace industry, he has been responsible for the development of a variety of multi-user simulation systems, including a virtual reality simulation used for vehicle design and analysis. Professor Miller has extensive instrument and weather flying experience. Most of this experience was obtained while flying his Mooney for business purposes. Currently Professor Miller is involved in the research and development of a virtual reality flight simulator for teaching and flight technique analysis.

Other Flights of "13MIKE"

BOOK ONE

Flights of "13MIKE" - LEVEL A

"Competitive", "Challenging", "Fun", "Exciting", "Thrilling", and "Nerve Racking" are words that have been used to describe flying these scenarios. Non-pilots, student pilots, and commercial pilots are all hooked on the challenge and adventure of 13MIKE. You do not have to be a pilot to enjoy the thrill and adventure of flying through the LA Class B Airspace Corridor. Professor Calfior is seated at your right for the entire flight. Drawing on years of flight training has enabled Professors Miller and Calfior to bring you the most authentic and realistic selection of flight scenarios that you have ever encountered. You feel like you are actually in the cockpit, with Professor Calfior giving you friendly advice in his humorous fashion.

BOOK THREE   (Coming Winter 1995)

Airienteering™ with "13MIKE" - LEVEL A

What would it be like to do a little orienteering with an airplane? Well, jump into old 13MIKE, get out the map, and let's hit the sky. We need to find all the marks and get back to our home field as fast as we can. The clock is ticking and it looks like a storm is brewing. How good are you at map reading and flying at the same time? Come fly with 13MIKE and find out.

Order form in back of book

Preface

After flying "13MIKE" around for the hundredth time, Professor Calfior and I, Professor Miller, decided we wanted more challenges, more thrills, and **MORE** white knuckle flying! So we started this next set of adventures for our fun loving 13MIKE flyers, **IFR Flights of "13MIKE"**. This collection of foul weather and wind cross countries give 13MIKE a run for its money. We have included eight dynamos of power packed scenarios for your yukky weather flying pleasure. The procedures are as realistic as we can make them, from the **FULL** weather brief down to the Ground Control clearance to taxi to the destination terminal. All enroute charts, airport diagrams, departure information, and approach plates are authentic in every detail.

NOTE: The charts and plates are intended for use with this book only, in flying the scenarios utilizing Microsoft's Flight Simulator program. Please do not try to use these navigational charts for actual flight purposes. Reason - they are no longer current.

By drawing on our experience and background in teaching flying and aviation concepts, we have been able to bring to you a very authentic and realistic set of cross country flights.

This is the second book of a vast series of upcoming action books for the Microsoft Flight Simulator program. The books have been designed to be flown in sequence, even though it is not required. The action books come in two levels. Level A is primarily visual flight (VFR), keeping the non-pilot and student pilot well challenged but within reach of everyone's flying ability. Level B, on the other hand, is a book geared to anyone who has completed the first book or is an experienced pilot. This book deals with cloud overcast, shifting winds, and developing weather instrument flights, sometimes right down to a missed approach (go to another place!) condition. It will challenge you and feel so realistic that your body will sway with your airplane motion!

6   IFR Flights of "13MIKE"

This action book has eight flight scenarios covering five geographic areas. You do not need to fly the scenarios in sequence, though it is advisable to do so. The areas are:

San Diego/Los Angeles, California

1. San Diego to Los Angeles
2. Oceanside to Van Nuys

San Francisco, California

1. San Francisco to South Lake Tahoe
2. Watsonville to Oakland

Chicago, Illinois

1. Kankakee to Champaign

New York City, New York

1. Islip to Westchester County
2. Block Island to Marthas Vineyard

Seattle, Washington

1. Port Angeles to Seattle-Tacoma

You will notice that there are scoring points throughout the flight scenarios. They are weighted according to their degree of importance in the IFR flying arena. The purpose of the scoring is so you may have a target of proficiency to shoot for . We'll tell you, based upon your score, what category of pilot you **REALLY, REALLY** are! The answers for each scenario are provided in the back of the book, so that you can tell how close your skills are to whatever goals you've set for yourself.

IFR Flights of "13MIKE" - Book Two - Level B has been prepared and written so that it challenges the non-pilot, student pilot, instrument pilot, and commercial pilot. It is assumed the student is familiar and versatile with Microsoft Flight Simulator Versions 4.0 or 5.0. This is not a teaching aid on how to fly the simulator - we assume that you have already practiced using the Microsoft Flight Simulator's own manual and guide. So whether you have version 4.0 or 5.0, this companion provides you with a custom program geared for your needs no matter what version you own.

The airplane in which you will be practicing is a Cessna 182 RG, a retractable gear airplane. We recommend that you use the map display very sporadically - more for curiosity sake than anything else. The areas are default areas which come automatically with your original Microsoft program. You won't have to build any scenery, locations or navaids unless you want to do so for your own personal thrill. We also recommend that you follow all the steps in each scenario so you can build a habit pattern of awareness in procedural techniques, especially in the preflight area. If you do skip a step, you won't fall out of the sky and die in simulation, but you will fail to utilize this action book to its full benefit!

You may fly each one of these flight scenarios using your keyboard, mouse, or joystick. There is no specific preference. The transfer of learning will be attained by the application and practice of the standardized procedures which are a foundational part of each and every flight scenario. These procedures are practiced and accepted worldwide. We recognize that there will be differences of opinion based upon Fixed Base Operator (FBO) or flight school methods of instruction. For example, the magneto checks which we have you do are performed with "**LEFT**" first then with "**RIGHT**", so that at the end of the final magneto check one click will bring it back to "**BOTH**". If the "**LEFT**" magneto was checked last, then one click would rest on the "**RIGHT**" magneto, and a pilot could then quite inadvertently take off with only one magneto in operation!

So, start up your computers! **CESSNA 13MIKE** is ready to fly with you to the exciting and challenging IFR world in a totally hands on, you're in control, plan ahead style of airplane navigation! Happy flying!!!!!

8   IFR Flights of "13MIKE"

****

As you progress through this companion, we would enjoy hearing about your triumphs, thrills, and any other comments you may wish to share with us. We are always eager to hear from our fellow flyers. All comments are appreciated. Please send them to CalMil Publishing, 2224 Katahn Drive, Prescott AZ, 86301.

> Professor Douglas W. Miller
> Professor Fred John Calfior

Table of Contents

ABOUT THE AUTHORS 3

OTHER FLIGHTS OF "13MIKE" 4

PREFACE 5

PREFLIGHT
   About This Action Book 11
   Flying The Scenarios 12
   The Instrument Environment and You 17

Flight Scenario One (Islip to Westchester County) 23

Flight Scenario Two (San Diego to Los Angeles) 49

Flight Scenario Three (Kankakee to Champaign) 75

Flight Scenario Four (San Francisco to South Lake Tahoe) ... 101

Flight Scenario Five (Port Angeles to Seattle-Tacoma) 127

Flight Scenario Six (Oceanside to Van Nuys) 153

Flight Scenario Seven (Watsonville to Oakland) 179

Flight Scenario Eight (Block Island to Marthas Vineyard) 205

10   IFR Flights of "13MIKE"

ANSWERS 229

APPENDIX A (Flight Plan Form and Worksheet)

Flight Plan Form 255
Flight Plan Worksheet 256

APPENDIX B (Low Altitude Enroute Charts)

B1 - New York (L-28) 257
B2 - San Diego/Los Angeles (L-3) 259
B3 - Chicago (L-23) 261
B4 - San Francisco (L-2) 263
B5 - Seattle (L-1) 267
B6 - New York (L-25) 269

APPENDIX C (Airport Diagrams and Approach Plates)

C1 - Scenario 1 (Islip to Westchester County) 271
C2 - Scenario 2 (San Diego to Los Angeles) 277
C3 - Scenario 3 (Kankakee to Champaign) 283
C4 - Scenario 4 (San Francisco to South Lake Tahoe) 287
C5 - Scenario 5 (Port Angeles to Seattle-Tacoma) 293
C6 - Scenario 6 (Oceanside to Van Nuys) 299
C7 - Scenario 7 (Watsonville to Oakland) 305
C8 - Scenario 8 (Block Island to Marthas Vineyard) 311

NOTES 314

ORDER FORM 320

PreFlight

ABOUT THIS ACTION BOOK

The flight scenarios in this action book have been written with the assumption that you are familiar with the operation and control of Microsoft Flight Simulator 4.0 or 5.0.

Hi! My name is Professor Miller. Professor Calfior and I will be helping you fly "N9413M", referred to as "13MIKE" (pronounced "ONE THREE MIKE"), through the scenarios in this action book. It is to your advantage to read the Microsoft Flight Handbook and understand all the keyboard controls for operating the instruments, engine, and flap controls on the Cessna 182 RG instrument panel before starting. An excellent way to acquire this knowledge is by going through Microsoft's "Flight School".

The following Flight School sections are recommended: 1) "Ground School", 2) "Basic Flight Training", 3) "Advanced Flight Training", and 4) "Navigation Course". It is best to complete all lessons in each of these sections. Flying the scenarios in this action book without the Flight School experience is possible. We try to provide as much help as we can in areas where you may run into problems. You can also refer to the Microsoft Flight Handbook for help. We highly recommend that you have a good understanding of how the following instruments work: 1) VOR and OBI, 2) DME, and 3) VSI.

Flight Simulator version 5.0 comments

The latest version of Microsoft Flight Simulator is something to behold. The scenery is fantastic, and the instruments and controls are very realistic. There are a few differences between versions 4.0 and 5.0. We have used a bold square bracket "[ ]" to indicate any 5.0 version specific command or answer. **If you are flying version 5.0, please use the numbers in the square brackets.**

Make sure that your propeller is set to **"fixed pitch"**. Airspeed indicator to **"indicated"**. Aircraft position will need to be set using **Latitude** and **Longitude** settings. 5.0 also displays NAV 1 and NAV 2 DME simultaneously. When you come across a command that tells you to switch to NAV 2 DME, just revert your attention to your second DME display.

Due to the slant range consideration given in version 5.0, the minimum DME for station passage over a VOR will be different from that of version 4.0, and is also noted in brackets.

The power settings are directly linked to the airspeed indicator. In other words, as your airspeed increases, your RPM will increase, and vice versa. You will have to closely watch your RPM settings as your airspeed changes, in order to maintain the commanded RPM setting.

When setting up winds and clouds, each level must be created in sequence to mimic the version 4.0 levels.

FLYING THE SCENARIOS

The "Competitive", "Challenging", "Fun", "Exciting", "Thrilling", and "Nerve Racking" experiences of 13MIKE are back! Along with "White Knuckle" and "Yukky" weather! All levels of flyers have agreed that these scenarios are, by far, the most challenging series of intensely packed instrument flights they have ever encountered. From the zero-zero takeoff to the instrument landing approach with a two hundred foot ceiling, and everything in between, Professors Calfior and Miller keep you busy and on the edge of your seat from startup to shutdown. All procedures are authentic, from the flight plan and weather brief, to the low altitude enroute charts and instrument approach plates.

The flight scenarios we created in this action book are the results of our many years of actual flying and flight instructor experiences. We hope you will benefit from the great effort we expended to assure the authenticity of each and every scenario, and the realism that we ingrained into each flight.

As you progress through the flights, you will get a sense of repetitiveness from scenario to scenario. Because of the authentic nature of each flight, it was necessary to step through the repetitive procedures that are an inherent part of every real flight. Flight instructors spend hours upon hours trying to get the student to be able to repeat these procedures in their sleep. Welcome to the real world of instrument flying!

Okay, here is an overview of the setup procedures, COM dialog, questions format, simulator flying techniques, and general hints.

SETUP

<u>Aircraft</u> - It is important to select the Cessna 182 RG aircraft. All performance and position parameters are based on the 182 RG. If another aircraft is used, your answers will not match the answers in the back of the book.

<u>Winds</u> - The winds are set by levels. The wind changes speed and direction as your altitude changes. Double check the level settings and make sure that the wind speeds and directions indicated in the SETUP section of the scenario match your settings, as well as the turbulence levels. Your distance, timing, and position answers will be off if the winds are not set correctly.

<u>Clouds</u> - The clouds are set by levels. Thunderstorms are also found in this section. Make sure you have the proper level settings, which become especially important when shooting an instrument approach to your destination airport.

<u>Position</u> - When the simulator starts, you are placed at a default airport and runway. Do not be concerned about this. The SETUP section of the scenario takes you through a repositioning series of steps. Just follow the instructions and you will be repositioned at the correct airport for the departure part of the scenario. The aircraft positioning sequence has four parts, "NORTH", "EAST", "ALTITUDE", and "HEADING". Be sure that all parts have been set correctly. You do not need to set the "Control Tower" position. ***Caution***, your position will be different at each airport. You will need to read the TAXI section to determine how to get to the runup area for the departure end of the runway in the scenario.

14 IFR Flights of "13MIKE"

COM SETTINGS and DIALOG

This action book is based on realistic flight procedures which include weather briefs and radio communications. Unfortunately, the radio dialog of the Microsoft Flight Simulator is limited, therefore we have inserted full radio communications dialog within the scenarios where they would normally occur. This dialog will appear after you have changed COM frequencies, and a transmission on your part or a broadcast message would normally take place. At times, you will tune in an ATIS frequency and see a message run across your outside view screen. Microsoft Flight Simulator has ATIS broadcast messages at selected airports only. To make the scenarios as realistic as possible, we have included ATIS messages in the action book for all airports that are used. These ATIS messages will not necessarily match those that Microsoft displays. You only need to be concerned with those in the book.

Some of the frequencies listed in the Microsoft Flight Simulator are different from those you'll notice in the IFR low altitude enroute charts and instrument approach plates. Please use the frequencies listed in the scenarios. Also, you will notice that all radials given in the book are even numbered, which differ from some of the instrument approach plates and Victor airway tracks. This is due to Microsoft Flight Simulator version 4.0's two degree gradation for the OBS.

QUESTIONS and ANSWERS

One of the objectives in flying the scenarios is to obtain the highest score possible by performing the listed procedures as precisely as you can. At different times during the execution of the scenario, you will be asked to "pause" the simulator. Write down specific flight parameters or answer certain questions pertaining to the flight (all questions are indicated with a double "**"). After you have written the information down, you will be asked to continue the simulation. Each question has a certain point value assigned to it. Some questions are more important than others, and therefore have a higher point value. At the end of the flight, you add up the points to find out what kind of pilot you are. You will need to study the questions you missed so you can do better the next time you fly that scenario.

THE PATH TO THE PERFECT SCORE

Obviously, you are interested in gaining the maximum number of points for each flight scenario. The level of flight difficulty increases as you get deeper into the book. For the most part, it will take you at least three to five attempts before you can nail each flight scenario with a maximum score! The harder flights may even require more than five flights! So don't feel discouraged at a low score for your first flight. That's what makes these series of flight scenarios so dynamically alive and heart pounding! You keep trying to better your previous attempt, being ready for a required quick reaction that you may have missed before, or keeping your VOR needle centered so you can accurately meet a checkpoint.

We recommend the following five steps when you're ready to fly:

1. READ THE ENTIRE SCENARIO FROM START TO FINISH WITH CHARTS IN FRONT OF YOU. THE FLIGHT CANNOT BE UNDERSTOOD UNLESS YOU WALK IT THROUGH.

2. ENJOY BEING IN THE AIR DURING YOUR FIRST FLIGHT. TRY TO STAY A PAGE AHEAD SO YOU CAN ANTICIPATE WHAT IS COMING UP. GO FROM DEPARTURE TO DESTINATION FOLLOWING EACH SERIES OF NOTES AND TASKS METHODICALLY.

3. THE SECOND FLIGHT, YOU KNOW WHAT TO EXPECT. STABILIZE YOUR FLYING BY BEING SHARPLY ON ALTITUDE - PROPER POWER SETTINGS - RECOMMENDED OR PREVIOUSLY DISCOVERED DESCENT RATES, ETC. SEARCH TO SPECIFICALLY BETTER THE AREAS WHICH YOU MISSED THE FIRST TIME.

4. THE THIRD FLIGHT, SKIP PROFESSOR CALFIOR'S NOTES (YOU'VE BEEN THROUGH THEM TWICE NOW!) AND CONTINUE WITH THE RADIO CALLS. HUNT FOR THOSE ELUSIVE CORRECT NUMBERS, BUT KEEP THE FLOW NONSTOP FOR THE ENTIRE FLIGHT RIGHT TO THE LANDING.

16 IFR Flights of "13MIKE"

5. THE FOURTH FLIGHT AND ANY ADDITIONAL FLIGHTS, PAY SHARP ATTENTION TO ALL THE NUMBERED NOTES. THESE FLIGHTS WILL BE QUITE DYNAMIC BECAUSE YOU WON'T BE NEEDING TO READ AHEAD TO PREPARE FOR THE NEXT STEP! YOU'VE GOT THE SCENARIO PRACTICALLY MEMORIZED. WHEN YOUR TIMING IS ON, AND YOU KNOW THE ROAD, IT BECOMES ONE THRILLING MANEUVER AFTER ANOTHER.

HINTS and SIMULATOR TECHNIQUES

The following is a list of flying techniques that will help in performing the scenarios with more accuracy and precision, thereby increasing your score:

a) You may need to adjust your power setting from the one stated in the scenario. This is due to deviations from the correct approach speed and altitude.

b) Watch your VSI (vertical speed) on approach. Try to maintain a constant vertical speed.

c) Watch your heading. The winds will make your airplane fly a different ground track than your heading would indicate. You may need to set in a crab to compensate.

d) Watch overbanking and over controlling. It is easy to over control the simulator. After putting in a roll control, you will need to put in an opposite control to stop the roll. Do not overdo it. The airplane will oscillate back and forth if you do. Gentle on the controls.

The following hints will help you in flying the scenarios in the beginning. After you become more proficient, try to fly without the aid of these hints.

a) For finding the airport and taxiing around the airport, use the "Num Lock" key.

b) To determine orientation to the airport and other landmarks, use the "Scroll Lock" along with key pad numbers 1 through 9 (except 5) to change your view of the outside to the different windows of the aircraft.

c) To provide more stability to the aircraft and minimize the aircraft's tendency to wander, you may want to fly with the autopilot "wing leveler" on.

d) To help maintain your orientation, follow your flight on the IFR low altitude enroute charts in Appendix B.

e) You should fly the scenarios more than once, trying to improve your performance, accuracy, and score each time. Remember timing is important.

f) You may want to save your approach or landing configuration so you can practice these sections without having to fly the entire scenario again.

g) For the best scanning technique, use a round pattern around the six-pack of instruments. These are the airspeed indicator, attitude indicator, altimeter, VSI, heading indicator, and turn and bank indicator. Other scanning methods are the "L", "T", or "X". Don't disregard your other instruments, but these six are the meat of basic attitude instrument flying.

THE INSTRUMENT ENVIRONMENT AND YOU

The following section consists of some helpful instructional aids, methods, and knowledge of how to operate in an instrument environment, so as to allow you to accomplish the basic instrument procedures given throughout your flight scenarios. It will help you acquire a high flight score.

PREFLIGHT

Notice to Airmen System:

Called NOTAMs, there are three categories possible.
 1. NOTAM (D) which is distant
 2. NOTAM (L) which is local
 3. Flight Data Center (FDC) NOTAM

18 IFR Flights of "13MIKE"

A representative sample of information found in NOTAMs are:
- i. airport equipment outages
- ii. runway or taxiway closures
- iii. change in instrument approach procedures
- iv. temporary flight restrictions
- v. construction or movement on runways

Flight Plan for IFR Flights:

IFR flight plans need to be filed at the least, thirty minutes before planned departure, so that the controlling agency has plenty of time to prepare your brief.

When using Victor airways, designate each and every one in the **Route of Flight** block of your Flight Plan Form. If there are several VORs in a line along a similar Victor airway, just the first and last needs to be identified as endpoints of that Victor airway. When going direct from one fix to another, not using a Victor airway, each checkpoint must be designated.

Special equipment codes used for Block 3 of your Flight Plan Form are as follows:

1. /X - no transponder
2. /T - transponder, no altitude encoding
3. /U - transponder, altitude encoding
4. /D - DME, no transponder
5. /B - DME, transponder, no alt encoding
6. /A - DME, transponder, altitude encoding
7. /M - TACAN, no transponder
8. /N - TACAN, transponder, no altitude encoding
9. /P - TACAN, transponder, alt encoding
10. /C - RNAV, transponder, no altitude encoding
11. /R - RNAV, transponder, alt encoding
12. /W - RNAV, no transponder
13. /G - Flight Management System

13MIKE is slash A equipped, even though the transponder on the instrument panel does not have an ALT indicator.

DEPARTURE

Departure Control:

If taking off from a controlled airport, (one which has a tower) do not switch to a Departure Control frequency until advised to do so. If taking off from an uncontrolled airport, you may switch to the Departure Control frequency once airborne and at your discretion.

In a flight plan clearance, both the departure frequency and the transponder code will be given. Pilots are advised to not activate their transponders until just prior to the takeoff roll. This is so that radar does not have to pick up any unnecessary clutter.

Standard Instrument Departures (SIDs):

You cannot accept a SID unless you have, as a minimum, a textual description of it with you, and that you can meet the required performance parameters necessary to execute that SID. By flying a SID, and following its track, you are ensured of obstacle clearance straight through to the minimum enroute altitude. You may enter a SID at any portion of that SID, as long as you are cleared for it. In other words, it does not always have to be flown from its designated start point all the way through to its end point.

ENROUTE

Low Altitude Enroute Charts:

Some altitudes of interest when analyzing a low altitude enroute chart are:

1. **Minimum enroute altitude (MEA)** - this is the minimum IFR altitude under normal circumstances, where navigational signal coverage is constant from the VOR at one end of the airway to the VOR at the other end of the airway. There are three methods of determining when to switch from the navigational facility behind you to the one in front of you on the airway. (called changeover points or COP)
   - A) when it is symbolized by a three line right angled symbol
   - B) when a course change occurs at an intersection to bring you to the navaid in front of you
   - C) with no symbol given, or course change present, the changeover point will occur at the halfway point along the Victor airway

2. **Minimum obstruction clearance altitude (MOCA)** - this is the minimum emergency IFR altitude which guarantees navigational signal coverage only within twenty two nautical miles of a facility. It does ensure one thousand feet obstacle clearance in non-mountainous, and two thousand feet obstacle clearance in mountainous areas.

3. **Minimum crossing altitude (MCA)** - this is an altitude designated to cross a specific fix at or above. What will follow is a higher MEA than the one you just came from.

4. **Minimum reception altitude (MRA)** - this is the altitude at a certain fix which you must be at or above in order to be guaranteed a way to identify that fix via an off airway navigational facility. Most of the time, that will be a VOR.

VOR Tracking on a Radial:

When you have intercepted your desired course, the CDI needle should be centered with either a "TO" or a "FROM" indication. If there were no winds to blow you off course, that needle would stay centered. But that generally does not happen, so something called tracking and bracketing is done.

Whenever you notice you're drifting off course, (that is, the CDI needle is moving from its center position), make a **twenty** degree correction in the direction that the needle is moving. Hold that **twenty** degree correction until you see that the needle is back to its centered position.

Now take **ten** degrees out of your heading correction, and watch that needle. If it remains centered, your **ten** degree crab angle is the correction you need to hold that desired radial. But if the needle starts moving now in the opposite direction, the **ten** degrees is too much of a correction. So turn to the heading which parallels your radial and drift back to a centered needle.

When the needle centers, make a **five** degree correction in the original direction and that should keep your needle centered.

If the first **twenty** degrees of heading change does not force your CDI needle to head back towards the center, then put in another **twenty** degrees in the same direction. You're obviously in a strong crosswind. When the needle finally centers, take out **twenty** of those degrees and see how your needle reacts.

Reading the VOR CDI:

The VOR OBI has a needle which moves to the left or right of center, depending on whether you are left or right of your intended radial. There are four visible dots to the right and left with a small circle between them. The circle is covering the first dot which would be to the left and right of the center of the circle. Therefore, when the needle, called the CDI, is over the left edge of the circle, it is one dot to the left of center. Each dot represents two degrees of radial.

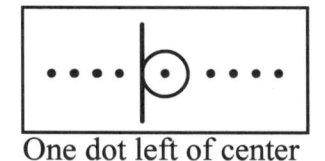

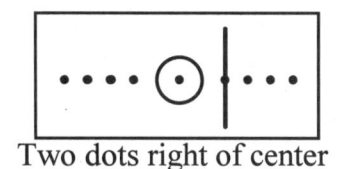

One dot left of center   Two dots right of center

When you are flying these scenarios, and a command tells you to turn to a specific heading when your NAV 1 or 2 CDI is two dots RIGHT of center, you must count the circle's edge as dot one.

Holding Patterns:

Holding at some designated position will be necessary whenever you are given a clearance to a fix other than your destination, and a further clearance has not been received at the time of your arrival at the fix.

There are three methods of entering a holding pattern:

1. **Direct** - where you turn directly to the outbound leg of the holding pattern
2. **Teardrop** - where you turn to the far corner of the outbound leg by way of a thirty degree intercept
3. **Parallel** - where you turn to parallel the inbound leg

Most holding patterns are designed from one minute inbound legs, and the outbound leg is adjusted accordingly based on winds. A rule of thumb is that whatever wind correction angle you need to track properly on the inbound leg, double that correction for the outbound leg.

If an expect further clearance time (EFC) has been received, you must plan your holding pattern so as to be at the holding fix on the inbound leg at that time, and then continue your flight to the destination.

22 IFR Flights of "13MIKE"

ARRIVAL

Standard Terminal Arrival Routes (STARs):

This is a programmed track which brings you to your destination. As in a SID, you cannot accept a clearance with a STAR in it unless you have at least a textual description of it. Also, a STAR can be entered at any portion of that STAR, if cleared for it.

Instrument Approach Procedure Charts (IAPs):

An instrument approach procedure chart is made up of five sections when using the NOS charts.

1. **Planview** - this gives a bird's eye view of the approach from above, and is found in the upper panel.
2. **Profile view** - this gives an edgewise view of the approach, depicting altitudes to descend to at various portions of the instrument approach.
3. **Minimums section** - this gives the landing minimums by way of visibility, and the lowest altitude you can descend to or arrive at, without having the field in sight. It can change when approach lights are inoperable, or when another altimeter source other than the destination's must be used. Also when not landing straight in - but having to circle to land.
4. **Geographic view** - this displays the airport itself and the orientation of the final approach course to the runway. It shows the runway lights that are available.
5. **Timing and Remarks section** - this is necessary when the only way to know when you've arrived at the missed approach point (MAP) is by timing from the final approach fix (FAF) to the missed approach point, based on your ground speed. Pertinent notes are often present.

Visual approach:

ATC (Air Traffic Center) may opt to assign you a visual approach to the airport. This is to relieve their workload and allow more airplanes to land in a shorter period of time, than if instrument approaches are executed.

You must remain VFR and have either the airport in sight, or the traffic which precedes you in sight.

Flight Scenario One

Islip to Westchester County

(New York Area - estimated flying time 60 minutes)

Well, here we go again! Hi, Professor Miller here! Let's jump right into the first IFR flight and get our feet wet. This flight departs Islip which is on Long Island, New York and arrives at Westchester County which is northwest of Islip across the Long Island Sound. First we will trace our route of flight, fill out the flight plan, and play 20 questions or something like that! Afterwards, Professor Calfior will help you with a rather extensive weather brief, followed by my skillful guidance through the initial setup. By this time you will be ready for Professor Calfior to assist you with the Preflight, Taxi, Runup, Departure, Cruise, Descent, and Approach to your destination airport. Remember to listen to Professor Calfior, he is trying to help you obtain the best possible score.

Let's look at our route of flight for this scenario. It has some interesting instrument procedures and an unusual approach.

24 IFR Flights of "13MIKE"

FLIGHT PLAN -

This route of flight follows well established departure, climb, cruise, descent, and landing procedures. You will depart Islip, Long Island MacArthur Airport (**Airport diagram and Takeoff Minimums in Appendix C1**) on runway 6 at 1430 Zulu. With radar vector assistance from New York Departure Control, you will track inbound to Calverton VOR. Cruise altitude will be 5000 feet with a computed true airspeed of 130 knots.

From Calverton, you will slip into the BOUNO TWO ARRIVAL (**STAR diagram in Appendix C1**), which is a Standard Terminal Arrival Route, or STAR, into White Plains, Westchester County Airport, New York. You will be in contact with Boston Center as you fly the Calverton 002 radial through ZAHNN intersection, turning inbound on Bridgeport's 104 radial at EILEN intersection. Track inbound to Bridgeport until station passage, and then proceed outbound on the Bridgeport 288 radial. You'll go through ALIXX intersection until arriving at RYMES intersection. The weather seems to look good over Westchester County, so you will request a vectored descent from New York Approach Control, and when you see the field, you will cancel your IFR clearance. With a fuel on board of 6 hours, and enroute time of 55 minutes, that's plenty of fuel for an alternate plus 45 minutes FAA minimum. Danbury Municipal is a good alternate airport.

Looking at your airport diagram for Westchester County Airport (**Appendix C1**), you will come in visually for landing either on a left 45 degree traffic pattern entry or a left base to runway 16, depending on Westchester County Tower's instructions. Keep in mind it is a Class D airspace, so you can't come within 5 nautical miles of it until you have established radio communications and been cleared to continue inbound.

FILLING OUT THE FLIGHT PLAN -

Fill out the following Flight Plan completely, carefully paying attention to your route of flight. Trace out your route using the IFR low altitude enroute chart L-28 given to you in **Appendix B1**.

Islip to Westchester County

FLIGHT PLAN

1. TYPE	2. AIRCRAFT IDENTIFICATION	3. AIRCRAFT TYPE/ SPECIAL EQUIPMENT	4. TRUE AIRSPEED	5. DEPARTURE POINT	6. DEPARTURE TIME		7. CRUISING ALTITUDE
IFR					PROPOSED (Z)	ACTUAL (Z)	
VFR							
DVFR			KNOTS				

8. ROUTE OF FLIGHT

9. DESTINATION (Name of airport and city)	10. EST. TIME ENROUTE		11. REMARKS
	HOURS	MINUTES	

12. FUEL ON BOARD		13. ALTERNATE AIRPORT(S)	14. PILOT'S NAME, ADDRESS, TELEPHONE NO. AND AIRCRAFT HOME BASE	15. NO. ABOARD
HOURS	MINUTES			

16. COLOR OF AIRCRAFT

CLOSE FLIGHT PLAN WITH _____ FSS

Now answer these questions from your flight plan and enroute chart.

** a) What is in block 8, Route of Flight, of your flight plan?
_____(10 pts)

** b) The leg from Bridgeport to RYMES intersection crosses what Victor Airway?_____(10 pts)

** c) From Long Island MacArthur to Calverton, what NDB do you pass to the right of you?_____(10 pts)

** d) What is the minimum reception altitude at RYMES intersection?
_____(10 pts)

** e) List the Victor airways that RYMES intersection is on.
_____(10 pts)

26 IFR Flights of "13MIKE"

"If you make believe that the Long Island Sound is the Atlantic Ocean, and Westchester County is Paris, France, then this will become a fun intensive transatlantic IFR cross country flight! Before we get too deep into the nuts and bolts of this specific jaunt, I want to brief you on proper Flight Service Station etiquette when calling them, and what they expect to hear from you. You are expected to supply them with a certain amount of background data, so that they can input it into their computers in a logical and no nonsense fashion. I'll write the desired sequence of information in order for you on this white board, and you will, after our eight flights together, be able to verbalize it in your sleep! Here we go!"

1. Type of flight (whether IFR or VFR)
2. Aircraft ID
3. Type of aircraft
4. Departure airport
5. Proposed time of departure
6. Desired cruise altitude
7. Route of flight
8. Destination
9. Estimated time enroute
10. Remarks

"What I want you to do is go and visit Islip Flight Service Station right here, and enjoy the luxury of a face to face briefing. Practice this background data that I've shown you, and get yourself a weather brief and file our flight plan that we discussed a little while ago. Hup, two, three, four, what are you waiting for? We've got an ocean to cross!"

WEATHER BRIEF

You:

"WOW! This is a real nice Flight Service Station you have here! It's quite a palatial layout! Well, this will be fun getting a weather brief from you here, with all those charts, and computers, and - is that a real live satellite image over there?"

Islip to Westchester County

Islip FSS:

"Sure is! Would you like to get a tour of what's here? I'll be more than glad to schedule you for one. We get many pilots to simply come in and visit, or learn what exactly we do! They're busy, as we are, but it's sure a treat to have visitors!"

You:

"I'll take a rain check on that offer, I absolutely promise! My instructor is waiting for me to get a brief for this cross country, so I can't take the time now. It's a training introduction into instrument flying, and I'm too excited for words! Could I get a weather brief from you?"

Islip FSS:

"Okay! You're a private pilot working on an instrument rating, huh? Let's get this screen up right. I'm ready."

You:

"It's to be IFR, Tail number November 9413MIKE, Cessna 182 RG. I'm departing Islip, departure time in one hour. Altitude five thousand feet. It'll be a round-ish circuit through Calverton, Bridgeport, and down to White Plains, Westchester County. ETE will be one hour."

Islip FSS:

"There are no flight precautions for you, so no adverse conditions current or forecast.
A high pressure system dominates in your area.
Currently at Islip, there is a measured two thousand overcast, visibility six, temperature six two, wind zero niner zero at one zero, altimeter three zero three three.
Enroute: generally two to three thousand broken to overcast.
Westchester County is reporting measured ceiling three thousand broken, visibility seven, temperature six zero, wind zero eight zero at eight, altimeter three zero three two.
No PIREPs.

28 IFR Flights of "13MIKE"

> Forecast for Islip at one five zero zero Zulu is ceiling one thousand eight hundred overcast, unrestricted visibility. Enroute, ceilings are forecast three thousand broken to overcast.
> Westchester County forecasts ceiling two thousand five hundred overcast, visibility niner, wind zero niner zero at one two.
> No echoes being displayed on the Radar Weather scope.
> You said five thousand feet for cruise, right?"

You:

> "Right!"

Islip FSS:

> "Winds aloft for that altitude are forecast one one zero at two six.
> No NOTAMs D or L for you today.
> And that's what I have for you! Anything else I can do for you?"

FILING THE FLIGHT PLAN -

You:

> "Boy, I'll have to do this more often! This is a much more personal way to obtain weather, seeing it all happen in such a lively manner. Computers are nice, and phone calls are convenient, but being here in person could really be fun to the end of being spoiled! Let me give you the flight plan then, as I see it. Professor Calfior, my instructor, told me I'd get a kick out of this face to face brief, and was he ever right!"

Islip FSS:

> "I'll go to this screen then! Go ahead!"

You :

> "IFR, November 9413 MIKE, Cessna 182 RG - slash A, one three zero true airspeed, Departure - Islip (ISP), fourteen thirty Zulu, five thousand feet, Route - Direct Calverton (CCC), BOUNO TWO Arrival - Destination - Westchester County Airport (HPN). ETE is zero plus five five. Fuel on board six plus zero. Alternate - Danbury, Connecticut, [YOUR NAME - CONTACT PHONE NUMBER - HOME BASE], two on board, Red over white."

Islip to Westchester County

Islip FSS:

"Flight plan is filed! You're set!"

You:

"This has been spectacular! I will be doing this again! And next time, I'll have more time! I'd love a tour! Take care!"

SETUP

Aircraft:
   1) Choose "**Cessna Skylane RG**"

Weather:

Winds
   1) Set Surface winds "**DEPTH**" to "**1000**"
   2) Set Surface winds "**DIR**" to "**090**"
   3) Set Surface winds "**SPEED**" to "**8**"
   4) Set Level 1 "**TOPS**" to "**6000**"
   5) Set Level 1 "**BASE**" to "**1000**"
   6) Set Level 1 "**DIR**" to "**100**"
   7) Set Level 1 "**SPEED**" to "**20**"

Clouds
   1) Set Bottom Level - **TOPS** to "**6000**"
   2) Set Bottom Level - **BASE** to "**2200**"
   3) Set Bottom Level - **COVER** to "**overcast**"

Aircraft Position:

   1) "**NORTH**" to "**17129.6865**" — [N040° 47' 31.1462]
   2) "**EAST**" to "**21278.5049**" — [W073° 05' 57.6042]
   3) "**ALTITUDE**" to "**104**" — [0]
   4) "**HEADING**" to "**010**"

note: At this point you may wish to save this setup for future use.

30   IFR Flights of "13MIKE"

PREFLIGHT

note: Set **ZOOM** to "1.0"
Set **TIME** to "10:30"

"You know how a dog loves to be scratched under the ear, and nuzzles you into scratching its tummy? Well, 13MIKE loves thorough preflights, with plenty of petting and cooing, soft words of encouragement, like 'Good boy! You've got plenty of oil!', and stuff like that! Well, if you're all settled in, before getting started with the interior checks, let's call Islip Clearance Delivery and get our IFR flight clearance taken care of. It's within thirty minutes from our expected departure time, so it's waiting for us here right now! Frequency is one two one point eight five. Get your master switch on first!"

Departure Clearance:

1) Tune **COM** to "121.85" (Long Island Clearance)

You:

"LONG ISLAND CLEARANCE, NOVEMBER 9413MIKE WOULD LIKE TO ACTIVATE ITS IFR FLIGHT PLAN FROM ISLIP TO WESTCHESTER COUNTY AT THIS TIME, PLEASE."

Long Island Clearance:

"NOVEMBER 9413MIKE, LONG ISLAND CLEARANCE, CLEARED TO WESTCHESTER COUNTY AIRPORT AS FILED. MAINTAIN FIVE THOUSAND. NEW YORK DEPARTURE FREQUENCY WILL BE ONE ONE EIGHT POINT ZERO, SQUAWK TWO THREE THREE ONE."

Islip to Westchester County

You:

"ROGER! CLEARED AS FILED. MAINTAIN FIVE THOUSAND. DEPARTURE ONE ONE EIGHT POINT ZERO, SQUAWK TWO THREE THREE ONE."

Long Island Clearance:

"READBACK CORRECT. GOOD DAY!"

"That's right! Write down that clearance as they give it to you in whatever shorthand notation you want. Just as long as you understand it! And I enjoyed your snappiness in reading it back to them, because in case you've missed something or heard it wrong, they can then correct you and your departure will become nice and smooth. Well, let's crank up the airplane - yeah, it's purring nicely, isn't it? Getting ATIS is next on our list of priorities, so look at Islip's airport diagram and dial in the ATIS frequency."

Instruments:

1) Tune **COM** to "**128.45**" (Islip ATIS)

"LONG ISLAND MacARTHUR AIRPORT, INFORMATION ECHO, ONE THREE FIVE FIVE ZULU WEATHER, ESTIMATED CEILING TWO THOUSAND OVERCAST, VISIBILITY FIVE, TEMPERATURE SIX ONE, DEWPOINT FOUR NINER. WIND ZERO NINER ZERO AT ONE ZERO. ALTIMETER THREE ZERO THREE TWO. ILS RUNWAY SIX IS IN USE. LANDING AND DEPARTING RUNWAY SIX. ADVISE ON INITIAL CONTACT YOU HAVE INFORMATION ECHO."

32 IFR Flights of "13MIKE"

"Now comes the strategy part of setting up your navaids and such, because you will be juggling from one navaid frequency to another, but you want to be organized about it. Look at your BOUNO TWO Arrival plate. Notice how Calverton is our first VOR of use, and then Bridgeport, right? You bet ya! So put Calverton on the top, and Bridgeport on the bottom Omni Bearing Indicators. Now simply note that you'll probably be using Carmel, and perhaps even La Guardia."

2) Set **"Altimeter"** and **"Heading Indicator"**
3) Set **XPDR** to "**2331**" (assigned IFR code)
4) Tune **NAV 1** to "**117.2**" (CCC)
5) Set **NAV 1 OBS** to a **centered** "**TO**" needle
6) Tune **NAV 2** to "**108.8**" (BDR)
7) Set **NAV 2 OBS** to "**284**"
8) Set the **DME** to "**NAV 1**" and "**DIST**"
9) Check **CARB HEAT** is "**OFF**"
10) Check **GEAR** "**DOWN**"
11) Turn **STROBE** "**ON**"
12) Check **LIGHTS** are "**OFF**"

"Did you know that most ground frequencies are one two one point seven? You'll see some point eights and other varieties often enough, but if you're ever making a bet on what the frequency for Ground is, always stab at one two one point seven first! Chances are that's it. In this case, you'd win. Even though ATIS didn't tell us, give Ground what our intended departure direction will be. At least I feel it's a courtesy more than anything else."

13) Tune **COM** to "**121.7**" (Islip Ground)

You:
"ISLIP GROUND, THIS IS CESSNA 9413MIKE AT CHARLIE PAD, READY TO TAXI TO RUNWAY SIX WITH INFORMATION ECHO. NORTHEAST BOUND DEPARTURE."

Islip to Westchester County

Islip Ground:

> "CESSNA 9413MIKE, ISLIP GROUND, TAXI TO RUNWAY SIX. NEW WEATHER ESTIMATED CEILING ONE THOUSAND EIGHT HUNDRED OVERCAST, VISIBILITY FOUR. ALTIMETER THREE ZERO THREE ONE."

You:

> "13MIKE, THREE ZERO THREE ONE, TAXI TO RUNWAY SIX."

"Now, don't you dare go off anywhere without resetting your altimeter to three zero three one! The information was given you to use, and it's not something any pilot should blow off! Just tweak it to that 'one'."

      14) Set **"Altimeter"**

TAXI -

"Take a look at the Takeoff Minimums and airport diagram again! From the information that's given:

**   1. What is the standard takeoff minimums for runway 6?
      _____(5 pts)

**   2. How much of runway 6's length is usable for landing?
      _____(5 pts)

**   3. Which runway is only 75 feet wide?_____(5 pts)

**   4. What is the field elevation?_____(5 pts)

**   5. To the nearest whole number, what is the variation at Islip?
      _____(5 pts)

**   6. Does runway 6 have an upslope, downslope, or no slope to it?
      _____(5 pts)

34 IFR Flights of "13MIKE"

This is all part of what you must be aware of as a guest at any airport you visit, or is home to you. Nicely done! Well, let's turn left and float on tires of blessing to the hold short line of runway six!"

RUN UP -

        1) Set brake (hold down to prevent aircraft from moving)
        2) Advance power to about "**1700**" RPM
**   3) Select **CARB HEAT "ON"**, record RPM drop_____(5 pts)
        4) Select **CARB HEAT "OFF"**
**   5) Select "**LEFT**" Mag, record RPM drop_____(5 pts)
        6) Select "**BOTH**" Mags
**   7) Select "**RIGHT**" Mag, record RPM drop_____(5 pts)
        8) Select "**BOTH**" Mags
        9) Reduce power to **idle**
        10) Set **FLAPS** to **first notch** (10 degrees takeoff configuration)

"Do you know why Noah, in the Bible, couldn't play cards during the flood? It says he sat on the deck! Yuk - yuk! I'm ready to get off this deck, so let's call Tower on one one niner point three. Check your clearance so you know what to anticipate. It's always a job to stay ahead of the airplane in the IFR environment. You'll see as we go, but I know you'll love it as much as I do!"

        11) Tune **COM** to "**119.3**" (Islip Tower)

You:

    "ISLIP TOWER, CESSNA 9413MIKE IS READY FOR IFR DEPARTURE RUNWAY SIX."

Islip Tower:

    "CESSNA 9413MIKE, ISLIP TOWER, RUNWAY SIX, CLEARED FOR TAKEOFF. FLY RUNWAY HEADING. LEAVING ONE THOUSAND ONE HUNDRED, CONTACT NEW YORK DEPARTURE."

Islip to Westchester County 35

You:

"13MIKE, RUNWAY SIX, CLEARED FOR TAKEOFF. RUNWAY HEADING. LEAVING ONE THOUSAND ONE HUNDRED, CONTACT NEW YORK DEPARTURE."

FLIGHT

Takeoff:

"That's nice! I like it when I'm forewarned when to switch to Departure Control. It's no big deal one way or the other. What's important is that you never make your own decision as to when to switch. In this case, if Tower hadn't said anything, you'd simply stay on Tower frequency until they then tell you to switch. All right! Nice simple straight out departure, so you know vectors are coming our way! Let's roll out, and while that's occurring, check your flaps at ten degrees, fuel, trimmed for takeoff, oil temperature and pressure are greenies, and I can't think of anything else!"

1) Record TIME_____
2) Release brakes and taxi onto runway 6
3) Advance power to **"FULL"**
4) Maintain centerline of runway
5) At **50 knots** airspeed, lift nose wheel off runway
6) At **70 knots,** ease back on the yoke to establish a 10 degree pitch up attitude
7) Maintain a climb **AIRSPEED** of **80 knots**
8) Raise **Gear** when there is no more runway to land on
9) At **"500"** feet above the ground, raise the **FLAPS** to **"0"**

** 10) At what MSL altitude were you when **FLAPS** were raised? _____(25 pts)
11) Reduce power to about **"2300"** RPM at **"1000"** feet above the ground (AGL)
12) Tune **COM** to **"118.0"** (New York Departure)

36   IFR Flights of "13MIKE"

"Hey, I'm impressed! You remembered to switch perfectly when you reached your cleared altitude! Press on, Watson!"

Climb out:

1) Lower nose to establish a **100 knot** climb airspeed

You:

"NEW YORK DEPARTURE, CESSNA 9413MIKE IS WITH YOU, PASSING ONE THOUSAND FOUR HUNDRED FOR FIVE THOUSAND."

New York Departure:

"CESSNA 9413MIKE, NEW YORK DEPARTURE, RADAR CONTACT. TURN RIGHT HEADING ZERO EIGHT ZERO UNTIL RECEIVING CALVERTON, THEN PROCEED DIRECT."

You:

"13MIKE IS TURNING RIGHT ZERO EIGHT ZERO, DIRECT CALVERTON."

2) Turn **RIGHT** to a heading of "**080**" (standard rate)
3) **Re-center** the NAV 1 CDI needle
4) Turn to that heading
5) Track inbound on the centered **CALVERTON VOR** radial

"Now anticipate your entrance into the clouds, because this will become your common environment from now on. I think of it as being warmed inside a toaster! Okay, falling into a vat of Q-tips! How about you just received the shock of your life and you better get to scanning with a purpose now!"

6) When the altimeter reads "**2000**" feet, press "**P**" to pause the simulation

**   7) Record your:

         AIRSPEED_____(30 pts)
         RPM_____(25 pts)
         HEADING_____(25 pts)
         VSI_____(20 pts)
         NAV 1 DME DIST_____(20 pts)
         GEAR_____(15 pts)
         FLAPS_____(15 pts)
         COM FREQUENCY_____(10 pts)

8) Press "**P**" to continue the simulation

"Now here is what I call a quiet zone. When flying IFR, you have four stages according to the proverbs of Calfior! They are number one - takeoff. That's quite active and you're busy. Number two is radio madness! You always have to attune your senses to listen to the radio and be assimilating all the chatter that's taking place, plus recognize when you're being talked to. Number three is the quiet zone. That's when not much is happening, but you should then be planning your next couple of moves ahead in the flight. Number four is approach and landing, when so much is going on that you don't feel you've stopped juggling until wheels are on the deck!"

Level off:

1) Begin to level off when the altimeter reads "**4900**" feet
2) Maintain "**5000**" feet
3) Reduce power to about "**2200**" [**2400**] RPM

4) When established, press "**P**" to pause the simulation

**   5) Record your:

         NAV 1 CDI POSITION_____(30 pts)
         HEADING for centered NAV 1 CDI_____(30 pts)
         NAV 1 DME DIST_____(25 pts)
         CALVERTON VOR's IDENT
         _____(5 pts)

6) Press "**P**" to continue the simulation

38   IFR Flights of "13MIKE"

New York Departure:

"CESSNA 13MIKE, CONTACT BOSTON CENTER ONE TWO FOUR POINT FIVE."

You:

"CESSNA 13MIKE, SWITCHING ONE TWO FOUR POINT FIVE. SEE YOU!"

    7) Tune **COM** to "**124.5**" (Boston Center)

You:

"BOSTON CENTER, CESSNA 9413MIKE WITH YOU AT FIVE THOUSAND."

Boston Center:

"CESSNA 13MIKE, IDENT."

You:

"13MIKE, IDENT."

    8) Press the IDENT button (simulate)

**

"All that the IDENT button does is supply some vitamins to our radar image on the controller's scope, so that they know we are we! Pretty soon, we should have station passage, which means we've passed overhead of Calverton VOR. Station passage occurs when the 'TO' flips to 'FROM' on the OBI. How many miles will we go outbound on our new radial? _____(5 pts) See? You just keep thinking ahead, just like in a chess game."

Boston Center:

"CESSNA 13MIKE, RADAR CONTACT."

Course change 1:

    1) When the **DME** on **NAV 1** reads "**0.4**" **[0.8]**, turn left to a heading of "**002**"
    2) Set **NAV 1 OBS** to "**002**"

Islip to Westchester County

      3) Track outbound on the **CALVERTON VOR 002** radial that your **NAV 1 OBI** is displaying

      4) When the **NAV 1 DME DIST** reads "**5.5**", press "**P**" to pause the simulation

**   5) Record your:

           NAV 1 CDI POSITION_____(40 pts)
           HEADING_____(35 pts)
           ALTITUDE_____(25 pts)
           AIRSPEED_____(15 pts)
           COM FREQUENCY_____(10 pts)
           NAME OF INTERSECTION YOU'RE ALMOST AT_____(5 pts)

**   6) Press "**P**" to continue the simulation

"What is the name of the next intersection off of this Calverton radial? _____(5 pts)

By the way, we're over the Atlantic Ocean, I mean Long Island Sound now!"

Course change 2:

      1) When the **NAV 2 CDI** needle is 2 dots **RIGHT** of center, start your **LEFT** turn to a heading of "**284**"

      2) When your heading indicator reads "**295**", start to roll out

      3) When wings are level, press "**P**" to pause the simulation

**   4) Record your:

           NAV 1 DME DIST_____(30 pts)
           VSI_____(25 pts)
           ALTITUDE_____(20 pts)
           BRIDGEPORT VOR's IDENT
           _____(15 pts)

      5) Press "**P**" to continue the simulation

      6) Track inbound on the **BRIDGEPORT VOR 104** radial

40 IFR Flights of "13MIKE"

Boston Center:

"CESSNA 9413MIKE, CONTACT BOSTON CENTER ONE THREE THREE POINT TWO."

You:

"ROGER, CESSNA 9413MIKE, BOSTON CENTER ONE THREE THREE POINT TWO. GOOD-BYE!"

    7) Tune **COM** to "**133.2**" (Boston Center)

You:

"BOSTON CENTER, CESSNA 9413MIKE AT FIVE THOUSAND."

Boston Center:

"CESSNA 9413MIKE, ROGER."

**

"A lot of times, you are transitioning through different sectors of a Center's jurisdiction. A castle wall looking rectangular box in the low altitude enroute charts shows you approximately where those sector transitions are. What is the name of the remote site which is in this sector of Boston Center? (mistakenly labeled 'New York')
_____(5 pts)
How many miles is it from this latest turnoff to Bridgeport VOR?
_____(5 pts)
Based on your cruise winds and a computed true airspeed of about one hundred and thirty knots, how long will it take to arrive at Bridgeport from the turnoff?_____(5 pts)
Start jazzing up yourself for the approach and landing phase of this flight, because soon you'll feel you're in the swamp up to your rear end with alligators and otters (OTTERS?)!"

Course change 3:

    1) When the **NAV 2 OBI** flips from "**TO**" to "**FROM**", turn **RIGHT** to a heading of "**288**"

Islip to Westchester County

    2) Set **NAV 2 OBS** to "**288**"
    3) Track outbound on the **BRIDGEPORT VOR 288** radial

"Before you get too close to Westchester County Airport, I'd suggest you excuse yourself from Boston Center temporarily and get some ATIS information. Because pretty soon, they'll want to flag you over to Approach Control, and I first would like to know what the deck is over the airport. It'd be fun to show you what it takes to cancel an IFR clearance and finish up this flight with a visual entry to the traffic pattern. ATIS frequency will be one one eight point six."

You:

    "BOSTON CENTER, CESSNA 9413MIKE WOULD LIKE TO SWITCH OFF THE FREQUENCY FOR A MOMENT."

Boston Center:

    "CESSNA 9413MIKE, APPROVED AS REQUESTED. REPORT BACK ON."

You:

    "CESSNA 13MIKE."

    4) Tune **COM** to "**118.6**" (Westchester County ATIS)

"WESTCHESTER COUNTY AIRPORT, INFORMATION LIMA, ONE FOUR FIVE FIVE ZULU WEATHER, ESTIMATED CEILING TWO THOUSAND FIVE HUNDRED OVERCAST, VISIBILITY FOUR, TEMPERATURE FIVE EIGHT, DEWPOINT FOUR SEVEN, WIND ONE ZERO ZERO AT NINER. ALTIMETER THREE ZERO TWO NINER. ALL ARRIVING VFR TRAFFIC CONTACT TOWER ON ONE ONE NINER POINT SEVEN. ALL ARRIVING IFR TRAFFIC CONTACT NEW YORK APPROACH ON ONE TWO SIX POINT EIGHT. ILS RUNWAY ONE SIX IN USE. ADVISE ON INITIAL CONTACT YOU HAVE INFORMATION LIMA."

42 IFR Flights of "13MIKE"

> 5) Set **ALTIMETER**, set **HI**, and check **FUEL**

"I like it! I like it! Altimeter setting is given, and you've automatically made it so and verified that your magnetic compass is lined up with your heading indicator. You've just received two important frequencies from ATIS - one one niner point seven Tower and one two six point eight Approach. When you feel it's appropriate, after we're passed over to Approach, let them know we'd like to get below that twenty five hundred foot deck, cancel IFR, and proceed visually. All right! Quit gabbing Professor Calfior! I know!"

> 6) Tune **COM** to "**133.2**" (Boston Center)

You:

> "BOSTON CENTER, CESSNA 9413MIKE IS BACK WITH YOU."

Boston Center:

> "CESSNA 9413MIKE, ROGER."

> 7) Tune **NAV 1** to "**116.6**" (CMK)
> 8) Set **NAV 1 OBS** to "**348**"

Boston Center:

> "CESSNA 9413MIKE, CONTACT NEW YORK APPROACH ONE TWO SIX POINT FOUR."

You:

> "CESSNA 13MIKE, SWITCHING ONE TWO SIX POINT FOUR. THANKS FOR YOUR HELP."

> 9) Tune **COM** to "**126.4**" (New York Approach)

Islip to Westchester County

You:

"NEW YORK APPROACH, CESSNA 9413MIKE IS WITH YOU AT FIVE THOUSAND, ONE TWO MILES WEST OF BRIDGEPORT."

New York Approach:

"CESSNA 9413MIKE, NEW YORK APPROACH, SQUAWK FOUR FOUR SIX SEVEN, AND IDENT."

You:

"CESSNA 13MIKE, SQUAWK FOUR FOUR SIX SEVEN. IDENT."

10) Set **XPDR** to "**4467**" (and simulate pressing the IDENT button

New York Approach:

"CESSNA 13MIKE, RADAR CONTACT. EXPECT RADAR VECTORS TO INTERCEPT THE FINAL APPROACH COURSE INBOUND FOR THE ILS RUNWAY ONE SIX APPROACH WESTCHESTER COUNTY."

You:

"NEW YORK APPROACH, CESSNA 13MIKE WOULD LIKE TO DROP DOWN BELOW THE OVERCAST LAYER FOR A VISUAL TO RUNWAY ONE SIX. WILL CANCEL IFR WHEN FIELD IS IN SIGHT."

New York Approach:

"CESSNA 13MIKE, HAVE YOUR REQUEST! OVER RYMES, TURN LEFT HEADING TWO FIVE ZERO, THEN DESCEND AND MAINTAIN TWO THOUSAND. REPORT FIELD IN SIGHT."

44   IFR Flights of "13MIKE"

You:

> "CESSNA 13MIKE, AT RYMES, TURN LEFT HEADING TWO FIVE ZERO, THEN DESCEND AND MAINTAIN TWO THOUSAND. REPORT FIELD IN SIGHT."

"Now see what your constant thinking activity did for you? You had set Carmel's frequency up on the VOR, and it's easy now to wait until RYMES intersection happens. Otherwise, now you'd have to tap dance a little, quickly set up the frequency and radial, and become breathless trying to do a hundred yard dash to catch up with the eight ball!"

Enroute Descent:

1) When your **NAV 1 CDI** is **centered**, turn **LEFT** to a heading of **"250"**
2) Reduce power to about **"1500"** [**1800**] RPM
3) Set **CARB HEAT "ON"**
4) Establish a **"1500" FPM** rate of descent
5) Descend to and maintain **"2000"** feet
6) When below the clouds, and the field is in sight:

You:

> "NEW YORK APPROACH, CESSNA 13MIKE, FIELD IN SIGHT. CANCEL MY IFR."

New York Approach:

> "CESSNA 13MIKE, RADAR SERVICE IS TERMINATED. SQUAWK ONE TWO ZERO ZERO. CONTACT TOWER ON ONE ONE NINER POINT SEVEN. GOOD DAY!"

You:

> "CESSNA 13MIKE, GOOD BEING WITH YOU!"

"From my point of view, it looks like we are five to six miles from the field. Let's circle right here, get set up, call Tower and take our time, because we don't want to encroach upon the Class C airspace without establishing radio communications."

Islip to Westchester County   45

       7) Make a 360° standard **RIGHT** turning series of circles until radio contact and clearance from Tower
       8) Set **XPDR** to "**1200**" (VFR code)
       9) Tune **COM** to "**119.7**" (Westchester County Tower)
     10) Select **GEAR** "**DOWN**"

You:

    "**WESTCHESTER COUNTY TOWER, CESSNA 9413MIKE, SIX NORTHEAST WITH INFORMATION LIMA FOR LANDING.**"

Westchester Tower:

    "**CESSNA 9413MIKE, WESTCHESTER COUNTY TOWER, ENTER LEFT BASE RUNWAY ONE SIX. REPORT A TWO MILE LEFT BASE. FULL STOP OR TOUCH AND GO?**"

You:

    "**FULL STOP. WILL REPORT TWO MILE LEFT BASE.**"

"Boy, isn't that nice of them! Rather than drag this thing (Oh, sorry 13MIKE! How could I ever have allowed myself to call you a 'thing'!) to a left forty five position, they're helping expedite us to the field. Now you can descend down to some altitude that'll seem comfortable for a base entry. Your choice!"

     11) Turn **RIGHT** and establish a **LEFT BASE** to runway 16
     12) When airspeed is "**90**" knots, continue descent to "**1200**" ft.
**   13) What heading is an established **LEFT BASE**?_____(30 pts)

    Approach:

      1) Set **FLAPS** to **first notch** (10 degrees)
      2) Try and maintain a **400** ft per minute descent on your Vertical Speed Indicator (VSI)
      3) When runway 16 is at your 11 o'clock position:

You:

    "**WESTCHESTER COUNTY TOWER, CESSNA 13MIKE TWO MILE LEFT BASE.**"

IFR Flights of "13MIKE"

Westchester County Tower:

>"CESSNA 13MIKE, NUMBER TWO. FOLLOW MOONEY SHORT FINAL, RUNWAY ONE SIX. CLEARED TO LAND."

You:

>"CESSNA 13MIKE IS CLEARED TO LAND."

4) Set **FLAPS** to **second notch** (20 degrees)
5) When runway 16 is at your 10 o'clock position, start a **"90"** degree **LEFT** turn to establish your **FINAL** leg
6) When established on the **FINAL** leg, set **FLAPS** to **third notch** (30 degrees)
7) Airspeed should be **70 knots**

"You're in a beautiful position to land. Plant that approach end of runway one six on your windscreen right where you see it best, about an inch or two from the bottom lip. Now keep that perspective and allow the runway to get bigger and bigger and bigger!"

8) When you are 10 to 20 feet off the runway, reduce power to about **"1000"** RPM and start to slowly pitch the nose of the aircraft up to slow your descent and establish a touchdown attitude
9) When you are five feet off the runway, hold the nose of the aircraft up and allow the airspeed to **SLOWLY** bleed off. Your aircraft will <u>settle</u> onto the runway while you follow the centerline
10) After touchdown, reduce power to **idle**
11) Apply the brakes

Westchester County Tower:

>"CESSNA 13MIKE, TURN LEFT SECOND INTERSECTION. CONTACT GROUND EXITING THE RUNWAY."

Islip to Westchester County   47

You:

    "CESSNA 13MIKE, SECOND INTERSECTION."

    12) Taxi the aircraft off the active runway to the **LEFT**
    13) When the aircraft has stopped, set **CARB HEAT** to "**OFF**"
    14) Set **FLAPS** to "**0**"
    15) Tune **COM** to "**121.8**" (Westchester County Ground)

You:

    "WESTCHESTER COUNTY GROUND, CESSNA 9413MIKE ON BRAVO. REQUEST TAXI TO THE TERMINAL."

Westchester County Ground:

    "CESSNA 13MIKE, WESTCHESTER COUNTY GROUND, TAXI TO THE TERMINAL."

You:

    "13MIKE TO THE TERMINAL."

"For an introduction into the IFR arena, I am exceedingly impressed with the way you stayed cool, calm, and in control. I'll help you tie down 13MIKE and we'll debrief at the restaurant over a nice cup of hot chocolate and some jelly beans!"

**   16) Record the **TIME**_____(5 pts)

    TOTAL POINTS POSSIBLE FOR THIS FLIGHT___**645**___

48 IFR Flights of "13MIKE"

Flight Scenario Two

San Diego to Los Angeles

(Southern California Area - estimated flying time 70 minutes)

Congratulations on your first venture into the world of no-see-um flying! It's not easy flying that AI is it? Well, the next flight is full of no-see-ums, so let's get at it.

This flight departs beautiful San Diego Lindbergh Field in the southernmost part of California, utilizing a SID, and concludes by shooting a VOR approach into smoggy Los Angeles International. You will need to plot your course on the Low Altitude Enroute Chart, fill out your flight plan, and answer a few questions. Then Professor Calfior will help you with the weather brief. I will step you through the setup where you will be setting the cloud level down to 1100 feet. Looks like you will be in the no-see-um conditions right after takeoff. Then back to Professor Calfior for the remainder of the adventure where he will entertain you with his easy going and humorous instruction. You need to listen to Professor Calfior's witty dialog (the jokes you can ignore) for all the good information that will help you become a better pilot and achieve a better score.

Our route of flight for this scenario has some interesting instrument procedures, so you will need to keep sharp.

50   IFR Flights of "13MIKE"

FLIGHT PLAN -

This route of flight follows well established departure, climb, cruise, descent, and landing procedures. You will depart San Diego International, Lindbergh Field (**Airport diagram in Appendix C2**) on runway 27 at 2100 Zulu. You will fly a standard instrument departure procedure, or SID, called the HARBR TWO DEPARTURE. (**Appendix C2**)

As soon as practicable, you'll make a climbing right turn to a heading of 290 degrees, switch to San Diego Departure Control, and intercept Oceanside VOR's 154 radial inbound. Stay at or below 4000 feet until crossing CLSTR intersection, then continue your climb out to 7000 feet. You will be switched over to Los Angeles Center. You computed your true airspeed as 120 knots.

When intercepting the Mission Bay VOR 314 radial, turn left and track outbound until arriving at LNSAY intersection. At LNSAY, you should be at 7000 feet, and you will turn left, tracking inbound on the Santa Catalina 090 radial. Continue that track until arriving at HARBR intersection. From HARBR, proceed inbound on the Seal Beach VOR 148 radial to Seal Beach. Notice the coded name of this transition to Seal Beach.

Now Seal Beach VOR is the initial approach fix (IAF) for the VOR or TACAN or GPS RWY 25L/R instrument approach into Los Angeles. (**Appendix C2**) Under South California Approach Control's umbrella, you will descend to 4000 feet, flying outbound on the Seal Beach VOR 326 radial to FITON intersection, where the intermediate segment of the approach begins.

You'll turn inbound onto Los Angeles VOR's 068 radial (248 course inbound) and descend to 2000 feet by FREBY intersection. This is the final approach fix, and begins the final segment of the instrument approach procedure. At some point, you'll go to Los Angeles Tower. As long as you have DME capability, you'll descend to 620 feet by NOELE intersection, and then to your minimum descent altitude of 540 feet by the 2.7 DME missed approach point. If the field is in sight, you'll land straight in to runway 25L. If the field is not in sight, you will execute the missed approach procedure given in the profile view of the approach plate. Fuel on board is 5 hours and 50 minutes, and you've planned this out to be a 70 minute flight, so fuel is no problem. You've made a good choice in having Ontario International as your alternate.

Los Angeles International Airport's diagram is shown in **Appendix C2**.

San Diego to Los Angeles

FILLING OUT THE FLIGHT PLAN -

Fill out the following Flight Plan completely, carefully paying attention to your route of flight. Trace out your route using the IFR low altitude enroute chart L-3 given to you in **Appendix B2**.

FLIGHT PLAN						
1. TYPE ☐ IFR ☐ VFR ☐ DVFR	2. AIRCRAFT IDENTIFICATION	3. AIRCRAFT TYPE/ SPECIAL EQUIPMENT	4. TRUE AIRSPEED KNOTS	5. DEPARTURE POINT	6. DEPARTURE TIME PROPOSED (Z) | ACTUAL (Z)	7. CRUISING ALTITUDE
8. ROUTE OF FLIGHT							
9. DESTINATION (Name of airport and city)		10. EST. TIME ENROUTE HOURS | MINUTES		11. REMARKS		
12. FUEL ON BOARD HOURS | MINUTES		13. ALTERNATE AIRPORT(S)		14. PILOT'S NAME, ADDRESS, TELEPHONE NO. AND AIRCRAFT HOME BASE		15. NO. ABOARD
16. COLOR OF AIRCRAFT				CLOSE FLIGHT PLAN WITH_____ FSS		

Now answer these questions from your flight plan and enroute chart.

** a) What is in block 8, Route of Flight, of your flight plan?
_____(10 pts)

** b) What restricted airspaces are to the right of you about 40 miles out from San Diego?_____(10 pts)

** c) How many miles is it from Seal Beach VOR to Los Angeles VOR along Victor 23?_____(10 pts)

** d) The name of the compass locator beacon southwest of Seal Beach VOR is what?_____(10 pts)

** e) The minimum enroute altitude from Seal Beach VOR along Victor 8 to WILMA intersection is what?_____(10 pts)

52   IFR Flights of "13MIKE"

"Take a look at your airport diagram for San Diego International Lindbergh Field. On the left top corner, you will find that Lindbergh Clearance Delivery has a frequency of one two five point niner. At this airport, there is a pre-taxi clearance procedure available. That means pilots who are departing IFR can, if they want, receive an IFR clearance before even taxiing. It's not mandatory, but if one participates, they would call Clearance Delivery about ten minutes before they taxi, and the IFR clearance will be issued right then and there!

You will do just that. Before you even preflight the aircraft, you'll call up and get our clearance. Then you'll make your rounds about 13MIKE, and a taxiing we will go!

To start, you must call San Diego's Flight Service Station, and here's the local phone number: 277-3493. I happen to have it because it's listed, but from anywhere in the United States, you can always get a hold of a Flight Service Station by dialing 1-800-WX-BRIEF. You'll get relayed to the one closest to where you're calling from.

Okay! Have some fun, get the weather for this cross country flight, and file our flight plan as we've discussed."

WEATHER BRIEF

You:

"Hello! I'm calling in next door from Lindbergh Field and would like to request an IFR weather brief. Tail number November 9413MIKE which is a Cessna 182 RG. Departure point is Lindbergh Field with a departure around twenty one hundred Zulu. I guess that's one hour from now. I'd like to fly at seven thousand feet and I'll go by way of Oceanside and Seal Beach. Destination is Los Angeles and ETE should be about one hour and ten minutes."

San Diego FSS:

"I have no flight precautions for your flight.

San Diego to Los Angeles

There is a weakening cold front across southern California.

Currently at Lindbergh, weather is reported as a measured ceiling one thousand five hundred broken, four thousand overcast, visibility one five, temperature five seven, wind two four zero at eight, and altimeter three zero zero niner.

Enroute ceilings are generally two thousand broken to overcast, and that's all!

Los Angeles is currently reporting measured ceiling two thousand broken, visibility one zero, temperature six zero, wind two seven zero at one five, altimeter three zero one one.

No PIREPs for you. No echoes on the Radar Summary.

Lindbergh's terminal forecast is ceiling one thousand overcast, unrestricted visibility

Enroute ceilings are forecast two thousand overcast.

Los Angeles' terminal forecast for your arrival is ceiling one thousand two hundred overcast, visibility unrestricted, wind two three zero at one zero, and that's the end of that!

Wind at seven thousand feet is forecast - we'll use two seven zero at two one.

NOTAMs that are in effect are a few I can see. At LA runway two four Left, ILS DME is out of service. Runway two five Right, ILS middle marker is reported out of service. Runway six Left's ILS middle marker also is out of service.

An FDC NOTAM is in effect in the Van Nuys airspace. Effective immediately and until further notice, pursuant to FAR 91.137A(2), temporary flight restrictions are in effect three nautical miles radius of the Van Nuys zero two zero degree radial, nine DME position, at and below three thousand feet AGL, to provide a safe environment for rescue operations. No local NOTAMs.

That's the gist of what I have for you. Is there anything else you'd like to know, or that I can do for you?"

FILING THE FLIGHT PLAN -

You:

"I'm ready to file, unless do I have to call somebody else to do that?"

54 IFR Flights of "13MIKE"

San Diego FSS:

"No, no! I can do that too! I'll just let my fingers do the typing, of which I'm ready to get your flight plan now."

You:

"IFR, November 9413MIKE, Cessna 182 RG - slash A, one twenty true, Departure - SAN, twenty one hundred Zulu, seven thousand feet, Route - HARBR TWO Departure, Seal Beach transition - Destination LAX. ETE is one plus one zero. Fuel on board is five plus fifty. Alternate - Ontario International. [YOUR NAME - CONTACT PHONE NUMBER - HOME BASE], two on board, Red over white."

San Diego FSS:

"Sounds like it should be a blast! Wish you the best!"

You:

"Same to you! Good-bye!"

SETUP

Aircraft:
  1) Choose **"Cessna Skylane RG"**

Weather:

  Winds
  1) Set Surface winds **"DEPTH"** to **"800"**
  2) Set Surface winds **"DIR"** to **"240"**
  3) Set Surface winds **"SPEED"** to **"6"**
  4) Set Level 1 **"TOPS"** to **"4000"**
  5) Set Level 1 **"BASE"** to **"850"**
  6) Set Level 1 **"DIR"** to **"290"**
  7) Set Level 1 **"SPEED"** to **"16"**
  8) Set Level 2 **"TOPS"** to **"7000"**
  9) Set Level 2 **"BASE"** to **"4000"**

San Diego to Los Angeles

       10) Set Level 2 "**DIR**" to "**270**"
       11) Set Level 2 "**SPEED**" to "**21**"

Clouds
       1) Set Bottom Level - **TOPS** to "**3500**"
       2) Set Bottom Level - **BASE** to "**1100**"
       3) Set Bottom Level - **COVER** to "**overcast**"
       4) Set Top Level - **TOPS** to "**7000**"
       5) Set Top Level - **BASE** to "**4300**"
       5) Set Top Level - **COVER** to "**overcast**"

Aircraft Position:
       1) "**NORTH**" to "**14761**" [N032° 43' 57.6575]
       2) "**EAST**" to "**6102**" [W117° 11' 25.8622]
       3) "**ALTITUDE**" to "**8**" [0]
       4) "**HEADING**" to "**000**"

note: At this point you may wish to save this setup for future use.

PREFLIGHT

note: Set **ZOOM** to "**1.0**"
       Set **TIME** to "**1400**"

"I sure do enjoy our flights together! And isn't it a unique challenge to be working the details of the IFR environment, while at the same time sharpening up your instrument scanning pattern? When flying the T-2 Buckeye and A-4 Skyhawk in the Navy, one of the first lessons that had to be accomplished before getting into the airplane was to pass a blindfold cockpit check. Sitting inside the cockpit, you couldn't see anything and the instructor would ask you to point to the airspeed indicator, so you would. NAV 1 receiver - you would. Air conditioning switch - you would. Well, I won't have you do that, but it's not a bad idea to know exactly where each of your gauges are, so that your scan will be smooth. Let's use the pre-taxi clearance program, and get our clearance on one two five point niner."

56   IFR Flights of "13MIKE"

Departure Clearance:

    1) Tune **COM** to "125.9" (Lindbergh Clearance)

You:

"LINDBERGH CLEARANCE, CESSNA 9413MIKE, EAST TERMINAL, IFR. I'D LIKE TO ACTIVATE MY IFR FLIGHT PLAN FROM SAN DIEGO INTERNATIONAL TO LOS ANGELES, PLEASE."

Lindbergh Clearance:

"CESSNA 9413MIKE, LINDBERGH CLEARANCE, CLEARED TO LOS ANGELES INTERNATIONAL AS FILED. MAINTAIN SEVEN THOUSAND. SAN DIEGO DEPARTURE FREQUENCY WILL BE ONE TWO FIVE POINT THREE, SQUAWK SIX FOUR FIVE TWO."

You:

"NOVEMBER 9413MIKE IS CLEARED AS FILED. MAINTAIN SEVEN THOUSAND. DEPARTURE ONE TWO FIVE POINT THREE, SQUAWK SIX FOUR FIVE TWO."

Lindbergh Clearance:

"READBACK CORRECT. ENJOY YOUR FLIGHT!"

"You remember what our 'as filed' is now, right? This is your first attempt at a Standard Instrument Departure, SID, and it's a beautiful one! I can't tell you how thrilling these instrument flights are to me! When I instructed in the Navy, I used to trade my spin flights for another instructor's instrument flights. Two reasons! One, I loved the puzzle challenge of the instrument world of flying. Two, I hated spins!"

Instruments:

    1) Tune **COM** to "134.8" (Lindbergh ATIS)

San Diego to Los Angeles 57

"SAN DIEGO INTERNATIONAL AIRPORT, LINDBERGH FIELD, INFORMATION PAPA, TWO ZERO FIVE FIVE ZULU WEATHER, ESTIMATED CEILING ONE THOUSAND ONE HUNDRED OVERCAST, VISIBILITY ONE TWO. TEMPERATURE FIVE EIGHT, DEWPOINT FOUR EIGHT, WIND TWO FOUR ZERO AT SIX. ALTIMETER THREE ZERO ZERO NINER. LOCALIZER RUNWAY TWO SEVEN IS IN USE. LANDING AND DEPARTING RUNWAY TWO SEVEN. ADVISE ON INITIAL CONTACT YOU HAVE INFORMATION PAPA."

**

"Okay! We know runway two seven, so look over the HARBR TWO departure from runway two seven. You'll need Oceanside VOR to get where you want to go, and interestingly enough, Mission Bay to identify certain fixes. What's the first heading you are interested in once you get airborne? Check your SID_____(5 pts)
And what is the first critical altitude you want to be aware of?
_____(5 pts)."

2) Set "**Altimeter**" and "**Heading Indicator**"
3) Set **XPDR** to "**6452**" (assigned IFR code)
4) Tune **NAV 1** to "**115.3**" (OCN)
5) Set **NAV 1 OBS** to "**334**"
6) Tune **NAV 2** to "**117.8**" (MZB)
7) Set **NAV 2 OBS** to "**298**"
8) Set the **DME** to "**NAV 1**" and "**DIST**"
9) Check **CARB HEAT** is "**OFF**"
10) Check **GEAR** "**DOWN**"
11) Turn **STROBE** "**ON**"
12) Check **LIGHTS** are "**OFF**"

"We've got our clearance, we've got ATIS, we've got our navaid panel set, and we've got us about to go flying! I can tell Ground is anxious to see us depart because I see the signal flag being flown, 'Go 13MIKE!' Actually, that's the emergency Quebec flag to warn the airport users we're just about ready to fly! Ground is on one two three point niner - remember I told you not all Ground frequencies are one two one point something?"

58 IFR Flights of "13MIKE"

13) Tune **COM** to "**123.9**" (San Diego Ground)

You:

"SAN DIEGO GROUND, CESSNA 9413MIKE AT EAST TERMINAL, READY TO TAXI TO RUNWAY TWO SEVEN WITH INFORMATION PAPA. NORTHBOUND DEPARTURE."

San Diego Ground:

"CESSNA 9413MIKE, SAN DIEGO GROUND, TAXI TO RUNWAY TWO SEVEN."

You:

"RUNWAY TWO SEVEN FOR 13MIKE."

"So, you'll need to turn right and proceed down along the south taxiway until approaching the hold short line at the very end with a snappy left turn. A safe rule of thumb is to taxi no faster than a fast walk, just to stay in absolute control at all times. I'd like for you to always abide by that safety procedure."

TAXI -

"Don't ever depart from any airport with blinders (like a race horse) on. Be knowledgeable of its idiosynchrasies. Let's see what you know by way of utilizing your San Diego Lindbergh Field airport diagram!

**   1. What is the variation around this geographic area to the nearest whole number?_____(5 pts)
2. What is the length of runway 9-27?_____(5 pts)
3. What is the elevation of the approach end of runway 27?
   _____(5 pts)
4. From where you're sitting here at the ramp, is the control tower in front of you and to the LEFT, or in front of you and to the RIGHT?
   _____(5 pts)
5. What is the name of the north taxiway paralleling runway 9-27?
   _____(5 pts)

San Diego to Los Angeles 59

6. The alignment of runway 27 is actually what magnetic course?
_____(5 pts)

And away we go, Alice! Isn't that something Jackie Gleason said in the Honeymooners? Am I dating myself or what? What! You're a diplomat!"

RUN UP -

             1) Set brake (hold down to prevent aircraft from moving)
             2) Advance power to about "**1800**" RPM
**   3) Select **CARB HEAT** "**ON**", record RPM drop_____(5 pts)
             4) Select **CARB HEAT** "**OFF**"
**   5) Select "**LEFT**" Mag, record RPM drop_____(5 pts)
             6) Select "**BOTH**" Mags
**   7) Select "**RIGHT**" Mag, record RPM drop_____(5 pts)
             8) Select "**BOTH**" Mags
             9) Reduce power to **idle**
             10) Set **FLAPS** to **first notch** (10 degrees takeoff configuration)

"Are you committed to excellence? Enjoy the view on takeoff for about one thousand feet, because it looks like that's all you'll have to sightsee! Handle our Tower communications then on one one eight point three."

             11) Tune **COM** to "**118.3**" (San Diego Tower)

You:

    "SAN DIEGO TOWER, CESSNA 9413MIKE IS READY FOR IFR DEPARTURE RUNWAY TWO SEVEN."

San Diego Tower:

    "CESSNA 9413MIKE, SAN DIEGO TOWER, HOLD SHORT. TRAFFIC IS ON THREE QUARTER MILE FINAL."

You:

    "13MIKE, HOLDING SHORT."

60 IFR Flights of "13MIKE"

"Man, oh man! That's a nice approach they're doing! I try to recommend to all my students that they sit somewhere by an approach end of an active runway, and watch incoming aircraft. You can so easily see high landing attitudes, low landing attitudes, power juggling, wind effects, so many, many great things. It can get downright scary, I'll tell you!"

San Diego Tower:

> **"CESSNA 13MIKE, RUNWAY TWO SEVEN, CLEARED FOR TAKEOFF."**

You:

> **"CESSNA 13MIKE, TWO SEVEN, CLEARED FOR TAKEOFF."**

"You go through the drill! Flaps - yup! Ten degrees. Fuel is topped. Yeah, that takeoff trim setting sure is vital. Green oil temperature and green oil pressure. Oh, that beautiful runway length and it's all ours! Light the afterburners and let's show them 13MIKE's awesome two hundred and thirty five horsepower output!"

FLIGHT

Takeoff:

1) Record TIME_____
2) Release brakes and taxi onto runway 27
3) Advance power to **"FULL"**
4) Maintain centerline of runway
5) At **50 knots** airspeed, lift nose wheel off runway
6) At **70 knots,** ease back on the yoke to establish a 10 degree pitch up attitude
7) Maintain a climb **AIRSPEED** of **80 knots**
8) Raise **Gear** when there is no more runway to land on
9) When **GEAR** is **UP**, turn **RIGHT** to a heading of **"290"**
10) At **"500"** feet above the ground, raise the **FLAPS** to **"0"**

San Diego to Los Angeles 61

       11) Reduce power to about "**2300**" RPM at "**1000**" feet above the ground (AGL)

San Diego Tower:

    "CESSNA 13MIKE, CONTACT SAN DIEGO DEPARTURE. GOOD DAY!"

You:

    "ROGER! 13MIKE SWITCHING ONE TWO FIVE POINT THREE. THANKS!"

       12) Tune **COM** to "**125.3**" (San Diego Departure)

You:

    "SAN DIEGO DEPARTURE, CESSNA 9413MIKE IS WITH YOU, PASSING ONE THOUSAND FOUR HUNDRED FOR FOUR THOUSAND."

San Diego Departure:

    "CESSNA 9413MIKE, SAN DIEGO DEPARTURE, RADAR CONTACT."

"Great job! Just keep your scan going. Hit that attitude indicator more often than anything else, but keep your eyes moving. Don't fixate, but as you're moving, mentally highlight what the gauges are telling you as you swing by them. At any time, I should be able to ask you anything regarding your six pack of instruments, and you can tell me what they said."

Level off:

    1) Begin to level off when the altimeter reads "**3900**" feet
    2) Maintain "**4000**" feet
    3) Reduce power to about "**2250**" **[2450]** RPM

62 IFR Flights of "13MIKE"

San Diego Departure:

> "CESSNA 13MIKE, CONTACT LOS ANGELES CENTER ONE THREE FOUR POINT FIVE."

You:

> "CESSNA 13MIKE, SWITCHING LA CENTER, ONE THREE FOUR POINT FIVE."

    4) Tune **COM** to "**134.5**" (Los Angeles Center)

You:

> "LOS ANGELES CENTER, CESSNA 9413MIKE WITH YOU AT FOUR THOUSAND."

Los Angeles Center:

> "CESSNA 9413MIKE, LOS ANGELES CENTER, IDENT."

You:

> "CESSNA 13MIKE, IDENT."

    5) Press the IDENT button (simulate)

Los Angeles Center:

> "CESSNA 13MIKE, RADAR CONTACT."

"Keep popping your vision over to the NAV 1 CDI because you want to turn to the northwest when it centers, right? You've got excellent heading control - I also love your level off at four thousand feet as the departure calls for! Concentrate on what you're doing now, and be aware of your next step always."

Course change 1:

    1) When the **NAV 1 CDI** is **centered**, turn **RIGHT** to a heading of "**334**"

San Diego to Los Angeles — 63

**
2) When wings are level, press "**P**" to pause the simulation
3) Record your:
- NAV 1 DME DIST_____(25 pts)
- ALTITUDE_____(20 pts)
- AIRSPEED_____(15 pts)
- RPM_____(15 pts)
- VSI_____(15 pts)
- COM FREQUENCY_____(15 pts)
- XPDR_____(10 pts)

4) Press "**P**" to continue the simulation

5) Track inbound on the **OCEANSIDE VOR 154** radial that your **NAV 1 OBI** is displaying
6) When the **NAV 2 CDI** centers, increase power to about "**2300**" [**2500**] RPM
7) Commence climb to "**7000**" feet

**

"We're in no rush to get to seven thousand feet, since the departure calls for us to be at or above six thousand five hundred by what intersection? _____(5 pts)
From your present position, at CLSTR, how many miles is it to the above intersection?_____(5 pts)
So let's climb at a speed that's closer to our cruise speed, one hundred knots, so we can travel forward at a good pace, while at the same time climbing sufficiently to meet the standard instrument departure altitude restriction."

8) Maintain a **100 knot** climb airspeed
9) Set **NAV 2 OBS** to "**314**"
10) Begin to level off when the altimeter reads "**6900**" feet
11) Maintain "**7000**" feet
12) Reduce power to about "**2250**" [**2450**] RPM

Course changes 2:

1) When the **NAV 2 CDI** is ½ dot **RIGHT** of center, turn **LEFT** to a heading of "**314**"

64   IFR Flights of "13MIKE"

      2) Track outbound on the **MISSION BAY VOR 314** radial that your **NAV 2 OBI** is displaying

**

*"Is there something you could be doing in order to get a feel for when you'll intercept your Santa Catalina track? Yeah, get that Number two DME to working for you! **LNSAY** intersection is identified by twelve DME from Mission Bay, right? TRUE or FALSE?_____(5 pts) Darn right, it's wrong! How many miles is **LNSAY** intersection from Mission Bay VOR?_____(5 pts) As an instrument pilot, I guarantee you that you want to use all the sources of information you can ever get your throttle and yoke skilled hands on!"*

      3) Set **DME** to "**NAV 2**"
      4) Tune **NAV 1** to "**111.4**" (SXC)
      5) Set **NAV 1 OBS** to "**270**"

**   6) What is the heading which is maintaining your 314 degree radial track?_____(30 pts)
      7) When **NAV 1 CDI** is **centered**, turn **LEFT** to a heading of "**270**"

      8) When wings are level, press "**P**" to pause the simulation
**   9) Record your:
           NAV 2 DME DIST_____(25 pts)
           NAV 1 DME DIST_____(20 pts)
           ALTITUDE_____(20 pts)
     10) Press "**P**" to continue the simulation

     11) Track inbound on the **SANTA CATALINA VOR 090** radial
     12) Set **DME** to "**NAV 1**"

"There! You're learning! Now that Mission Bay is useless, take advantage of Santa Catalina's thirty DME fix at HARBR intersection. Whoops! Hold that seven thousand feet! Don't get too excited at my praise, because it can turn to colorful negative metaphors without even breathing in between!"

San Diego to Los Angeles   65

Course change 3:

    1) Tune **NAV 2** to "**115.7**" (SLI)
    2) Set **NAV 2 OBS** to "**328**"

**   3) Write out the 'dit-dah' Morse code for **SEAL BEACH VOR** as you identify it_____(20 pts)

    4) When the **NAV 2 CDI** is **centered**, turn **RIGHT** to a heading of "**328**"
    5) Track inbound on the **SEAL BEACH VOR 148** radial

"Now once again, begins the time when you want to concentrate on your instrument approach procedure plate for Los Angeles. Sometimes, Los Angeles will just arbitrarily assign the ILS approach to you, but you never have to accept what they give you. In our case, I want you to practice a VOR approach, the one that's into runways two five left and right. So start briefing yourself on that approach plate."

    6) Set **DME** to "**NAV 2**"
    7) Tune **NAV 1** to "**113.6**" (LAX)
    8) Set **NAV 1 OBS** to "**248**"

Los Angeles Center:

    "**CESSNA 13MIKE, STATE YOUR INTENTIONS INTO LOS ANGELES INTERNATIONAL.**"

You:

    "**CESSNA 13MIKE WOULD LIKE TO EXECUTE THE VOR APPROACH RUNWAY TWO FIVE. REQUEST PERMISSION TO SWITCH OFF THE FREQUENCY FOR A SHORT TIME.**"

Los Angeles Center:

    "**CESSNA 13MIKE, APPROVED AS REQUESTED. REPORT BACK ON SO-CAL APPROACH ONE TWO FOUR POINT FIVE.**"

66   IFR Flights of "13MIKE"

You:

> "CESSNA 13MIKE. SO-CAL APPROACH ONE TWO FOUR POINT FIVE. SEE YOU!"

    9) Tune **COM** to "**135.65**" (Los Angeles ATIS)

> "LOS ANGELES INTERNATIONAL AIRPORT, INFORMATION SIERRA, TWO ONE FOUR ZERO ZULU WEATHER, ESTIMATED CEILING ONE THOUSAND FIVE HUNDRED BROKEN, THREE THOUSAND FIVE HUNDRED OVERCAST, VISIBILITY THREE IN HAZE. TEMPERATURE SIX TWO, DEWPOINT FOUR SIX. WIND TWO SEVEN ZERO AT EIGHT. ALTIMETER THREE ZERO ONE ONE. ILS RUNWAYS TWO FOUR LEFT AND TWO FIVE LEFT IN USE. LANDING RUNWAYS TWO FOUR AND TWO FIVE. RUNWAY TWO FOUR LEFT ILS DME IS OUT OF SERVICE. RUNWAY TWO FIVE RIGHT MIDDLE MARKER IS OUT OF SERVICE. ADVISE ON INITIAL CONTACT YOU HAVE INFORMATION SIERRA."

    10) Set **ALTIMETER**, set **HI**, and check **FUEL**
    11) Tune **COM** to "**124.5**" (South California Approach)

You:

> "SO-CAL APPROACH, CESSNA 9413MIKE IS TWO EIGHT MILES SOUTH OF SEAL BEACH AT SEVEN THOUSAND. I'D LIKE TO REQUEST A VOR APPROACH RUNWAY TWO FIVE LEFT OR RIGHT IF POSSIBLE. I HAVE INFORMATION SIERRA."

South California Approach:

> "CESSNA 9413MIKE, SO-CAL APPROACH, SQUAWK FIVE FIVE FIVE TWO, AND IDENT."

You:

> "CESSNA 13MIKE, SQUAWK FIVE FIVE FIVE TWO, AND IDENT."

San Diego to Los Angeles 67

        12) Set **XPDR** to "**5552**" (new assigned IFR code)
        13) Press the IDENT button (simulate)

South California Approach:

> "CESSNA 13MIKE, RADAR CONTACT. CLEARED FOR VOR RUNWAY TWO FIVE LEFT APPROACH. OVER SEAL BEACH, DESCEND AND MAINTAIN FOUR THOUSAND TO FITON INTERSECTION."

You:

> "CESSNA 13MIKE, VOR RUNWAY TWO FIVE LEFT. OVER SEAL BEACH, DESCEND AND MAINTAIN FOUR THOUSAND."

**   14) When the **NAV 2 DME DIST** reads "**20.0**", record:
            HEADING for centered NAV 2 CDI_____(30 pts)
            GROUND SPEED_____(25 pts)
            XPDR_____(20 pts)
            COM FREQUENCY_____(20 pts)

"WOW! I'd certainly say that you have your radio communications well under control! Do you know what the real key to good radio communications is? Self confidence! You are aware of what ATC wants and when they want it, and as long as you know where you are and where you want to go and do, simply tell them! Making requests, verifying information, changing plans, acknowledging instructions, they all spring from your awareness that you are absolutely in control of your airplane in the ATC system."

        15) When the **NAV 2 DME DIST** reads "**0.6**" [**1.3**], set **NAV 2 OBS** to "**326**"
        16) When the **NAV 2 DME DIST** reads "**0.4**" [**1.1**], track outbound on the **SEAL BEACH VOR 326** radial

"That's right! ATC didn't have to tell you what radial to pick, because it's the desired track on your instrument approach plate in a bold black line. Good thinking! That's using your personal heads up display!"

68   IFR Flights of "13MIKE"

Initial Approach Fix inbound:

1) Reduce power to about "**1700**" **[2000]** RPM
2) Establish an "**800**" **FPM** rate of descent
3) Begin to level off when the altimeter reads "**4100**" feet
4) Maintain "**4000**" feet
5) Hold power at about "**1700**" **[2000]** RPM to decelerate

6) When at **4000** feet, press "**P**" to pause the simulation

** 7) Record your:
   - NAV 2 DME DIST_____(25 pts)
   - RPM_____(20 pts)
   - AIRSPEED_____(20 pts)
   - HEADING_____(20 pts)
   - NAME of intersection you are heading to_____(15 pts)

8) Press "**P**" to continue the simulation

9) When the **NAV 2 DME DIST** reads "**9.0**", switch **DME** to "**NAV 1**"

"There is a mathematical method of leading the radial properly to Los Angeles' inbound track, but for right now, just watch the needle movement rate, and gauge when you need to lead it for eighty degrees worth of turn, right? That's the experience which you will build for yourself as you fly steadily in the instrument environment."

10) When the **NAV 1 CDI** is 1 dot **RIGHT** of center, turn **LEFT** to a heading of "**248**"
11) Track inbound on the **LOS ANGELES VOR 068** radial
12) Select **GEAR "DOWN"**
13) Set **CARB HEAT "ON"**

14) Press "**P**" to pause the simulation

** 15) Answer the following questions by referencing the VOR or TACAN or GPS RWY 25L/R instrument approach plate:

San Diego to Los Angeles

A. What five airports can be found on the south side of your inbound track and north of Victor 64? (Use L-3)
   1. _____
   2. _____
   3. _____
   4. _____
   5. _____ (25 pts)
B. What's the next altitude to descend to? _____ (5 pts)
C. What is the altitude restriction prior to reaching NOELE intersection? _____ (5 pts)
D. If you didn't have DME or a second VOR, what would be your minimum descent altitude for this approach? _____ (5 pts)
E. How many miles is it from NOELE to the missed approach point? _____ (5 pts)
F. If you didn't have DME, how would you know when you've arrived at the missed approach point with a 90 knot ground speed? _____ (5 pts)

16) Press "**P**" to continue the simulation

Final Approach to Landing:

1) Reduce power to about "**1500**" [**1800**] RPM
2) Descend to "**2000**" feet

South California Approach:

"CESSNA 13MIKE, CONTACT LOS ANGELES TOWER ONE TWO ZERO POINT NINER FIVE."

You:

"CESSNA 13MIKE, SWITCHING TOWER ONE TWO ZERO POINT NINER FIVE. THANKS FOR YOUR ASSISTANCE."

3) Tune **COM** to "**120.95**" (Los Angeles South Complex Tower)

IFR Flights of "13MIKE"

You:

> "LOS ANGELES TOWER, CESSNA 9413MIKE AT THIRTEEN DME INBOUND, VOR RUNWAY TWO FIVE APPROACH, FULL STOP. I HAVE INFORMATION SIERRA."

Los Angeles Tower:

> "CESSNA 9413MIKE, LOS ANGELES TOWER, RUNWAY TWO FIVE LEFT, CLEARED TO LAND. REPORT FREBY INTERSECTION."

You:

> "CESSNA 13MIKE WILL REPORT FREBY."

*"See that Maltese cross on the profile view of your instrument approach plate? That's at **FREBY** and it's the final approach fix, where your final approach course begins. For the Cessna 182 RG, the final approach course is flown at about one hundred knots. Keep your descents nice and relaxed. No rush to get down, yet you don't want to lollygag and muck about! I like your control on this approach!"*

    4) When the **NAV 1 DME DIST** reads "**7.5**", continue descent to "**620**" feet

You:

> "LOS ANGELES TOWER, CESSNA 13MIKE AT FREBY."

Los Angeles Tower:

> "CESSNA 13MIKE, REPORT FIELD IN SIGHT."

You:

> "ROGER, CESSNA 13MIKE WILL REPORT."

"In any instrument approach, be aware that there will be a disorienting transition from strictly instrument scanning to all of a sudden receiving visual inputs when you break out of the clouds. You have to be ready for the mental dizziness that can take place, and simply handle it within the circle of your self known limitations. Everybody experiences it, so it's not a macho thing to say you're not affected!"

San Diego to Los Angeles

** 5) Record your:
    COM FREQUENCY_____(15 pts)
    CARB HEAT_____(10 pts)
    AIRSPEED_____(10 pts)

6) When runway 25L is in sight, continue descent to "**540**" feet and reduce power to about "**1400**" [**1700**] RPM

You:

    "**LOS ANGELES TOWER, CESSNA 13MIKE HAS FIELD.**"

Los Angeles Tower:

    "**CESSNA 13MIKE, ROGER! WINDS ARE NOW TWO SEVEN ZERO AT ONE ONE.**"

"Pretty, huh? All right, just take a bit of power off, hold that nose up a tad to slow down from your hundred knots, so you can get some flaps in. Watch the VASI lights - makes you want to kiss them flying by when you see red over white, doesn't it? It doesn't give you that desire? Weirdo!"

7) When you have slowed to **90 knots**, set **FLAPS** to **first notch** (10 degrees)
8) Try to maintain a **400** ft per minute descent on your Vertical Speed Indicator (VSI)
9) Set **FLAPS** to **second notch** (20 degrees)
10) When altimeter reads "**300**" feet, set **FLAPS** to **third notch** (30 degrees)

11) Press "**P**" to pause the simulation

** 12) Record your:
    AIRSPEED_____(25 pts)
    VSI_____(25 pts)
    HEADING_____(25 pts)
    GEAR_____(15 pts)
    FLAPS_____(15 pts)
    NAV 1 DME_____(10 pts)
    STROBE_____(10 pts)

13) Press "**P**" to continue the simulation

72 IFR Flights of "13MIKE"

    14) Airspeed should be **70 knots**

"Super glue the approach end of the runway to the lower part of your windscreen, and hold that picture. That's a picture perfect transition to landing, and you are blowing my mind! Sweet and smooth!"

    15) When you are 10 to 20 feet off the runway, reduce power to about "**1000**" RPM and start to slowly pitch the nose of the aircraft up to slow your descent and establish a touchdown attitude

    16) When you are five feet off the runway, hold the nose of the aircraft up and allow the airspeed to **SLOWLY** bleed off. Your aircraft will **settle** onto the runway while you follow the centerline

    17) After touchdown, reduce power to **600 RPM**

    18) Apply the brakes

Los Angeles Tower:

> "CESSNA 13MIKE, TURN LEFT FIRST INTERSECTION, HIGH SPEED TWO ZERO GOLF. CONTACT GROUND EXITING THE RUNWAY."

You:

> "CESSNA 13MIKE, FIRST INTERSECTION."

    19) Taxi the aircraft off the active runway to the **LEFT**

    20) When the aircraft has stopped, set **CARB HEAT** to "**OFF**"

    21) Set **FLAPS** to "**0**"

"Didn't Frank Sinatra sing a song about leaving his heart in Los Angeles or something? Tony Bennett? You're kidding! And San Francisco? What'd he have against Los Angeles? Well, I'm sure I'm not wrong now - Ground is one two one point seven five, and I'll bet they park us at the Imperial Terminal!"

    22) Tune **COM** to "**121.75**" (Los Angeles South Complex Ground)

San Diego to Los Angeles

You:

> "LOS ANGELES GROUND, CESSNA 9413MIKE ON TWO ZERO GOLF HIGH SPEED FOR TAXI."

Los Angeles Ground:

> "CESSNA 9413MIKE, LOS ANGELES GROUND, CONTINUE STRAIGHT AHEAD TO THE GENERAL AVIATION RAMP."

"Doggone it!"

You:

> "CESSNA 13MIKE, THANK YOU. STRAIGHT AHEAD GENERAL AVIATION RAMP."

"Do you realize what you've accomplished this flight? A standard instrument departure, ending up with a VOR approach into one of the busiest airports in the nation! I applaud you! Your radio discipline made me want to cry a few times - from joy, not tribulation! Take a well deserved break!"

**   23) Record the **TIME**_____(5 pts)

TOTAL POINTS POSSIBLE FOR THIS FLIGHT IS __765__

74 IFR Flights of "13MIKE"

Flight Scenario Three

Kankakee to Champaign

(Chicago Area - estimated flying time 45 minutes)

Have you had enough of the no-see-ums? Okay, let's do a see-um takeoff with a no-see-um approach. Sound good? Let's do it! We'll depart Greater Kankakee Airport, in the northeast part of Illinois, VFR. We will get a pop up IFR clearance, when the weather starts to close in, and continue the flight under no-see-um rules to Willard-Champaign Airport, in the central east part of Illinois. Before we start, we need to do our flight plan, because we need to give this information to FSS. After we do the flight plan, I'm going to hand you over to Professor Calfior so he can take you through the weather brief and filing of your flight plan. I will step you through the setup phase. That's where we set in those nasty clouds! Professor Calfior will then leap into the right seat (ouch) and assist you through the yuk! Listen to what Professor Calfior has to say about flying techniques. He is not only trying to help you obtain the best possible score but he also has a wealth of information and trivia. Some of his jokes are rather good, if I do say so myself!

Okay, let's look at our route of flight and get smart on all the specifics associated with this flight.

FLIGHT PLAN -

This route of flight follows well established departure, climb, cruise, descent, and landing procedures. You will depart Greater Kankakee Airport (**Airport diagram in Appendix C3**) on runway 34, and the departure time will be as we thought, 1300 Zulu. This will start off on a VFR flight plan, but the weather further south will be deteriorating enough to where it becomes necessary to file a pop up IFR flight plan.

The departure out of Kankakee will be a left crosswind departure to Roberts VOR, climbing to and maintaining 4500 feet. Your true airspeed is 120 knots. About 10 miles or so short of Roberts VOR, you will cancel your VFR flight plan and file an IFR one with Kankakee Radio.

Since Roberts VOR is the initial approach fix for the VOR/DME RWY 22R instrument approach into Willard-Champaign Airport (**Appendix C3**), you will be filing to VINEY intersection. The intent is to circle to land on runway 32L. Radar vectors might be given by Champaign Approach Control that are slightly different, so be ready for that eventuality.

You will be on the final approach course inbound on Champaign VOR's 028 radial, having descended to 2400 feet, where you will remain until crossing STADI intersection at 6 DME, which is the final approach fix. Champaign Tower should then pick you up. Then with DME capability, you will descend to 1400 feet by the 2.7 DME fix, which is called a stepdown fix. You can then descend further to a minimum descent altitude of 1160 feet which is a circling altitude minimum.

With the weather as expected, the field will come into sight before arriving at Champaign VOR. For landing on runway 32L, you will turn left to circle, in order to set up what looks like a right base, remaining at 1160 feet until your turn to final. Willard-Champaign's airport diagram is in **Appendix C3**. The weather being as it is, use Bloomington-Normal Airport as the alternate. You've shown how fuel on board is 6 hours and enroute time is about 50 minutes, so you're fat.

Kankakee to Champaign

FILLING OUT THE FLIGHT PLAN -

Fill out the following Flight Plan completely, carefully paying attention to your route of flight, remembering that it's starting out as a VFR flight plan. Trace out your original route using the IFR low altitude enroute chart L-23 given to you in **Appendix B3**.

FLIGHT PLAN

| 1. TYPE
☐ IFR
☐ VFR
☐ DVFR | 2. AIRCRAFT IDENTIFICATION | 3. AIRCRAFT TYPE/ SPECIAL EQUIPMENT | 4. TRUE AIRSPEED

KNOTS | 5. DEPARTURE POINT | 6. DEPARTURE TIME
PROPOSED (Z) / ACTUAL (Z) | 7. CRUISING ALTITUDE |

8. ROUTE OF FLIGHT

| 9. DESTINATION (Name of airport and city) | 10. EST. TIME ENROUTE
HOURS / MINUTES | 11. REMARKS |

| 12. FUEL ON BOARD
HOURS / MINUTES | 13. ALTERNATE AIRPORT(S) | 14. PILOT'S NAME, ADDRESS, TELEPHONE NO. AND AIRCRAFT HOME BASE | 15. NO. ABOARD |

16. COLOR OF AIRCRAFT

CLOSE FLIGHT PLAN WITH _____ FSS

Now answer these questions from your flight plan and enroute chart.

** a) What is in block 8, Route of Flight, of your flight plan?
_____(10 pts)

** b) The length of Greater Kankakee Airport's longest runway is what?
_____(10 pts)

** c) If intercepting NEWTT intersection to the west of Kankakee VOR, what is the remaining distance to Willard-Champaign Airport along Victor 191 and Victor 429? _____(10 pts)

** d) Around Roberts VOR, what is Chicago Center's sector name and frequency? _____(10 pts)

** e) What are the geographical coordinates of Champaign VOR?
_____(10 pts)

78   IFR Flights of "13MIKE"

"There's nothing like a good morning start to a day with a solid breakfast and another cross country flight in our buddy, 13MIKE! You've worked on all the preflight planning stuff already, and from what weather we know, it might get a little bit soupy heading south. But I purposely want you to experience the need to acquire an IFR clearance while enroute. So we'll depart here VFR and take it as far as we can.

Let me say a few things about the flight plan form itself. Do you see number five - Departure Point? And number nine - Destination? Because they're there, it won't be necessary to repeat them in the number eight block - Route of Flight. The Route of Flight block should have the components of your enroute portion of flight, but minus the departure and destination. This is so that blocks five, eight, and nine are then the whole cross country unit. Prima, hey!

Something else that comes to my mind concerns going direct to a point or navaid or place. Many times you'll notice that pilots put a 'D' with a horizontal arrow through it, in order to show it's a direct route. There's nothing wrong with that, but it really is not necessary at all! Because if nothing is shown, then it must be direct. If you are taking a Victor airway to a point, navaid or place, then 'V__' would be written before its designation. Without that Victor series of letters and numbers, the only other option is that it's direct! Make sense? Small point, but I'm allowed to have pet peeves if I want them, and I've got them!

The last time I was in Kankakee, I went north. So I'm excited to be with you heading south in the direction of the Confederacy! Why don't you get what weather we need, and file to depart out of Kankakee VFR. It's a gorgeous day! Eight o'clock will be as good a time as any to split out of here."

WEATHER BRIEF

You:

"Good morning to you! May I please have a weather briefing for a VFR cross country flight? Tail number is November 9413MIKE, and it's a Cessna 182 RG. Leaving Kankakee Airport, with an estimated time of departure in about an hour, nah - make it two from now. My cruise altitude will be four thousand five hundred feet. I'll be going by way of Roberts VOR to Willard-Champaign Airport. ETE will be one hour. I'm a private pilot with an instrument rating."

Kankakee FSS:

"Convective Sigmet One Central is in effect for thunderstorms one hundred miles either side of a line from twenty nautical miles west of South Bend to Terre Haute, moving east northeast at fifteen knots.

A low pressure center over central Indiana with a cold front extends south from that low.

Currently at Kankakee, there is an estimated ceiling eight thousand overcast, visibility one zero, temperature three eight, wind three three zero at one zero, altimeter two niner eight four.

Enroute, clouds are generally three thousand five hundred scattered, with ceiling eight thousand overcast.

Champaign is reporting an estimated ceiling five thousand broken, niner thousand overcast, visibility one five, temperature four zero, wind three one zero at one two.

Forecast for Kankakee at one three zero zero Zulu is ceiling seven thousand overcast, unrestricted visibility.

Enroute, ceilings are forecast five thousand broken.

Champaign's terminal forecast for one four zero zero Zulu is four thousand thin broken, ceiling eight thousand overcast, visibility unrestricted, wind three two zero at eight.

Let's see! You're at four thousand five hundred, so interpolating winds aloft, expect wind three five zero at two zero.

There are no NOTAMs D or L relevant to your flight.

That about wraps up the information I have for you! Any questions you have, or anything I can do for you?"

80   IFR Flights of "13MIKE"

FILING THE FLIGHT PLAN -

You:

"I might as well file now. Wish I could go right now, but my instructor has a lot of wisdom, as he calls it, to bless my aviation oriented brain with!"

Kankakee FSS:

"Okay! My fingers are ready to type, so give me your plan!"

You:

"VFR, November 9413MIKE, Cessna 182 RG - slash A, one twenty true, Departure - IKK, thirteen hundred Zulu, four thousand five hundred feet, Route - Roberts VOR (that's RBS), Destination - Champaign (CMI). ETE zero plus fifty. Fuel on board six plus no minutes. Alternate - Bloomington Normal Airport, [YOUR NAME - CONTACT PHONE NUMBER - HOME BASE], two on board, Red over white."

Kankakee FSS:

"Good! It's on file. Learn good wisdom! For enroute weather pilot reports, Flight Watch one two two point zero. Enjoy the trip!"

You:

"Thanks! See you later!"

SETUP

Aircraft:
   1) Choose "**Cessna Skylane RG**"

Weather:
   Winds
   1) Set Surface winds "**DEPTH**" to "**1200**"
   2) Set Surface winds "**DIR**" to "**310**"

3) Set Surface winds "**SPEED**" to "**10**"
4) Set Surface winds "**TURBULENCE**" to "**1**"
5) Set Level 1 "**TOPS**" to "**5500**"
6) Set Level 1 "**BASE**" to "**1850**"
7) Set Level 1 "**DIR**" to "**355**"
8) Set Level 1 "**SPEED**" to "**22**"
9) Set Level 1 "**TURBULENCE**" to "**2**"

Clouds
1) Set Bottom Level - **TOPS** to "**9000**"
2) Set Bottom Level - **BASE** to "**8000**"
3) Set Bottom Level - **COVER** to "**overcast**"

Aircraft Position:
1) "**NORTH**" to "**16845.3988**" — [N041° 04' 00.4519]
2) "**EAST**" to "**16596.3563**" — [W087° 51' 09.1356]
3) "**ALTITUDE**" to "**629**" — [0]
4) "**HEADING**" to "**125**"

note: At this point you may wish to save this setup for future use.

PREFLIGHT

note: Set **ZOOM** to "**1.0**"
Set **TIME** to "**08:00**"

"I've been reading some Louis L'Amour books where I've picked up on some common sayings which I feel pertain to the perspective of an instrument pilot! Here's one! Whenever you do acquire your instrument rating, I'd say you're at the place where:
1. 'You've been up the creek and over the mountain.'
There's a comfort in piloting an aircraft with capable instrument trained pilots, because no matter what the weather (to a point), you do what's necessary to work around it, in it, or through it. To me, this statement is what epitomizes the skill and drive of any serious instrument pilot.

2. 'You ever need help, you talk to that person there. If I was heading into grief, there's no person I'd rather have riding point for me. When that person wants to go somewhere and there ain't no hole, he just naturally makes himself one.'

Let's get some preliminary information from UNICOM on one two three point zero before we start too deeply into this wonderful excursion to Champaign!"

Instruments:

1) Tune **COM** to "**123.0**" (Kankakee UNICOM)

You:

"KANKAKEE UNICOM, CESSNA 9413MIKE IS AT THE RAMP. WOULD YOU LAY ON ME WHAT THE WINDS, RUNWAY IN USE, AND ALTIMETER SETTING IS, IF YOU DON'T MIND?"

Kankakee UNICOM:

"CESSNA 9413MIKE, WIND THREE ONE ZERO AT ONE ZERO, TAKEOFFS AND LANDINGS ARE ON RUNWAY THREE FOUR, AND THE ALTIMETER SETTING IS TWO NINER EIGHT FIVE."

2) Set "**Altimeter**" and "**Heading Indicator**"
3) Set **XPDR** to "**1200**" (VFR code)
4) Tune **NAV 1** to "**116.8**" (RBS)
5) Set **NAV 1 OBS** to a **centered** needle **TO** the station

"This is going to be another fantastic training hop for you! I'm wanting you to acquire a pop up IFR clearance when you feel that VFR conditions can no longer be met. I also want to do another VOR approach, but with a circle to land, so you can see what it takes to fly one of those. Therefore, I've chosen the VOR DME runway two two Right approach into Champaign, and you'll notice that the inbound track is two zero eight. So set up your NAV 2 to Champaign and that inbound track. Oh yeah! Good job on that VFR transponder code!"

Kankakee to Champaign

6) Tune **NAV 2** to "110.0" (CMI)
7) Set **NAV 2 OBS** to "208"
8) Set the **DME** to "NAV 1" and "DIST"
9) Check **CARB HEAT** is "OFF"
10) Check **GEAR** "DOWN"
11) Turn **STROBE** "ON"
12) Check **LIGHTS** are "OFF"

"Rid'em cowboy! Runway three four is what the dude said - or was it a dudess? Anyway, tell UNICOM we're taxiing and meanwhile, we'll watch out for deer and waterfowl which supposedly is in the vicinity of the airport!"

You:

"KANKAKEE UNICOM, CESSNA 13MIKE WILL BE TAXIING TO RUNWAY THREE FOUR FOR DEPARTURE, VFR."

Kankakee UNICOM:

"CESSNA 13MIKE, ROGER!"

TAXI -

"The approach end of runway three four is about ten o'clock, but we'll have to back taxi down runway three four to get to its runup area. Take a look at the Airport Diagram and notice how, from the terminal, we taxi to the left and intersect the runway about a third of the way down. We could do an intersection takeoff, and nobody would care, but for your experience, a back taxi will be marvelous."

1) Taxi to just short of runway 34 and brake to a stop

"Now look for traffic off of three four. Right! I don't see any either! So let's tell traffic that we're back taxiing down runway three four to the runup area."

84   IFR Flights of "13MIKE"

You:

"KANKAKEE TRAFFIC, CESSNA 13MIKE IS BACK TAXIING DOWN TO THE APPROACH END OF RUNWAY THREE FOUR."

"Okay! Go for it"

    2) Taxi down runway 34 to the right

"Now pull off the runway to the right there, and spin around one hundred and eighty degrees, and hold short on a heading of zero seven zero. Tell traffic you're clear."

You:

**

"KANKAKEE TRAFFIC, CESSNA 13MIKE CLEAR OF THREE FOUR."

"Here's a couple of quiz questions to familiarize you with the Airport Diagram.
1. What is the elevation of the ground where you're parked?
   _____*(5 pts)*
2. What is the width of runway 34?_____*(5 pts)*
3. Can Kankakee be used as an alternate airport in the IFR environment? (check notes below minimums section)_____*(5 pts)*
4. What are the intensity of the runway lights on 34? Low, Medium, or High?_____*(5 pts)*
5. What is the elevation at Greater Kankakee Airport?_____*(5 pts)*
6. What is the runway length of 34?_____*(5 pts)*
Great! Do what checks you need like the runup to check the magnetos, and we'll be soaring aloft in no time at all!"

RUNUP -

    3) Set brake (hold down to prevent aircraft from moving)
    4) Advance power to about "**2000**" RPM
**   5) Select **CARB HEAT "ON"**, record RPM drop_____*(5 pts)*
    6) Select **CARB HEAT "OFF"**
**   7) Select "**LEFT**" Mag, record RPM drop_____*(5 pts)*
    8) Select "**BOTH**" Mags

Kankakee to Champaign

**
       9) Select "**RIGHT**" Mag, record RPM drop_____(5 pts)
     10) Select "**BOTH**" Mags
     11) Reduce power to **idle**
     12) Set **FLAPS** to **first notch** (10 degrees takeoff configuration)

"Wait! Wait! My previous statement about soaring aloft was relatively speaking! We first need to activate our VFR flight plan, so that we are nestled in the ever loving arms of the ATC people concerned about our welfare. And that's good! Since the low altitude enroute chart shows a shadow box around Kankakee, FSS frequency will be one two two point two. Yup!"

     13) Tune **COM** to "**122.2**" (Kankakee Radio)

You:

    "**KANKAKEE RADIO, CESSNA 9413MIKE, ONE TWO TWO POINT TWO.**"

Kankakee Radio:

    "**CESSNA 9413MIKE, KANKAKEE RADIO, GO AHEAD.**"

You:

    "**KANKAKEE RADIO, CESSNA 13MIKE WOULD LIKE TO ACTIVATE ITS VFR FLIGHT PLAN TO WILLARD AIRPORT, CHAMPAIGN, ILLINOIS, PLEASE.**"

Kankakee Radio:

    "**CESSNA 13MIKE, FLIGHT PLAN ACTIVATED AT ZERO EIGHT. FOR ADDITIONAL ENROUTE WEATHER, FLIGHT WATCH ONE TWO TWO POINT ZERO.**"

You:

    "**KANKAKEE RADIO, ROGER.**"

     14) Tune **COM** to "**123.0**" (Kankakee UNICOM)

86 IFR Flights of "13MIKE"

"Boy, I've got to put a leash on you! I take these walks with my dog, Lindy, and pull, pull, pull, pull, pull! I applaud your enthusiasm! And to honor your excitement and gusto, don't let me stop you! Go for it! Left downwind departure! And because you're a veteran of VFR departures, I expect it to be perfectly executed! How's that for pressure on an instructional flight, huh?"

You:

"KANKAKEE TRAFFIC, CESSNA 13MIKE IS TAKING THE ACTIVE, RUNWAY THREE FOUR, FOR A LEFT DOWNWIND DEPARTURE."

FLIGHT

Takeoff:

"Never ever ever skip your last minute pre-takeoff checks, such as fuel, the takeoff trim setting, and green oil temperature and pressure, and flaps at ten. Something else to be aware of is when you go full power, make sure you're getting the RPMs you expect, such as in our case, twenty three hundred to twenty five hundred RPM. If you don't, then abort the takeoff because your engine is not producing the power it's supposed to according to the Operating Manual."

1) Record TIME_____
2) Release brakes and taxi onto runway 34
3) Advance power to "**FULL**"
4) Maintain centerline of runway
5) At **50 knots** airspeed, lift nose wheel off runway
6) At **70 knots,** ease back on the yoke to establish a 10 degree pitch up attitude
7) Maintain a climb **AIRSPEED** of **80 knots**
8) Raise **Gear** when there is no more runway to land on
9) At "**500**" feet above the ground, raise the **FLAPS** to "**0**"

Kankakee to Champaign

10) At "**700**" feet above the ground, begin a **LEFT** "**90**" degree CROSSWIND turn (standard rate)
11) Reduce power to about "**2300**" RPM at "**1000**" feet above the ground (AGL)
12) With wings level, check your airspace and begin another **LEFT** "**90**" degree turn to the **LEFT** DOWNWIND

"You know, the tendency in these turns is to let the nose drop, when in fact, some additional nose up pressure needs to be applied. That's because in the turn, some vertical lift is becoming horizontal lift (which is what allows you to turn), so you need to increase your nose attitude (angle of attack) to make up for the lost vertical lift."

Pattern Departure:

1) Hold the downwind course until abeam the approach end of Runway 34
2) When abeam the approach end of Runway 34, reset **NAV 1 OBS** to a **centered** needle **TO** the station
3) Turn to the OBS course, and track inbound on the **ROBERTS VOR** radial

4) When wings are level, press "**P**" to pause the simulation

** 5) Record your:

HEADING_____	(25 pts)
ALTITUDE_____	(25 pts)
NAV 1 DME DIST_____	(25 pts)
AIRSPEED_____	(20 pts)
RPM _____	(20 pts)
GEAR _____	(15 pts)
FLAPS_____	(15 pts)
XPDR _____	(10 pts)
COM FREQUENCY_____	(10 pts)

6) Press "**P**" to continue the simulation

88 IFR Flights of "13MIKE"

*"That was incredible! You must have flown all twelve cross countries of '13MIKE's' first book! We're VFR, so keep your head moving, looking for traffic, yet enjoy the scenery. One of the ten commandments for safe flying is '**Thou shalt cast thine eyes to thy right and to thy left as thou passeth through the firmament, lest thy fellow pilots bring flowers to thy widow and comfort her in other ways.**'! The only thing necessary now is a courtesy move. Let traffic know we're out of anybody's way!"*

You: **"KANKAKEE TRAFFIC, CESSNA 13MIKE IS DEPARTING THE AREA."**

Level off:

1) Begin to level off when the altimeter reads **"4400"** feet
2) Maintain **"4500"** feet
3) Hold the climb power setting of about **"2300"** RPM

"As we expected, it does have an appearance of being somewhat green pea soupier towards the south there, doesn't it? This is perfect for what I have in mind for your training. We're still safe, but watch how sneakily the weather can try to put you into a corner of desperation unless you're watching for it."

** 4) When the NAV 1 DME DIST reads **"17.0"**, record your ground speed_____(20 pts)

5) Press **"P"** to pause the simulation

** 6) Record your:
    HEADING with centered NAV 1 CDI_____(30 pts)
    AIRSPEED_____(25 pts)
    ALTITUDE_____(20 pts)
    RPM _____(10 pts)

7) Press **"P"** to continue the simulation

Kankakee to Champaign

"I agree! Enough is enough. We're thirteen DME north of Roberts, and it's pretty solid down below just past Roberts VOR, so let's cancel VFR and request an IFR clearance to finish out this flight. It always blesses me to fly and see weather from this perspective. We're a fortunate breed of people, you know that? One two two point zero is what Kankakee told us."

    8) Tune **COM** to "**122.0**" (Kankakee Radio)

You:

    "KANKAKEE RADIO, CESSNA 9413MIKE ON ONE TWO TWO POINT ZERO."

Kankakee Radio:

    "CESSNA 9413MIKE, KANKAKEE RADIO, GO AHEAD."

You:

    "KANKAKEE RADIO, CESSNA 13MIKE WOULD LIKE TO CLOSE ITS VFR FLIGHT PLAN, AND FILE A POP UP IFR FLIGHT PLAN TO WILLARD - CHAMPAIGN AIRPORT. CURRENTLY, I'M ONE TWO MILES NORTH OF ROBERTS VOR."

Kankakee Radio:

    "CESSNA 13MIKE, VFR FLIGHT PLAN IS CLOSED. IS THERE A DIFFERENT ROUTING YOU'D LIKE?"

You:

    "CESSNA 13MIKE, YES! HERE'S MY IFR FLIGHT PLAN REQUEST. IFR, CURRENT POSITION ROBERTS ZERO THREE ZERO RADIAL, ONE TWO DME DIRECT TO RBS, DIRECT VINEY, DESTINATION WILLARD - CHAMPAIGN, CMI. ETE ZERO PLUS THIRTY."

IFR Flights of "13MIKE"

Kankakee Radio:

> "CESSNA 13MIKE, MAINTAIN CURRENT POSITION NORTH OF ROBERTS WHILE WE PICK UP A CLEARANCE FROM CHICAGO CENTER."

You:

> "CESSNA 13MIKE, ROGER!"

"That means we can keep approaching Roberts, and I don't think it'll take long for them to come back. Meanwhile, I heard this joke the other day about a flea who wanted to be a dog - and he saw this - durn it! That's us!"

Kankakee Radio:

> "CESSNA 13MIKE, KANKAKEE RADIO, I HAVE YOUR IFR CLEARANCE."

You:

> "KANKAKEE RADIO, CESSNA 13MIKE IS READY TO COPY."

Kankakee Radio:

> "ATC CLEARS CESSNA 9413MIKE TO WILLARD, CHAMPAIGN AS FILED. MAINTAIN FOUR THOUSAND FIVE HUNDRED. CONTACT CHAMPAIGN APPROACH FREQUENCY ONE TWO ONE POINT THREE FIVE. SQUAWK FOUR FIVE SIX TWO. OVER."

You:

> "CESSNA 9413MIKE CLEARED CHAMPAIGN AS FILED. MAINTAIN FOUR THOUSAND FIVE HUNDRED. APPROACH ONE TWO ONE POINT THREE FIVE, SQUAWK FOUR FIVE SIX TWO."

Kankakee Radio:

> "CESSNA 13MIKE, READBACK CORRECT."

You:

> "KANKAKEE RADIO, CESSNA 13MIKE, THANKS FOR YOUR HELP. I'M SWITCHING APPROACH."

    9) Set **XPDR** to "**4562**"
    10) Tune **COM** to "**121.35**" (Champaign Approach)

You:

> "CHAMPAIGN APPROACH, CESSNA 9413MIKE IS WITH YOU, FOUR THOUSAND FIVE HUNDRED, IFR WILLARD, CHAMPAIGN."

Champaign Approach:

> "CESSNA 9413MIKE, CHAMPAIGN APPROACH, IDENT."

You:

> "CESSNA 13MIKE, IDENT."

    11) Press the IDENT button (simulate)

Champaign Approach:

> "CESSNA 9413MIKE, CHAMPAIGN APPROACH, RADAR CONTACT. CLEARED DIRECT ROBERTS, VICTOR FOUR TWENTY NINE. EXPECT VECTORS VOR DME RUNWAY TWO TWO RIGHT APPROACH."

You:

> "CHAMPAIGN APPROACH, CESSNA 9413MIKE, OVER ROBERTS, OUTBOUND VICTOR FOUR TWENTY NINE FOR VECTORS VOR DME TWO TWO RIGHT. MAINTAIN FOUR THOUSAND FIVE HUNDRED."

"Doesn't it bring tears to your eyes to realize how easy all that was? Is there any Kleenex handy? Now check your low altitude enroute chart, so you have the macro picture of what you're doing. Also start dragging out the VOR DME approach into runway two two. Study it as you're flying, get a feel for it, and at the same time, start transitioning to an instrument scan frame of mind. Never mind the flea!"

92   IFR Flights of "13MIKE"

Course change:

1) When the **DME** on **NAV 1** reads "**0.4**" **[0.6]**, turn **LEFT** to a heading of "**186**"
2) Set **NAV 1 OBS** to "**186**"

3) Press "**P**" to pause the simulation

Weather:

Winds

a) Set Surface winds "**TURBULENCE**" to "**0**"
b) Set Level 1 "**TURBULENCE**" to "**1**"

Clouds

a) Set Bottom Level - **TOPS** to "**3000**"
b) Set Bottom Level - **BASE** to "**2000**"
c) Set Thunderstorm - **TOPS** to "**9000**"
d) Set Thunderstorm - **BASE** to "**3500**"
e) Set Thunderstorm - **COVERAGE** to "**widely scattered**"

4) Press "**P**" to continue the simulation

Enroute Intersection:

1) Track outbound on the **ROBERTS VOR 186** radial that your **NAV 1 OBI** is displaying

**

"Looking at the approach plate for the VOR DME runway two two Right approach, what potential initial approach fix did we just pass? _____(5 pts)
How many other initial approach fixes does this approach have anyway? Look carefully, because it's pretty tricky!_____(5 pts)
Nice thunderstorms, huh? Why not flip over to ATIS on one two four point eight five so we get a feel for whether runway three two is still the wind preferred runway? Whoa! Get permission from Approach."

Kankakee to Champaign

You:

"CHAMPAIGN APPROACH, CESSNA 9413MIKE WOULD LIKE TO SWITCH OFF THE FREQUENCY FOR A MOMENT."

Champaign Approach:

"CESSNA 9413MIKE, APPROVED AS REQUESTED. REPORT BACK ON."

You:

"CESSNA 13MIKE."

    2) Tune **COM** to "**124.85**" (Champaign ATIS)

"WILLARD - CHAMPAIGN AIRPORT, INFORMATION HOTEL, ONE TWO FIVE FIVE ZULU WEATHER, MEASURED CEILING TWO THOUSAND OVERCAST, VISIBILITY ONE ZERO, TEMPERATURE FOUR TWO, DEWPOINT THREE THREE, WIND THREE THREE ZERO AT ONE TWO. ALTIMETER TWO NINER EIGHT SIX. ILS RUNWAY THREE TWO LEFT IN USE. LANDING AND DEPARTING RUNWAY THREE TWO LEFT. CONTACT CHAMPAIGN TOWER ON ONE TWO ZERO POINT FOUR. ADVISE ON INITIAL CONTACT YOU HAVE INFORMATION HOTEL."

"Marvelous! Our circling plans are going to work! Check your instruments, get back to Approach, strap in, and put on your 13MIKE sweat band because you're going to work!"

    3) Set **ALTIMETER,** set **HI,** and check **FUEL**
    4) Tune **COM** to "**121.35**" (Champaign Approach)

You:

"CHAMPAIGN APPROACH, CESSNA 9413MIKE IS BACK WITH YOU."

Champaign Approach:

> "CESSNA 9413MIKE, ROGER."

**   5) When NAV 1 DME DIST reads "**10.5**", record:
HEADING for centered NAV 1 CDI_____(30 pts)
6) When the **DME** on **NAV 1** reads "**11.5**":

Champaign Approach:

> "CESSNA 9413MIKE, CHAMPAIGN APPROACH, TURN LEFT HEADING ONE FOUR FIVE. DESCEND AND MAINTAIN TWO THOUSAND FOUR HUNDRED."

You:

> "CESSNA 9413MIKE, LEFT TO ONE FOUR FIVE. DESCEND AND MAINTAIN TWO THOUSAND FOUR HUNDRED."

    7) Turn left to a heading of "**145**"
    8) Set **DME** to "**NAV 2**"

Enroute Descent:

    1) Reduce power to about "**1700**" **[2100]** RPM
    2) Descend to and maintain "**2400**" feet

"We're training, right? It's tempting to reset your NAV 1 to the Champaign approach frequency, but I want you to hold it on the NAV 2. Experience the need to execute an instrument approach using the bottom navaid. Scan pattern doesn't change any, but it'll feel weird until your eyes call it home! This will be some good in cloud weather flying!"

Champaign Approach:

> "CESSNA 9413MIKE, CHAMPAIGN APPROACH, CLEARED VOR DME RUNWAY TWO TWO RIGHT APPROACH, CIRCLE TO RUNWAY THREE TWO LEFT."

Kankakee to Champaign

You:

"CESSNA 9413MIKE IS CLEARED VOR DME RUNWAY TWO TWO RIGHT, CIRCLE TO RUNWAY THREE TWO LEFT."

3) When the **NAV 2 CDI** needle is 1 dot **LEFT** of center, start your **RIGHT** turn to a heading of **"208"**
4) Track inbound on the **CHAMPAIGN VOR 028** radial
5) When passing **"2500"** feet, begin level off, keeping power at about **"1700"** **[2100]** RPM

"Good thinking! That'll reduce your airspeed to about one hundred and ten knots or so, and I liked your pre-thought out turn to the inbound track. The orchestra will begin to play when you pop out of the clouds and the field is in sight! William Tell Overture - just get that picture in your sonic mind!"

6) Press **"P"** to pause the simulation

** 7) Answer the following from the VOR/DME RWY 22R approach plate:
   - **A.** At what DME is the arcing part of the procedure? _____(5 pts)
   - **B.** When can you leave 2400 feet?_____(5 pts)
   - **C.** Where is the missed approach point at? _____(5 pts)
   - **D.** If you didn't sight the field until right at the missed approach point, would you turn **LEFT** or **RIGHT** to begin circling?_____(5 pts)
   - **E.** What is the airport elevation?_____(5 pts)
   - **F.** At the 2.7 DME fix, what altitude should you be at if the altimeter setting you have is not Champaign's, but Decatur's?_____(5 pts)
   - **G.** If your approach speed is 90 knots, what is the minimum descent altitude for your circling approach with Champaign's altimeter setting?_____(5 pts)

8) Press **"P"** to continue the simulation

3

VOR Approach Inbound:

1) When the **NAV 2 DME DIST** reads "**9.0**", GEAR "**DOWN**"
2) Reduce power to about "**1600**" **[2000]** RPM
3) Set **CARB HEAT** "**ON**"

4) When the NAV 2 DME DIST reads "**7.5**", press "**P**" to pause the simulation

** 5) Record your:
    HEADING for a centered NAV 2 CDI_____(30 pts)
    ALTITUDE_____(25 pts)
    AIRSPEED_____(20 pts)
    XPDR _____(15 pts)
    GEAR _____(15 pts)
    CARB HEAT_____(15 pts)
    COM FREQUENCY_____(10 pts)

6) Press "**P**" to continue the simulation

Champaign Approach:

"CESSNA 9413MIKE, CHAMPAIGN APPROACH, CONTACT CHAMPAIGN TOWER ONE TWO ZERO POINT FOUR. GOOD DAY!"

You:

"CESSNA 9413MIKE, TOWER ONE TWO ZERO FOUR. THANKS!"

7) Tune **COM** to "**120.4**" (Champaign Tower)

You:

"CHAMPAIGN TOWER, CESSNA 9413MIKE IS SEVEN MILES INBOUND ON VOR DME RUNWAY TWO TWO RIGHT, CIRCLE TO LAND THREE TWO LEFT. FULL STOP WITH INFORMATION HOTEL."

Champaign Tower:

> "CESSNA 9413MIKE, CHAMPAIGN TOWER, REPORT FIELD IN SIGHT."

You:

> "CESSNA 9413MIKE WILL REPORT FIELD IN SIGHT."

    8) When the **NAV 2 DME DIST** reads "**6.0**", reduce power to about "**1500**" **[1900] RPM**
    9) Descend to and maintain "**1400**" feet

"In three point three miles, you need to lose one thousand feet of altitude. At one hundred knots, about one and a half miles per minute, that means a rate of descent of about five hundred feet per minute. It's nice to be there a little early, so make it six to seven hundred feet per minute. See the thinking that goes along with these approaches?"

    10) When airport environment is in sight:

"Dah dah dah dah dah dah dah - DAH DAH - KABOOM! Isn't it one of the prettiest sights you've seen? This is what instrument flying is all about - it never gets old for me! The end is always so exciting! Did you like my William Tell Overture solo?"

You:

> "CHAMPAIGN TOWER, CESSNA 9413MIKE HAS FIELD IN SIGHT."

Champaign Tower:

> "CESSNA 13MIKE, REPORT ONE MILE RIGHT BASE RUNWAY THREE TWO LEFT."

You:

> "CESSNA 13MIKE WILL REPORT ONE MILE RIGHT BASE, THREE TWO LEFT."

11) Continue inbound until **NAV 2 DME DIST** reads "**2.7**"

"Great judgment on that one! No need to make a great big wide circle. I see you're trying to set it up to look as normal to a visual maneuver as possible. Now, I'm going to shut up to the best of my ability and let you solo your way into the landing. I feel confident of your skills from all that I've seen to date!"

Circle to land:

1) Circle **LEFT** for a setup to final on Runway 32
2) Descend to and maintain "**1160**" feet
3) When you have slowed to **90 knots**, set **FLAPS** to **first notch** (10 degrees)
4) When runway 32's approach lights are at your 2 o'clock position, set **FLAPS** to **second notch** (20 degrees)

You:

"CHAMPAIGN TOWER, CESSNA 13MIKE ONE MILE RIGHT BASE, RUNWAY THREE TWO LEFT."

Champaign Tower:

"CESSNA 13MIKE, CHAMPAIGN TOWER, RUNWAY THREE TWO LEFT, CLEARED TO LAND."

You:

"CESSNA 13MIKE, CLEARED TO LAND."

5) Turn **RIGHT** to establish your **FINAL** leg of the circling approach
6) When established on the **FINAL** leg, set **FLAPS** to **third notch** (30 degrees)
7) Descend on **FINAL** at about a **700 FPM** rate of descent
8) Airspeed should be **70 knots**

9) When the altimeter reads "**900**" feet, press "**P**" to pause the simulation

** 10) Record your:

    VASI Lights color sequence_____over_____(40 pts)
    RPM _____(20 pts)
    HEADING_____(20 pts)
    VSI _____(20 pts)
    FLAPS_____(15 pts)
    COM FREQUENCY_____(15 pts)
    AIRSPEED_____(10 pts)

11) Press "**P**" to continue the simulation

"Brings to my mind another of the ten commandments for safe flying! 'Oft thou shalt confirm thy airspeed on final, lest the earth rise up and smite thee.' Don't relax until the tires stop turning!"

12) When you are 10 to 20 feet off the runway, reduce power to about "**1000**" RPM and start to slowly pitch the nose of the aircraft up to slow your descent and establish a touchdown attitude

13) When you are five feet off the runway, hold the nose of the aircraft up and allow the airspeed to **SLOWLY** bleed off. Your aircraft will **settle** onto the runway while you follow the centerline

14) After touchdown, reduce power to **600 RPM**

15) Apply the brakes

Champaign Tower:

    "CESSNA 13MIKE, TURN RIGHT SECOND INTERSECTION. CONTACT GROUND POINT EIGHT EXITING THE RUNWAY."

You:

    "CESSNA 13MIKE, SECOND INTERSECTION, RIGHT."

16) Taxi the aircraft off the active runway to the **RIGHT**

100   IFR Flights of "13MIKE"

17) When the aircraft has stopped, set **CARB HEAT** to "**OFF**"
18) Set **FLAPS** to "**0**"

"Tremendous! You are becoming quite an instrument pilot, and you should be very proud of your performance! You've been well prepared, excited, and bold in making decisions, not waiting on me to tell you every little thing! That's what an instructor likes to see with his students. All right! Wrap things up and I'll treat you to lunch and a five star debrief!"

19) Tune **COM** to "**121.8**" (Champaign Ground)

You:

"CHAMPAIGN GROUND, CESSNA 9413MIKE REQUEST TAXI TO THE TERMINAL."

Champaign Ground:

"CESSNA 9413MIKE, CHAMPAIGN GROUND, TAXI TO THE TERMINAL."

** 20) Record the **TIME**_____(5 pts)

TOTAL POINTS POSSIBLE FOR THIS FLIGHT__**715**__

Flight Scenario Four

San Francisco to South Lake Tahoe

(San Francisco Area - estimated flying time 85 minutes)

Have you ever taken off with your eyes closed? I don't mean as a passenger, I mean as the designated airplane driver! Well, get ready because that's almost what you will be doing in this departure. Hi, Professor Miller here with you again. WOW! A no-see-um takeoff. Now this I have to see! Sorry, I just could not resist that one! It looks like this is going to be some flight. It departs San Francisco International Airport using a SID with a transition and arrives at South Lake Tahoe doing a VOR approach with a procedure turn. Sounds very intense, busy, exciting, challenging, white knuckly, just down your alley, flight! So let's not dilly dally! Onward and upward into the yukky sky! First, Professor Calfior will help you with a rather extensive weather brief, followed by my modestly (I'm the best!) skillful guidance through the initial setup. By this time, you will be ready for Professor Calfior to assist you with the Preflight, Taxi, Runup, Departure, Cruise, Descent, and Approach to your destination airport. Listen to what Professor Calfior has to say about flying techniques. He is trying to help you obtain the best possible score.

102   IFR Flights of "13MIKE"

FLIGHT PLAN -

This route of flight follows well established departure, climb, cruise, descent, and landing procedures. You will depart San Francisco International Airport (**Airport diagram in Appendix C4**) around 1900 Zulu on runway 28L, with near zero-zero visibility and cloud deck. You will fly the SHORELINE NINE DEPARTURE (**Appendix C4**) with the Linden transition out of San Francisco.

Once airborne, and it's safe, turn right to a heading of 040 degrees. You will then go direct to Oakland VOR, having transitioned to Bay Departure Control. Your initial cruise altitude will be 11000 feet, with a true airspeed of 135 knots. Go outbound on the Oakland VOR 040 radial, and make sure to cross the 8 DME fix at or above 6000 feet. You'll be told to switch to Oakland Center at some point. Continue on that track until arriving at the 21 DME fix.

Then proceed inbound on the Linden VOR 240 radial until station passage. Now refer to your IFR low altitude enroute chart L-2 in **Appendix B4**. From Linden VOR, go outbound on the 028 radial, which is Victor 28. Now, because SPOOK intersection at 48 DME has a minimum crossing altitude of 15000 feet, you will start to climb from 11000 feet to 15000 feet after Linden VOR.

From SPOOK intersection, you will go inbound on the Mustang VOR 192 radial to RICHY intersection. From RICHY you will turn left to go inbound on the Squaw Valley VOR 116 radial to the initial approach fix, LAZEE intersection, for the VOR/DME-A instrument approach into South Lake Tahoe Airport. You will begin to descend out of 15000 feet for 11000 feet at LAZEE, execute the procedure turn as depicted on the approach plate, and then proceed inbound on the intermediate segment of your approach on the Squaw Valley VOR 116 radial.

You now descend to, but don't go below 10400 feet, until you have arrived back at LAZEE intersection, which is now the final approach fix inbound. Then commence a descent to 8800 feet until arriving at 18 DME from Squaw Valley. If the field isn't in sight, then execute missed approach as published, and go to your alternate which is Fallon Field in Nevada. But the field should be in sight if you look to the right, so you can execute the visual segment by turning to a heading of 166 for a visual landing on runway 18 at South Lake Tahoe Airport. (**Airport diagram in Appendix C4**)

It's a long flight, lasting close to 85 or 90 minutes, but with 6 hours and 10 minutes of fuel on board, it's a walk in the park.

✈ San Francisco to South Lake Tahoe 103

FILLING OUT THE FLIGHT PLAN -

Fill out the following Flight Plan completely, carefully paying attention to your route of flight. Trace out your route using the IFR low altitude enroute chart L-2 given to you in **Appendix B4**.

FLIGHT PLAN

| 1. TYPE (IFR / VFR / DVFR) | 2. AIRCRAFT IDENTIFICATION | 3. AIRCRAFT TYPE/ SPECIAL EQUIPMENT | 4. TRUE AIRSPEED (KNOTS) | 5. DEPARTURE POINT | 6. DEPARTURE TIME (PROPOSED (Z) / ACTUAL (Z)) | 7. CRUISING ALTITUDE |

8. ROUTE OF FLIGHT

| 9. DESTINATION (Name of airport and city) | 10. EST. TIME ENROUTE (HOURS / MINUTES) | 11. REMARKS |

| 12. FUEL ON BOARD (HOURS / MINUTES) | 13. ALTERNATE AIRPORT(S) | 14. PILOT'S NAME, ADDRESS, TELEPHONE NO. AND AIRCRAFT HOME BASE | 15. NO. ABOARD |

16. COLOR OF AIRCRAFT

CLOSE FLIGHT PLAN WITH _____ FSS

Now answer these questions from your flight plan and enroute chart.

** a) What is in block 8, Route of Flight, of your flight plan?
_____(10 pts)

** b) If going outbound on Victor 28 from Oakland VOR, and told to hold at ALTAM intersection, what kind of holding entry would be exercised? _____(10 pts)

** c) What is the minimum obstruction clearance altitude on the leg of Victor 28 from SPOOK intersection to RICHY intersection?
_____(10 pts)

** d) Without using Linden VOR or Mustang VOR, what two other ways can SPOOK intersection be identified?
   1. _____
   2. _____(10 pts)

** e) What is the total mileage from Linden VOR along Victor 28 to Mustang VOR? _____(10 pts)

104   IFR Flights of "13MIKE"

"This would probably be one of the most picturesque cross countries to fly if it was available to see below us. The entrance to the South Lake Tahoe area is a view of paradise. From looking at your low altitude enroute chart, you notice how fifteen thousand feet is where we need to cruise later on due to the minimum enroute altitude from SPOOK intersection to RICHY? That stretches '13MIKE' very closely to its absolute altitude, plus it's in the oxygen area of flying, so we'll bring some bottles of oxygen along with us to meet the FAR requirements. It's good for you to see how this airplane flies near its top altitude limits.

*Also, did you notice on the Shoreline Nine Departure that for props, the weather minimums are shown to be a one thousand five hundred foot ceiling with three miles prevailing visibility? I can see by looking out this window that we don't even come close to having those minimums. But I've already talked to departure control and for training purposes, I have obtained a special [**for this book only!**] permission to have you do an almost zero zero takeoff and departure. So we're spreading our wings and you are becoming very well versed in the various degrees of instrument flying happenings! I'm excited to get started, as I'm sure you are, so call Oakland and get your brief, plus file us an IFR flight plan. There are a lot of new things to see with this trip!"*

WEATHER BRIEF

You:

"What a day for a weather brief, huh? It's great for us IFR, commercial, instrument rated lovebirds, even if it is a bit soupy! I'm planning an IFR flight in aircraft Tail Number November 9413MIKE, which is a Cessna 182 RG. Departing San Francisco International about forty five minutes or so from now. I'll be at eleven thousand feet, then fifteen thousand feet. Route will be by way of Oakland and Linden to South Lake Tahoe Airport, and it should take an hour and a half to get there. Let's have the exciting news!"

Oakland FSS:

"You do have some flight precautions. Airmet Tango for occasional light to moderate turbulence below flight level two zero zero associated with moderate westerly to southwesterly wind flow aloft. Also there are a few widely scattered thunderstorms along your area of flight, causing some mountain obscuration. In addition, there is Airmet Zulu for light to occasionally moderate rime or mixed icing between niner thousand and one five thousand.

There is a low pressure system off the southern Oregon, northern California coast, with a cold front approaching the coast causing this weather.

Currently at San Francisco, estimated ceiling five hundred broken, three thousand overcast, visibility one half mile, rain and fog, temperature four seven, dewpoint four three, wind two niner zero at one five. Altimeter two niner eight one.

Enroute, ceilings are generally one thousand five hundred broken with scattered rain showers and thunderstorms.

South Lake Tahoe is reporting estimated ceiling seven thousand five hundred broken, one five thousand overcast, visibility two zero. Temperature three seven, wind two four zero at one six, and altimeter two niner eight six.

San Francisco's terminal forecast for two zero zero zero Zulu calls for ceiling four hundred broken, three thousand overcast, visibility one half mile, wind three one zero at one zero.

Enroute, you'll start off with two thousand broken, seven thousand overcast with scattered rain showers and thunderstorms. Cumulonimbus tops are at one seven thousand. Then as you go further north, two thousand scattered to thin broken, ceiling five thousand broken, one one thousand overcast.

South Lake Tahoe's terminal forecast is for ceiling six thousand broken, one two thousand overcast, visibility unrestricted, wind one niner zero at one five.

Winds aloft initially around San Francisco for one two thousand, two niner zero at three two. As you approach South Lake Tahoe, they're forecast two seven zero at two six.

106 IFR Flights of "13MIKE"

> There are no local NOTAMs. There is one NOTAM regarding the landing directional aid approaches at South Lake Tahoe are not authorized through the day.
>
> That wraps up what I have for you. Can I do anything else for you?"

FILING THE FLIGHT PLAN -

You:

> "It looks like a good solid IFR flight, with things shaping up to the north. I'd like to go ahead and file an IFR flight plan with you now, if that's okay with you."

Oakland FSS:

> "By all means! I'm at your service! Go and give me the details - I'm ready!"

You:

> "IFR, November 9413MIKE, Cessna 182 RG - slash A, one three five true airspeed, Departure - SFO, one niner zero zero Zulu, eleven thousand feet, Route - SHORELINE NINE DEPARTURE, Linden transition (SHOR9.LIN), Victor two eight to RICHY intersection, direct LAZEE intersection, Destination - South Lake Tahoe (TVL). ETE is one plus thirty five. Fuel on board six plus ten. Alternate - Fallon, Nevada. [YOUR NAME - CONTACT PHONE NUMBER - HOME BASE], two on board, Red over white."

Oakland FSS:

> "Marvelous! Red over white, huh? Must be quite a handsome little airplane you have! Enjoy the flight and have a great one! Flight Watch one two two point zero for enroute weather and pilot reports."

You:

> "Thanks for the brief! I always enjoy these things so much!"

San Francisco to South Lake Tahoe 107

SETUP

Aircraft:
1) Choose **"Cessna Skylane RG"**

Weather:

Winds
1) Set Surface winds **"DEPTH"** to **"900"**
2) Set Surface winds **"DIR"** to **"300"**
3) Set Surface winds **"SPEED"** to **"12"**
4) Set Level 1 **"TOPS"** to **"5000"**
5) Set Level 1 **"BASE"** to **"920"**
6) Set Level 1 **"DIR"** to **"260"**
7) Set Level 1 **"SPEED"** to **"19"**
8) Set Level 1 **"TURBULENCE"** to **"1"**
9) Set Level 2 **"TOPS"** to **"11000"**
10) Set Level 2 **"BASE"** to **"5000"**
11) Set Level 2 **"DIR"** to **"250"**
12) Set Level 2 **"SPEED"** to **"27"**
13) Set Level 3 **"TOPS"** to **"15500"**
14) Set Level 3 **"BASE"** to **"11000"**
15) Set Level 3 **"DIR"** to **"230"**
16) Set Level 3 **"SPEED"** to **"36"**

Clouds
1) Set Bottom Level - **TOPS** to **"8000"**
2) Set Bottom Level - **BASE** to **"20"**
3) Set Bottom Level - **COVER** to **"overcast"**
4) Set Top Level - **TOPS** to **"15000"**
5) Set Top Level - **BASE** to **"9500"**
6) Set Top Level - **COVER** to **"overcast"**
7) Set Thunderstorms - **TOPS** to **"16000"**
8) Set Thunderstorms - **BASE** to **"4000"**
9) Set Thunderstorms - **COVERAGE** to **"widely scattered"**

108 IFR Flights of "13MIKE"

Aircraft Position:

1) **"NORTH"** to **"17338.5959"** [N037° 36' 47.6534]
2) **"EAST"** to **"5057.0449"** [W122° 22' 49.2214]
3) **"ALTITUDE"** to **"9"** [0]
4) **"HEADING"** to **"100"**

note: At this point you may wish to save this setup for future use.

PREFLIGHT

note: Set **ZOOM** to **"1.0"**
Set **TIME** to **"12:00"**

"You are going to see a magnificent style of doing a takeoff, which is called an instrument takeoff! With the localizer positioned down the runway centerline, you make sure that the CDI needle stays centered. But that's not the primary way to accomplish this takeoff. You'll make sure you're lined up on the centerline, then with full power added and control movements being teeny tiny small, you'll hold the runway heading. It'll be thrilling! San Francisco also has a pre-taxi clearance program, so now it's time to get our IFR clearance. According to the airport chart, frequency is one one eight point two, right?"

Departure Clearance:

1) Tune **COM** to **"118.2"** (San Francisco Clearance)

You:

"SAN FRANCISCO CLEARANCE DELIVERY, CESSNA 9413MIKE, INTERNATIONAL TERMINAL, IFR. I'D LIKE TO ACTIVATE MY IFR FLIGHT PLAN FROM SAN FRANCISCO INTERNATIONAL TO SOUTH LAKE TAHOE, PLEASE."

San Francisco to South Lake Tahoe 109

San Francisco Clearance:

> "CESSNA 9413MIKE, SAN FRANCISCO CLEARANCE DELIVERY, CLEARED TO SOUTH LAKE TAHOE AIRPORT SHORELINE NINE DEPARTURE, LINDEN TRANSITION THEN AS FILED. MAINTAIN ONE ONE THOUSAND. BAY DEPARTURE FREQUENCY WILL BE ONE TWO ZERO POINT NINER, SQUAWK TWO SEVEN THREE FOUR."

You:

> "CESSNA 13MIKE IS CLEARED AS FILED. MAINTAIN ONE ONE THOUSAND. DEPARTURE ONE TWO ZERO POINT NINER, SQUAWK TWO SEVEN THREE FOUR."

San Francisco Clearance:

> "CESSNA 13MIKE, READBACK CORRECT. HAVE A SAFE FLIGHT!"

"For expectation purposes, realize that whenever you leave an airport area by way of a standard instrument departure, ATC will always clear you to the destination airport, and relate what that SID is as well as its transition. If we were to just boot out and go, then we'd simply be cleared to South Lake Tahoe Airport as filed. And the 'as filed' does not include altitude, so ATC must follow with an altitude. You're right! Let's get ATIS now and you have the frequency on your notes, I see!"

Instruments:

1) Tune **COM** to "**135.45**" (San Francisco ATIS)

> "SAN FRANCISCO INTERNATIONAL AIRPORT, INFORMATION JULIETTE, ONE EIGHT FIVE FIVE ZULU WEATHER, MEASURED CEILING ONE HUNDRED OVERCAST, VISIBILITY ONE QUARTER MILE, FOG, TEMPERATURE FOUR EIGHT, DEWPOINT FOUR FIVE, WIND THREE ZERO ZERO AT ONE TWO. ALTIMETER TWO NINER EIGHT ZERO. ILS RUNWAYS TWO EIGHT LEFT AND RIGHT ARE IN USE. LANDING AND DEPARTING RUNWAYS TWO EIGHT LEFT AND RIGHT. ADVISE ON INITIAL CONTACT YOU HAVE INFORMATION JULIETTE."

110 IFR Flights of "13MIKE"

    2) Set **"Altimeter"** and **"Heading Indicator"**
    3) Set **XPDR** to **"2734"** (assigned IFR code)

"Now here's where you put your NAV 1 setup to the localizer for runway two eight Left, since that's where I think they'll steer us for takeoff. It's a secondary method of maintaining a straight line takeoff for such a low cloud deck as we've got today. See, I raise my arm and look, Mom! No hands! Now that's a low cloud deck!!!!"

    4) Tune **NAV 1** to **"109.5"** (ISFO)
    5) Set **NAV 1 OBS** to **"280"**
    6) Tune **NAV 2** to **"116.8"** (OAK)
    7) Set **NAV 2 OBS** to **"040"**
    8) Set the **DME** to **"NAV 2"** and **"DIST"**
    9) Check **CARB HEAT** is **"OFF"**
    10) Check **GEAR "DOWN"**
    11) Turn **STROBE "ON"**
    12) Check **LIGHTS** are **"OFF"**

"Let me ask you this! Once we're airborne and proceeding outbound away from San Francisco, what would you do if in trying to raise Departure Control, you got nothing but silence over the radio? You can't see, so no visual landing to the airport is possible. Think about it, because it could really happen, right? And the first time it happens is not the time to be considering it for the first time! Stay tuned, but meanwhile, let's talk to Ground Control."

    13) Tune **COM** to **"121.8"** (San Francisco Ground)

You:

    "SAN FRANCISCO GROUND, CESSNA 9413MIKE AT INTERNATIONAL TERMINAL, READY TO TAXI, IFR TO SOUTH LAKE TAHOE, WITH INFORMATION JULIETTE."

San Francisco Ground:

    "CESSNA 9413MIKE, SAN FRANCISCO GROUND, TAXI STRAIGHT AHEAD AND HOLD SHORT RUNWAY ONE LEFT."

San Francisco to South Lake Tahoe

You:

"CESSNA 13MIKE, HOLD SHORT RUNWAY ONE LEFT, STRAIGHT AHEAD."

"Well, we're not anticipating any arrivals on runways one left or right, but who knows? Wouldn't it be neat to all of a sudden see someone pop out and land? That would be a Category two or Category three type of instrument approach, where the minimums are lower than us type instrument pilots. Some day, you might be flying an aircraft which is computerized all the way down the final approach course, and you never even have to see the runway at all for a good landing!"

14) Taxi up to runway 1L

TAXI -

San Francisco Ground:

"CESSNA 13MIKE, SAN FRANCISCO GROUND, CROSS RUNWAYS ONE LEFT AND ONE RIGHT, TURN LEFT ON TAXIWAY LIMA AND HOLD SHORT OF RUNWAY TWO EIGHT LEFT FOR INTERSECTION TAKEOFF. PERFORM YOUR RUNUP THERE."

You:

"CESSNA 13MIKE, CROSS ONE LEFT AND RIGHT, LEFT TAXIWAY LIMA, HOLD SHORT RUNWAY TWO EIGHT LEFT, INTERSECTION TAKEOFF."

"Let's continue taxiing. You don't see intersection takeoffs too often, especially when it's just as practical to always start at the approach end of a runway. But it is a long travel and we certainly have plenty of runway for our takeoff needs, don't you agree? That also means San Francisco is not busy with a lot of inbounds, which tells me how crazy we are to begin with! But who wants a book with only three flight scenarios?"

112   IFR Flights of "13MIKE"

RUN UP -

        1) Set brake (hold down to prevent aircraft from moving)
        2) Advance power to about "**1800**" RPM
**   3) Select **CARB HEAT "ON"**, record RPM drop_____(5 pts)
        4) Select **CARB HEAT "OFF"**
**   5) Select "**LEFT**" Mag, record RPM drop_____(5 pts)
        6) Select "**BOTH**" Mags
**   7) Select "**RIGHT**" Mag, record RPM drop_____(5 pts)
        8) Select "**BOTH**" Mags
        9) Reduce power to **idle**
       10) Set **FLAPS** to **first notch** (10 degrees takeoff configuration)

"Back to the no radio contact problem I left you poring over! There's nothing to think about! Just read your lost communication procedures off of your Shoreline Nine Departure plate. One minute after crossing the three four two radial out of San Francisco VOR, we would then go to Oakland VOR and cross it at or above four thousand feet. Then continue along our filed route which we've been cleared to. The adventure begins with you switching to one two zero point five, San Francisco Tower!"

       11) Tune **COM** to "**120.5**" (San Francisco Tower)

You:

    "SAN FRANCISCO TOWER, CESSNA 9413MIKE IS READY FOR IFR DEPARTURE RUNWAY TWO EIGHT LEFT AT LIMA."

San Francisco Tower:

    "CESSNA 9413MIKE, SAN FRANCISCO TOWER, RUNWAY TWO EIGHT LEFT, CLEARED FOR INTERSECTION TAKEOFF."

You:

    "CESSNA 13MIKE, CLEARED FOR TAKEOFF."

San Francisco to South Lake Tahoe

FLIGHT

Takeoff:

"Don't bother looking around once you're lined up! All of your focused attention will be on the gauges, and I'll spot you with the lineup. If I say come right, just tap the right rudder, or come left, just tap the left rudder. We don't want to laterally oscillate down the runway. And you watch your heading indicator and keep the CDI on your number one Nav centered. Flaps at ten degrees, oodles of fuel, trimmed properly and oil information is all in the green. Our bridges are burned behind us - let us be worthy of Roman heritage and vamoose out of here!"

1) Record TIME_____
2) Release brakes and taxi onto runway 28L
3) Position and hold with **NAV 1 CDI** needle **centered**
4) Advance power to **"FULL"**
5) Maintain centerline of runway by keeping **NAV 1 CDI** needle **centered**
6) At **50 knots** airspeed, lift nose wheel off runway
7) At **70 knots,** ease back on the yoke to establish a 10 degree pitch up attitude
8) Maintain a climb **AIRSPEED** of **80 knots**

"Hey! Soup city! At least we know we're airborne and climbing, so get the gear up because that right turn needs to occur quickly!"

9) When the altimeter reads **"100"** feet, raise **GEAR**

"Don't wait on the flaps either. You're in control, so get those flaps up now, and after they're up, turn right out of here!"

10) When the altimeter reads **"200"** feet, raise the **FLAPS** to **"0"**
11) Turn **RIGHT** to a heading of **"040"**

114 IFR Flights of "13MIKE"

**

12) Reduce power to about "**2300**" RPM at "**1000**" feet above the ground (AGL)
13) Start to roll out when you see "**025**" in the heading indicator
14) When wings are level, press "**P**" to pause the simulation
15) Record your:

    ALTITUDE_____(30 pts)
    NAV 2 DME DIST_____(30 pts)
    NAV 2 CDI POSITION_____(25 pts)
    AIRSPEED_____(20 pts)
    GEAR _____(15 pts)
    FLAPS_____(15 pts)
    COM FREQUENCY_____(10 pts)

16) Press "**P**" to continue the simulation

San Francisco Tower:

"CESSNA 9413MIKE, SAN FRANCISCO TOWER, CONTACT BAY DEPARTURE."

You:

"CESSNA 13MIKE SWITCHING ONE TWO ZERO POINT NINER. IT'S PRETTY GOOEY UP HERE! SEE YOU!"

"Boy, oh boy! Nice takeoff run! Nice eighty knot climbout! Nice turn! Nice radio communications! Nice vertigo! I feel like I'm upside down, but the instruments tell me you're doing perfectly! How come you ain't screwed up like me?! Oh you are? Then I feel better! That's excellent, how you're believing your instruments over your body."

Departure Track:

1) Track inbound on the **OAKLAND VOR 220** radial
2) Tune **COM** to "**120.9**" (Bay Departure)

You:

"BAY DEPARTURE, CESSNA 9413MIKE IS WITH YOU, PASSING ONE THOUSAND SIX HUNDRED FOR ONE ONE THOUSAND."

San Francisco to South Lake Tahoe 115

Bay Departure:

> **"CESSNA 9413MIKE, BAY DEPARTURE, RADAR CONTACT."**

**   3) When the NAV 2 DME DIST reads "**3.0**", record:
HEADING for centered NAV 2 CDI_____(35 pts)
ALTITUDE_____(25 pts)
4) Maintain track when transitioning from a **TO** indication to a **FROM** indication on the **NAV 2 OBI**

**   5) What altitude did you pass when the NAV 2 flag flipped to a **FROM** indication?_____(30 pts)

"When climbing to a high cruise altitude, it becomes sluggish ground distance wise to maintain a best rate of climb airspeed. So what becomes prevalent is a transition to a cruise climb, which means a higher climb airspeed, resulting in a greater ground speed in the climb, so that you can feel like you're moving forward! And we're certainly not in any rush to reach eleven thousand feet."

     6) When passing "**6000**" feet, lower nose to establish a **100 knot** climb airspeed

**   7) Record your NAV 2 DME DIST at "**6000**" feet_____(30 pts)

Bay Departure:

> **"CESSNA 13MIKE, CONTACT OAKLAND CENTER ONE TWO FIVE POINT FOUR FIVE."**

You:

> **"CESSNA 13MIKE, SWITCHING OAKLAND CENTER, ONE TWO FIVE POINT FOUR FIVE."**

     8) Tune **COM** to "**125.45**" (Oakland Center)

You:

> **"OAKLAND CENTER, CESSNA 9413MIKE WITH YOU PASSING SIX THOUSAND FIVE HUNDRED."**

4

116   IFR Flights of "13MIKE"

Oakland Center:

"CESSNA 9413MIKE, OAKLAND CENTER, IDENT."

You:

"13MIKE, IDENT."

    9) Press the IDENT button (simulate)

Oakland Center:

"CESSNA 13MIKE, RADAR CONTACT."

Transition:

1) When the **DME** on **NAV 2** reads "**8.0**", tune **NAV 1** to "**114.8**" (LIN)
2) Set **NAV 1 OBS** to "**060**"
** 3) What heading now is necessary to keep centered the NAV 2 CDI? _____(35 pts)
4) When the **NAV 1 CDI** centers, turn **RIGHT** to a heading of "**060**"
5) Track inbound on the **LINDEN VOR 240** radial that your **NAV 1 OBI** is displaying
6) Set **DME** to "**NAV 1**"
7) Begin to level off when the altimeter reads "**10900**" feet
8) Maintain "**11000**" feet
9) Hold a power setting of about "**2300**" **[2500]** RPM
** 10) When reaching "**11000**" feet, what is the NAV 1 DME DIST? _____(25 pts)

** *"Step by step, you are flying this enroute portion of the Shoreline Nine Departure with amazing accuracy. But a SID comes to an end, as all good things do, to be replaced by even gooder things! In this case, you need to think ahead by way of your enroute chart because from Linden, we're flying Victor twenty eight to what intersection?*_____*(5 pts)*
*How many miles is it from Linden to this intersection?*_____*(5 pts)*

San Francisco to South Lake Tahoe

What additional two navaids could help to identify this fix?
1. _____
2. _____*(10 pts)*

In case you ran into any '13MIKE' mechanical problems, what airport can you put down to that's west northwest of this fix?
_____*(5 pts)*

What is this airport's elevation and runway length?
_____*(10 pts)*

Well, good done! Isn't that better than saying 'Well, well done!'? The moral of this exercise is that you could set yourself up so that you are prepared for the Victor twenty eight transition out of Linden."

 11) Tune **NAV 2** to "**115.2**" (SAC)
 12) Set **NAV 2 OBS** to "**080**"
** 13) When the NAV 1 DME DIST reads "**24.0**", record your Ground speed_____(25 pts)
** 14) When the NAV 1 DME DIST reads "**10.0**", what is your NAV 1 CDI needle position?_____(30 pts)

Oakland Center:

 "CESSNA 13MIKE, OAKLAND CENTER, AT PILOT'S DISCRETION CLIMB AND MAINTAIN ONE FIVE THOUSAND."

You:

 "CESSNA 13MIKE, AT PILOT'S DISCRETION, ONE FIVE THOUSAND."

"Do you see why that instruction has occurred? Look even further ahead to SPOOK intersection just southwest of South Lake Tahoe. The minimum crossing altitude which you'll need to be at when flying over SPOOK on Victor twenty eight is what? That's right! Fifteen thousand feet! But we'll use the 'At pilot's discretion' and wait until outbound from Linden. Because of our low performance capability at such high altitudes, I'd suggest a ninety knot climb to fifteen thousand feet."

118   IFR Flights of "13MIKE"

Enroute climb:

1) When the **NAV 1 DME DIST** reads "**0.4**" **[1.7]**, turn left to a heading of "**028**"
2) Set **NAV 1 OBS** to "**028**"
3) Track outbound on the **LINDEN VOR 028** radial
4) Establish a **90 knot** climb attitude at **FULL POWER [2400]** to "**15000**" feet

5) When the **NAV 2 CDI** is **centered**, press "**P**" to pause the simulation

** 6) Record your:
   NAV 1 DME DIST_____(35 pts)
   HEADING_____(25 pts)
   VSI _____(20 pts)
   NAV 2 DME DIST_____(20 pts)
   NAV 1 CDI POSITION_____(20 pts)
   AIRSPEED_____(15 pts)
   ALTITUDE_____(15 pts)
   COM FREQUENCY_____(10 pts)
7) Press "**P**" to continue the simulation

Oakland Center:

"CESSNA 9413MIKE, CONTACT OAKLAND CENTER ONE TWO SIX POINT EIGHT FIVE."

You:

"CESSNA 9413MIKE, OKAY! OAKLAND CENTER ONE TWO SIX POINT EIGHT FIVE. THANKS FOR YOUR SERVICE."

"The enroute chart shows you this frequency by the Oakland rectangular radio box near Linden VOR, doesn't it? Angel's Camp sector? I wasn't caught by surprise because of having studied the chart as a part of the preflight preparation. By the way, start sniffing some of that oxygen we brought along!"

San Francisco to South Lake Tahoe 119

       8) Tune **COM** to "**126.85**" (Oakland Center)

You:

    "OAKLAND CENTER, CESSNA 9413MIKE CLIMBING ONE FIVE THOUSAND."

Oakland Center:

    "CESSNA 9413MIKE, OAKLAND CENTER, ROGER."

"You've got two choices to help identify SPOOK intersection now, huh? Why choose Squaw Valley over Hangtown? That's right! It's because we will be using Squaw Valley to help us along the instrument approach procedure into South Lake Tahoe. That's thinking on your feet!"

       9) Tune **NAV 2** to "**113.2**" (SWR)
      10) Set the **NAV 2 OBS** to "**164**"
      11) Begin to level off when the altimeter reads "**14950**" feet
      12) Maintain "**15000**" feet
      13) Reduce power to about "**2300**" **[2500] RPM**

**   14) When established in cruise, record your:
          AIRSPEED_____(25 pts)
          GROUND SPEED_____(25 pts)

Pre-initial approach fix:

    1) When the **NAV 2 CDI** is **centered**, press "**P**" to pause the simulation

**   2) Record your:
         NAV 1 CDI POSITION_____(35 pts)
         NAV 1 DME DIST_____(30 pts)
         NAV 2 DME DIST_____(30 pts)
         NUMBER of Thunderstorms in sight_____(20 pts)
         RPM_____(15 pts)
         COM FREQUENCY_____(10 pts)
    3) Press "**P**" to continue the simulation

120 IFR Flights of "13MIKE"

    4) Turn **LEFT** to a heading of "**012**"

"Strategy once again rules! Since Squaw Valley VOR is going to be your emphasis for the entire instrument approach, then put that on your top or primary navaid. We now need to track inbound on Mustang's VOR, but you can handle that on VOR number two, the lower one, can't you?"

    5) Tune **NAV 2** to "**117.9**" (FMG)
    6) Set the **NAV 2 OBS** to "**012**"
    7) Track inbound on the **MUSTANG VOR 192** radial
    8) Tune **NAV 1** to "**113.2**" (SWR)
    9) Set the **NAV 1 OBS** to "**296**"

"There's twenty five miles to RICHY intersection, so you've now got the time to pick up ATIS information right? Wrong! Look at your approach chart for the VOR DME Alpha approach. There is no ATIS! So who's there to give you the information you'll need? Tahoe Tower, sure!"

You:

    "OAKLAND CENTER, CESSNA 13MIKE WOULD LIKE TO SWITCH OFF FREQUENCY FOR A SECOND."

Oakland Center:

    "CESSNA 13MIKE, OAKLAND CENTER, APPROVED AS REQUESTED. REPORT BACK ON OAKLAND CENTER EAST ONE TWO EIGHT POINT EIGHT."

You:

    "CESSNA 13MIKE, OAKLAND CENTER EAST ONE TWO EIGHT POINT EIGHT. BYE!"

    10) Press "**P**" to pause the simulation

Weather:
    <u>**Winds**</u>
    a) Set Surface winds "**DIR**" to "**180**"
    b) Set Surface winds "**SPEED**" to "**11**"
    c) Set Level 1 "**TOPS**" to "**11500**"

San Francisco to South Lake Tahoe

    d) Set Level 1 "**BASE**" to "**7300**"
    e) Set Level 1 "**DIR**" to "**210**"
    f) Set Level 1 "**SPEED**" to "**13**"
    g) Set Level 2 "**TOPS**" to "**15000**"
    h) Set Level 2 "**BASE**" to "**11500**"
    i) Set Level 2 "**DIR**" to "**220**"
    j) Set Level 2 "**SPEED**" to "**16**"
    k) Set Level 3 "**TOPS**" to "**0**"
    l) Set Level 3 "**BASE**" to "**0**"
    m) Set Level 3 "**SPEED**" to "**0**"

Clouds
    a) Set Bottom Level - **TOPS** to "**11000**"
    b) Set Bottom Level - **BASE** to "**9000**"
    c) Set Top Level - **BASE** to "**12000**"
    d) Set Thunderstorms - **TOPS** to "**0**"
    e) Set Thunderstorms - **BASE** to "**0**"

11) Press "**P**" to continue the simulation

Prior to initial approach fix:

1) Tune **COM** to "**118.4**" (Tahoe Tower)

You:

> "TAHOE TOWER, CESSNA 9413MIKE ABOUT ONE FIVE MILES SOUTHWEST. COULD YOU GIVE ME WHAT YOUR WEATHER IS LIKE DOWN THERE?"

Tahoe Tower:

> "CESSNA 9413MIKE, TAHOE TOWER, WE HAVE AN ESTIMATED CEILING AT NINER THOUSAND OVERCAST, VISIBILITY TWO FIVE. WIND ONE EIGHT ZERO AT NINER. ALTIMETER TWO NINER NINER THREE. RUNWAY ONE EIGHT IS IN USE."

IFR Flights of "13MIKE"

You:

"CESSNA 13MIKE, THANKS A HEAP! I'LL BE THERE IN A BIT! GOOD COMMUNICATION DISCIPLINE, HUH?"

2) Set **ALTIMETER**, set **HI**, check **FUEL**
3) Tune **COM** to "**128.8**" (Oakland Center East)

You:

"OAKLAND CENTER EAST, CESSNA 9413MIKE WITH YOU AT ONE FIVE THOUSAND. WOULD LIKE TO REQUEST A VOR DME ALPHA APPROACH INTO SOUTH LAKE TAHOE."

Oakland Center East:

"CESSNA 9413MIKE, OAKLAND CENTER EAST, RADAR CONTACT. CLEARED VOR DME ALPHA SOUTH LAKE TAHOE."

"This is going to prove to be a very active instrument approach procedure. Remember all the steps we saw during our briefing session? Simply follow your approach plate one segment at a time, knowing what the next two steps to accomplish need to be. As a side note, I'd like for you to stay at fifteen thousand feet until LAZEE intersection, then you can descend at a pretty decent clip!"

4) When the **NAV 1 CDI** is 1 dot **RIGHT** of center, turn **LEFT** to a heading of "**296**"
5) Track inbound on the **SQUAW VALLEY VOR 116** radial
6) When the **NAV 1 DME DIST** reads "**14.0**", note the time and continue inbound track for **1** minute
7) Reduce power to about "**1800**" [**2100**] RPM
8) Descend to and maintain "**11,000**" feet at a "**1000**" feet per minute rate of descent
9) Set **CARB HEAT** "**ON**"

San Francisco to South Lake Tahoe

Initial segment:

**

1) After **1** minute, press **"P"** to pause the simulation
2) Record your:
   - ALTITUDE_____(25 pts)
   - VSI _____(25 pts)
   - AIRSPEED_____(20 pts)
   - NAV 1 DME DIST_____(20 pts)
   - NAV 1 CDI POSITION_____(20 pts)
   - COM FREQUENCY_____(15 pts)
3) Press **"P"** to continue the simulation

4) Turn **RIGHT** to a heading of **"342"**
5) When wings are level on a **"342"** heading, time for **1** minute
6) Set the **NAV 1 OBS** to **"116"**

"There are many ways of doing a procedure turn, which is what you are on now. The important thing is that somehow or other, you reverse your course one hundred and eighty degrees in the opposite direction. From what I've seen, it's the 'United States' thing to do what we're doing, which is the forty five - one eighty method as depicted on your plate."

7) Turn **LEFT** to a heading of **"162"**
8) When the **NAV 1 CDI** is 1 dot **RIGHT** of center, turn **LEFT** to a heading of **"116"**
9) Track outbound on the **SQUAW VALLEY VOR 116** radial
10) Commence a descent to **"10400"** feet
11) Adjust power to hold **110 knots** throughout

Oakland Center East:

   "CESSNA 13MIKE, OAKLAND CENTER EAST, CONTACT TAHOE TOWER ONE ONE EIGHT POINT FOUR."

You:

   "CESSNA 13MIKE, SWITCHING TOWER ONE ONE EIGHT POINT FOUR. YOU'VE BEEN GREAT!"

124 IFR Flights of "13MIKE"

        12) Tune **COM** to "**118.4**" (Tahoe Tower)

You:

    "TAHOE TOWER, CESSNA 9413MIKE, APPROACHING FINAL APPROACH FIX INBOUND, VOR DME ALPHA, FULL STOP."

Tahoe Tower:

    "CESSNA 9413MIKE, TAHOE TOWER, RUNWAY ONE EIGHT, CLEARED TO LAND . REPORT FIELD IN SIGHT."

You:

    "CESSNA 13MIKE WILL REPORT FIELD IN SIGHT."

        13) Press "**P**" to pause the simulation

**

*"There is a visual segment to this approach, so as you near eighteen DME, where should you look for the airport? **RIGHT or LEFT?** (5 pts)*
And what is the distance from the missed approach point at eighteen to the approach end of runway one eight?_____(5 pts)
How much altitude do you need to lose on the visual segment in order to land at the approach end of runway 18?_____(5 pts)
At what altitude is the highest peak shown on the instrument approach procedure? (From the plan view)_____(5 pts)
If you never saw the field at South Lake Tahoe, a part of the missed approach procedure is to proceed inbound on what radial of what VOR? _____(5 pts)
From the airport diagram, which runway has the displaced threshold? _____(5 pts)"

        14) Press "**P**" to continue the simulation

Intermediate & Final Approach:

    1) When the **NAV 1 DME DIST** reads "**14.0**", descend to "**8800**" feet
    2) Select **GEAR "DOWN"**
    3) Transition to **100 knots**

San Francisco to South Lake Tahoe   125

    4) When the **NAV 1 DME DIST** reads "**18.0**", turn **RIGHT** to a heading of "**166**"
    5) Reduce power to about "**1450**" [**1750**] RPM

You:

    "TAHOE TOWER, CESSNA 13MIKE HAS FIELD."

Tahoe Tower:

    "CESSNA 13MIKE, ROGER! WIND ONE EIGHT ZERO AT ONE TWO."

    6) When you have slowed to **90 knots**, set **FLAPS** to **first notch** (10 degrees)
    7) Commence a descent to runway 18, holding **90 knots**
    8) When the altimeter reads "**7400**", set **FLAPS** to **second notch** (20 degrees)
    9) When the altimeter reads "**6900**", set **FLAPS** to **third notch** (30 degrees)
    10) Airspeed should be **70 knots**

"It is hard to approximate your descent rate from a long distance such as where we started. But the key is still to put the approach end of the runway about an inch or two above the bottom edge of your windscreen, and allow it to grow as you get closer, without it moving from that position."

    11) When you are 10 to 20 feet off the runway, reduce power to about "**1000**" RPM and start to slowly pitch the nose of the aircraft up to slow your descent and establish a touchdown attitude
    12) When you are five feet off the runway, hold the nose of the aircraft up and allow the airspeed to **SLOWLY** bleed off. Your aircraft will <u>settle</u> onto the runway while you follow the centerline
    13) After touchdown, reduce power to **600 RPM**
    14) Apply the brakes

126 IFR Flights of "13MIKE"

Tahoe Tower:

> "CESSNA 13MIKE, TURN RIGHT FIRST OR SECOND INTERSECTION. CONTACT GROUND POINT NINER."

You:

> "CESSNA 13MIKE, GROUND POINT NINER."

15) Taxi the aircraft off the active runway to the **RIGHT**
16) When the aircraft has stopped, set **CARB HEAT** to "**OFF**"
17) Set **FLAPS** to "0"
18) Tune **COM** to "121.9" (South Lake Tahoe Ground)

You:

> "TAHOE GROUND, CESSNA 9413MIKE, REQUEST TAXI TO THE RAMP."

Tahoe Ground:

> "CESSNA 9413MIKE, TAHOE GROUND, CONTINUE STRAIGHT AHEAD."

You:

> "CESSNA 13MIKE, STRAIGHT AHEAD. THANKS!"

"Another mission extremely well done! You are handling new concepts like a champion! Would you look at that golf course off the approach end of runway three six?!! It's beautiful! I'm game if you are, for rest and relaxation! Boy, my Dad would absolutely love it!"

** 19) Record the **TIME**_____(5 pts)

TOTAL POINTS POSSIBLE FOR THIS FLIGHT __990__

Flight Scenario Five

Port Angeles to Seattle

(Seattle Area - estimated flying time 50 minutes)

Professor Miller with you once again! You can open your eyes now! Have you had enough IFR mountain flying? Well, let's try a little northern flying. Let me tell you about this far north flight. It departs Port Angeles in the northernmost part of Washington State, using a SID and arrives in beautiful Seattle using a published Visual approach. This would be a gorgeous flight if you could see the ground but the cloud level is set at 800 feet. You will have the marvelous opportunity to see the waterways into Seattle-Tacoma International Airport, once you descend out of the clouds. But it's too bad you can't see the sparkling tint of the Puget Sound as you overfly it in this no-see-um weather. Oh well, maybe the next time you fly up in Washington, the weather will be better. Okay, enough wishing! Let's get on to the flight plan, fill it out, and go with Professor Calfior to get our yukky weather briefing. Then I will assist you in making the weather yukky for real! After we are finished, I will let Professor Calfior get you ready for a most interesting flight. You will need to be alert on this flight. Things happen rather quickly. If you have ever been to Washington State, you probably already know that this kind of weather is the norm, not the exception.

Listen to Professor Calfior and maybe, just maybe, you will see the space needle.

IFR Flights of "13MIKE"

FLIGHT PLAN -

This route of flight follows well established departure, climb, cruise, descent, and landing procedures. You will depart Port Angeles, Fairchild International Airport (**Airport diagram in Appendix C5**) at a departure time of 2230 Zulu, on runway 31.

For departing the area, you will fly the PORT ANGELES ONE DEPARTURE (**Appendix C5**) to intercept Victor 4 out of Tatoosh VOR, on the 080 radial outbound. Upon takeoff, you will make a right turn to a heading of 040 as soon as practicable, and Whidbey Departure Control will provide further instructions. Climb up to and maintain 9000 feet as a cruise altitude, where along the way you'll be handed off to Seattle Center. Your true airspeed will be close to 130 knots.

At JAWBN intersection, your IFR low altitude enroute chart L-1 in **Appendix B5** shows that you'll need to make a right turn to go inbound on the Seattle VOR 306 radial, which is still a part of the Victor 4 airway. When arriving at LOFAL intersection, now proceed inbound on the Olympia VOR 350 radial to CARRO intersection. You will descend to 7000 feet which is that segment's minimum enroute altitude.

Then you fly inbound on the Seattle VOR 228 radial, which is Victor 27. By now, you'll be under the jurisdiction of Seattle Approach Control. The expectation is to descend to 3000 feet for the Mall Visual Approach Runway 34R into Seattle-Tacoma International. (**Appendix C5**) Following the water course, you'll turn on final, which can be identified by the 338 inbound course off of the Seattle VOR or the localizer course. You cannot leave 3000 feet until at the water tank and SeaTac Mall at 7.5 DME. The airport diagram for SeaTac International Airport is in **Appendix C5**. From your worksheet in flight planning, this will take about 55 minutes, and fuel on board is 6 hours and 5 minutes. We don't need an alternate, since the weather at our destination is better than 2000 foot ceiling and 3 miles visibility. But, let's keep Olympia Airport in our back pocket, just for mental insurance.

Port Angeles to Seattle

FILLING OUT THE FLIGHT PLAN -

Fill out the following Flight Plan completely, carefully paying attention to your route of flight. Trace out your route using the IFR low altitude enroute chart L-1 (**Appendix B5**).

```
┌─────────────────────────────────────────────────────────────────────────┐
│                          FLIGHT PLAN                                    │
├──────────┬────────────┬─────────────┬────────┬──────────┬──────────────┬─────────────┤
│ 1. TYPE  │ 2. AIRCRAFT│ 3. AIRCRAFT │ 4. TRUE│ 5. DEPART│ 6. DEPARTURE │ 7. CRUISING │
│          │ IDENT.     │ TYPE/SPEC.  │ AIRSPD │ POINT    │    TIME      │   ALTITUDE  │
│   IFR    │            │ EQUIPMENT   │        │          │ PROP.  ACT.  │             │
│   VFR    │            │             │        │          │  (Z)    (Z)  │             │
│   DVFR   │            │             │  KNOTS │          │              │             │
├──────────┴────────────┴─────────────┴────────┴──────────┴──────────────┴─────────────┤
│ 8. ROUTE OF FLIGHT                                                                   │
│                                                                                      │
├──────────────────────────────┬─────────────────────┬─────────────────────────────────┤
│ 9. DESTINATION (airport/city)│ 10. EST TIME ENROUTE│ 11. REMARKS                     │
│                              │ HOURS    MINUTES    │                                 │
├──────────────┬───────────────┴─────────┬───────────┴───────────────┬─────────────────┤
│ 12. FUEL ON BOARD            │ 13. ALTERNATE AIRPORT│ 14. PILOT'S NAME, ADDR, etc    │ 15. NO. ABOARD│
│ HOURS   MINUTES              │                      │                                │               │
├──────────────────────────────┴──────────────────────┴────────────────────────────────┤
│ 16. COLOR OF AIRCRAFT              CLOSE FLIGHT PLAN WITH _____ FSS                 │
└─────────────────────────────────────────────────────────────────────────────────────┘
```

Now answer these questions from your flight plan and enroute chart.

** a) What is in block 8, Route of Flight, of your flight plan?
_____(10 pts)

** b) The NDB that is practically on Victor 4 to the west of Port Angeles is named what, and is on what frequency?_____(10 pts)

** c) What kind of altitude restrictions are found at LOFAL intersection? (Type and altitude)
      1._____
      2._____(10 pts)

** d) West of Seattle, Victor 287 has what two VORs at either end of its airway segment?_____(10 pts)

** e) What military operating area (MOA) is southwest of Seattle?
_____(10 pts)

130   IFR Flights of "13MIKE"

"The field of meteorology - weather, is a fascinating study! One of the things I believe you're beginning to see is that weather briefs, procedures for obtaining weather, and filing IFR flight plans are generally quite standardized and easy to understand.

The Flight Service Station folks have a certain flow of information that they are responsible to give to all pilots. There's a format, order, and style to their briefs. It gives us pilots a sense of constancy, knowing that we won't ever be given a half hearted 'who cares?' kind of brief, because these weather people are actively caring about your specific flight. They probably don't like being called weather people! Let's call them convective activity specialists! Of course, you know what pilots are called, don't you? Airheads!

Let me tell you a little bit about in flight weather advisories. One of them is convective SIGMETS. This is used for heavy weather stuff, like severe turbulence, icing, storms, and such ilks of doom and gloom! Three bulletins cover the geographic areas of Eastern, Central, and Western. They can be designated anything from November to Yankee, with three exceptions - 1) Sierra 2) Tango and 3) Zulu.

Those three fall under another in flight weather advisory, called an AIRMET. **Tango** *always deals with turbulence.* **Zulu** *deals with icing. And* **Sierra** *deals with instrument flight rules or mountain obscuration.*

Hey! I'm not bad for a meteorological ground school instructor, am I? Lecturing is fine, but I know you're anxious to fly the Seattle area, so call up Seattle FSS and receive another outstandingly professional weather brief. Looks foggy out there, but that makes for great flying! I'll buy you a cup of coffee or hot chocolate when you get back."

WEATHER BRIEF

You:
"Hello Seattle! I'm coming down there to visit you and I'd like to acquire an IFR weather brief. I'm in November 9413MIKE, which is a Cessna 182 RG. I'm departing from the booming metropolis of Port Angeles, Fairchild International Airport. It's three o'clock now - let's expect me airborne in thirty minutes. Cruising at nine

thousand feet. I'll go easterly first, then southeasterly to SEATAC airport. One hour to Seattle enroute. I've got to get down there quick in order to see the Seattle Supersonics play live! I'm an instrument rated pilot."

Seattle FSS:

"There is a flight precaution of a developing line of thunderstorms ten miles wide moving eastward at thirty knots, north and west of Seattle. Also, there is an Airmet Tango for light to moderate turbulence above six thousand feet, which is valid until zero zero zero zero Zulu - that's five o'clock our time.

The frontal system will develop into a low pressure system near evening.

Currently, at Fairchild International, estimated ceiling eight hundred broken, six thousand overcast, visibility two, light rain and fog, temperature five five, wind three one zero at one three, altimeter two niner eight eight.

Enroute, ceilings are generally five thousand broken with widely scattered thunderstorms.

Here in Seattle, we have a measured ceiling of five thousand overcast, visibility three zero, temperature six one, wind three two zero at one one, with altimeter two niner eight niner.

Fairchild's forecast calls for ceiling one thousand two hundred broken, visibility three, light rain showers and fog, wind three two zero at one five.

Enroute, you should encounter two thousand scattered to thin broken, ceiling five thousand overcast, with scattered rain showers and thunderstorms. Cumulonimbus tops are at one five thousand.

By the time you arrive in SEATAC - wait! I pushed the wrong button - high level significant weather prognosis isn't what I want! It's interesting, but unless you're flying a Lear jet, you won't care! Here it is! Terminal forecast says for two three zero zero Zulu weather, one thousand five hundred scattered, ceiling four thousand broken, seven thousand overcast, visibility unrestricted, wind three two zero at eight.

132   IFR Flights of "13MIKE"

>   Winds aloft for niner thousand, three five zero at two niner. Over Seattle, they're forecast three four zero at two two.
>   There are no local or distant NOTAMs.
>   They play the New York Knickerbockers tonight, don't they?"

FILING THE FLIGHT PLAN -

You:

>   "Yeah! Should be quite a game! Well, looks pretty good to me - so with your blessing, I'll give you my flight plan to glory and hoops heaven!"

Seattle FSS:

>   "All right, I don't want to be the one responsible for you missing your game, so I'll clear the board and then you give me your flight plan!"

You:

>   "IFR, November 9413MIKE, Cessna 182 RG - slash A, one three zero true airspeed, Departure - Port Angeles-Fairchild International, two two three zero Zulu, niner thousand feet, Route - PORT ANGELES ONE DEPARTURE, Victor four LOFAL intersection, Victor two eighty seven CARRO intersection, Victor twenty seven, Destination - SEATAC, SEA. ETE is zero plus five five, Fuel on board six plus oh five. Alternate - Olympia. [YOUR NAME - CONTACT PHONE NUMBER - HOME BASE], two on board, Red over white."

Seattle FSS:

>   "Well, then, go, go, go!! Your flight plan is on file. For enroute weather, contact Flight Watch on frequency one two two point one, and we'd appreciate pilot reports on any turbulence or thunderstorm activity you might encounter. By the time you preflight and kick the tires, your clearance will await you! Hope the Knicks win! Sorry!"

You:
> "I'll tell you what! If the Knicks win, I'll give you a flight in 13MIKE. If the Supersonics win, you give me a diamond studded tour of the Flight Service Station there. Deal?"

Seattle FSS:
> "Deal! Call me tomorrow. I'm on the morning shift, and my operating initials are Foxtrot Mike. Take care!"

You:
> "So long, FM!"

SETUP

Aircraft:
1) Choose **"Cessna Skylane RG"**

Weather:

Winds
1) Set Surface winds **"DEPTH"** to **"800"**
2) Set Surface winds **"DIR"** to **"310"**
3) Set Surface winds **"SPEED"** to **"13"**
4) Set Level 1 **"TOPS"** to **"3000"**
5) Set Level 1 **"BASE"** to **"1100"**
6) Set Level 1 **"DIR"** to **"330"**
7) Set Level 1 **"SPEED"** to **"18"**
8) Set Level 2 **"TOPS"** to **"6500"**
9) Set Level 2 **"BASE"** to **"3000"**
10) Set Level 2 **"DIR"** to **"340"**
11) Set Level 2 **"SPEED"** to **"24"**
12) Set Level 2 **"TURBULENCE"** to **"1"**
13) Set Level 3 **"TOPS"** to **"10000"**
14) Set Level 3 **"BASE"** to **"6500"**
15) Set Level 3 **"DIR"** to **"350"**
16) Set Level 3 **"SPEED"** to **"29"**

134   IFR Flights of "13MIKE"

Clouds

1) Set Bottom Level - **TOPS** to "**3500**"
2) Set Bottom Level - **BASE** to "**800**"
3) Set Bottom Level - **COVER** to "**overcast**"
4) Set Top Level - **TOPS** to "**10000**"
5) Set Top Level - **BASE** to "**6000**"
6) Set Top Level - **COVER** to "**overcast**"
7) Set Thunderstorms - **TOPS** to "**13000**"
8) Set Thunderstorms - **BASE** to "**7000**"
9) Set Thunderstorms - **COVERAGE** to "**widely scattered**"

Aircraft Position:

1) "**NORTH**" to "**21742.8441**"   [N048° 07'22.1921]
2) "**EAST**" to "**6374.1958**"   [W123° 30'05.0869]
3) "**ALTITUDE**" to "**295**"   [0]
4) "**HEADING**" to "**220**"

note: At this point you may wish to save this setup for future use.

PREFLIGHT

note: Set **ZOOM** to "**1.0**"
Set **TIME** to "**15:30**"

"You're stuck on what to do for clearance procedures, huh? This is a great example of making use of the various resources which are available to you. If you look at an Airport Facility Directory, or any kind of an airport guide, you'll see that the Clearance Delivery listed is Whidbey on frequency one two four point one five. Taking off from an airport that has no tower does not automatically mean that no clearance delivery is used! No, no, nah - ah - ngah! In other words, for sure not! Got the point? Go ahead and visitate with Whidbey Clearance then!"

Departure Clearance:

1) Tune **COM** to "**124.15**" (Whidbey Clearance Delivery)

You:

"WHIDBEY CLEARANCE DELIVERY, CESSNA 9413MIKE WOULD LIKE TO ACTIVATE ITS IFR FLIGHT PLAN FROM PORT ANGELES TO SEATAC AT THIS TIME."

Whidbey Clearance Delivery:

"CESSNA 9413MIKE, WHIDBEY CLEARANCE DELIVERY, CLEARED TO SEATTLE TACOMA INTERNATIONAL AIRPORT AS FILED. MAINTAIN NINER THOUSAND. WHIDBEY DEPARTURE FREQUENCY WILL BE ONE ONE EIGHT POINT TWO, SQUAWK TWO TWO TWO SIX."

You:

"OKAY! CESSNA 13MIKE IS CLEARED AS FILED. MAINTAIN NINER THOUSAND. DEPARTURE ONE ONE EIGHT POINT TWO, SQUAWK TWO TWO TWO SIX."

Whidbey Clearance Delivery:

"CESSNA 13MIKE, READBACK CORRECT. ENJOY THE FLIGHT!"

"From what I see, as a result of your weather brief, this is the flight where you'll learn about an IFR arrival procedure called the visual approach. Many times, when the weather is good enough, instrument traffic can blow off the instrument approach procedures and execute a visual arrival to the destination. 'Blow off' may be a rather uncouth way to state that! ATC will assign it to you! Since SEATAC has the Mall Visual Approach to runway three four right, that will be our golden opportunity. UNICOM for info, right?"

136 IFR Flights of "13MIKE"

Instruments:

1) Tune **COM** to "**123.0**" (Port Angeles UNICOM)

You:

"PORT ANGELES UNICOM, CESSNA 9413MIKE. COULD YOU PLEASE GIVE ME WINDS, ACTIVE RUNWAY, AND ALTIMETER SETTING?"

Port Angeles UNICOM:

"CESSNA 9413MIKE, WIND THREE ONE ZERO AT ONE THREE, TAKEOFFS AND LANDINGS ARE ON RUNWAY THREE ONE, ALTIMETER SETTING TWO NINER EIGHT SEVEN."

"Just to ease their curiosity, tell them why we're situated where we are. Daresay, they wondereth!"

You:

"CESSNA 13MIKE, I'VE BEEN TESTING MY BRAKES, WHICH IS WHY I'M MIDWAY DOWN RUNWAY ONE THREE - THREE ONE ON THE EXIT. I'LL CALL WHEN I'M READY TO TAXI."

Port Angeles UNICOM:

"ROGER!"

"Why look at me?! I've got nothing to say! Get set up! What do you mean, 'Will surprises never end?'"

2) Set "**Altimeter**" and "**Heading Indicator**"
3) Set **XPDR** to "**2226**" (assigned IFR code)
4) Tune **NAV 1** to "**112.2**" (TOU)
5) Set **NAV 1 OBS** to "**080**"
6) Tune **NAV 2** to "**116.8**" (SEA)
7) Set **NAV 2 OBS** to "**126**"

Port Angeles to Seattle   137

  8) Set the **DME** to "**NAV 1**" and "**DIST**"
  9) Check **CARB HEAT** is "**OFF**"
  10) Check **GEAR** "**DOWN**"
  11) Turn **STROBE** "**ON**"
  12) Check **LIGHTS** are "**OFF**"

**

"We're doing a standard instrument departure out of Fairchild, right? What kind is it? Well, there are only two kinds! There you go! A vector navigation, that's right! And the other kind is a pilot navigation. Look at the takeoff instructions from runway three one.
1) After takeoff, how soon do we start a turn?_____(5 pts)
2) What's the first heading to turn to?_____(5 pts)
3) When will you leave your heading?
    When given a_____(5 pts)
That's why it's called vector navigation! Witty, huh? In other words, you absolutely need vectors to get you going where you need to go. Whereas with a pilot navigation SID, vectors may be given, but you predominantly are able to fly the SID with no assistance other than what the graphical track shows. Well, let's go to a basketball game!"

You:

  "PORT ANGELES UNICOM, CESSNA 13MIKE TAXIING TO RUNWAY THREE ONE FOR IFR DEPARTURE."

Port Angeles UNICOM:

  "CESSNA 13MIKE, ROGER!"

TAXI -

"Let me tell you a little bit about my philosophy of flying. It's wonderful to learn mechanical procedures, but continuing to fly under the umbrella of mechanical procedures can be deadly. I'm an advocate of thinking! I'm an advocate of having many different ways to do the same job, like setting up for a landing - when to lower flaps. Or coming in on an ILS approach, when to lower gear. You need to be free in your judgmental thinking, so that any new experience which challenges your safety or togetherness can result in you getting out of trouble. As Winston Churchill used to say, 'Let's turn left and taxi down to the approach end!'"

138   IFR Flights of "13MIKE"

RUN UP -

          1) Set brake (hold down to prevent aircraft from moving)
          2) Advance power to about "**1700**" RPM
**   3) Select **CARB HEAT "ON"**, record RPM drop_____(5 pts)
          4) Select **CARB HEAT "OFF"**
**   5) Select "**LEFT**" Mag, record RPM drop_____(5 pts)
          6) Select "**BOTH**" Mags
**   7) Select "**RIGHT**" Mag, record RPM drop_____(5 pts)
          8) Select "**BOTH**" Mags
          9) Reduce power to **idle**
         10) Set **FLAPS** to **first notch** (10 degrees takeoff configuration)

"Now on this flight, I really want you to work on your scan techniques. You've been flying wonderfully, but for the next step, relax more without letting your scan flow deteriorate any. An instruction I received while in the Navy's flight school was to let my eyes flow over the displays. It took me a while to stop jerking my eyes from one instrument to another. But believe me, it's a relief to the eyes when you get the feel of it. I don't see any traffic, but always just in case, state our intentions and let's fly!"

You:

    "PORT ANGELES TRAFFIC, CESSNA 13MIKE IS TAKING THE ACTIVE, RUNWAY THREE ONE, FOR A RIGHT CROSSWIND DEPARTURE, DEPARTING EASTBOUND."

FLIGHT

Takeoff:

"Ah! To be lined up on yet another runway! It's a fine sight for an Irish pilot to cast his eyes upon! Of course, I'm German, but there's a blood relation between the Irish and the Germans, I'm sure! Good! Take it slow onto the runway, and you're looking for flaps at ten degrees, plenty of fuel, trim that up a little more for takeoff, oil temperature and oil pressure are in limits. Make sure you check that you have full RPM within Pilot Operating Handbook limits once you give it full power. Let's be went!"

Port Angeles to Seattle

1) Record TIME_____
2) Release brakes and taxi onto runway 31
3) Advance power to "**FULL**"
4) Maintain centerline of runway
5) At **50 knots** airspeed, lift nose wheel off runway
6) At **70 knots,** ease back on the yoke to establish a 10 degree pitch up attitude
7) Maintain a climb **AIRSPEED** of **80 knots**
8) Raise **Gear** when there is no more runway to land on
9) At "**500**" feet above the ground, raise the **FLAPS** to "**0**"
10) Turn **RIGHT** to a heading of "**040**"
11) Tune **COM** to "**118.2**" (Whidbey Departure)

You:

"WHIDBEY DEPARTURE, CESSNA 9413MIKE IS WITH YOU, PASSING ONE THOUSAND TWO HUNDRED FOR NINER THOUSAND."

Whidbey Departure:

"CESSNA 9413MIKE, WHIDBEY DEPARTURE, IDENT."

You:

"CESSNA 13MIKE, IDENT."

12) Press the IDENT button (simulate)
13) Reduce power to about "**2300**" RPM at "**1000**" feet above the ground (AGL)

"That's a beautiful example of thinking that you did on takeoff. When did you think it appropriate to turn onto your zero four zero course? Sometime after you raised flaps, so that there wouldn't be a need to be in a turn with flaps hanging down. And obviously, you need to raise your flaps once you've got a good flying speed, like your eighty knots. Any problem raising flaps at three hundred feet AGL? Not if you're established and safely set up. That's the non-mechanical problem solving skill that I like to see in my students! Well done!"

140 IFR Flights of "13MIKE"

Whidbey Departure:

"CESSNA 9413MIKE, WHIDBEY DEPARTURE, RADAR CONTACT. MAINTAIN CURRENT HEADING UNTIL INTERCEPTING VICTOR FOUR ON TATOOSH ZERO EIGHT ZERO RADIAL."

You:

"CESSNA 13MIKE. CURRENT HEADING TO TATOOSH ZERO EIGHT ZERO RADIAL, VICTOR FOUR."

"We've got a ways to go before we arrive at niner thousand feet, and we certainly don't want to be late for the Knicks game, so ignite the afterburners and let's horizontally swoop to a ninety knot cruise climb! Check that all your fittings on your G-Suit are properly plugged in!"

Climb out:

1) When the altimeter reads "**1800**" feet, establish a **90** kt climb
2) When the altimeter reads "**2500**" feet, turn **RIGHT** to a heading of "**080**"

3) When wings are level, press "**P**" to pause the simulation

** 4) Record your:

    HEADING_____(30 pts)
    ALTITUDE_____(30 pts)
    AIRSPEED_____(30 pts)
    NAV 1 DME DIST_____(25 pts)
    NAV 1 CDI POSITION_____(20 pts)
    RPM_____(20 pts)
    GEAR_____(15 pts)
    FLAPS_____(15 pts)
    TATOOSH IDENT_____(10 pts)
    COM FREQUENCY_____(10 pts)
    XPDR_____(10 pts)

5) Press "**P**" to continue the simulation

6) Track outbound on the **TATOOSH VOR 080** radial

Port Angeles to Seattle 141

Whidbey Departure:

> "CESSNA 13MIKE, CONTACT SEATTLE CENTER ONE TWO ZERO POINT THREE."

You:

> "CESSNA 13MIKE, SWITCHING ONE TWO ZERO POINT THREE. BYE!"

    7) Tune **COM** to "**120.3**" (Seattle Center)

You:

> "SEATTLE CENTER, CESSNA 9413MIKE WITH YOU PASSING THREE THOUSAND THREE HUNDRED FOR NINER THOUSAND."

Seattle Center:

> "CESSNA 9413MIKE, SEATTLE CENTER, RADAR CONTACT."

*"Have I told you why visual approaches are favored so much whenever possible? For one thing, ATC is more excited to give it to you than you are to receive it! That's because it relieves their workload by a load plus another load! More airplanes can land in a shorter period of time when visual approaches are underway [**Navy term**] than when instrument approach procedures are accomplished. Meanwhile, it's a great view of the inside of clouds here, isn't it?! It's like checking the back of your eyelids!"*

Level off:

**   1) When the NAV 1 DME DIST reads "**60.0**", record:
       HEADING for centered NAV 1 CDI_____(35 pts)
       AIRSPEED_____(30 pts)
    2) Begin to level off when the altimeter reads "**8900**" feet
    3) Maintain "**9000**" feet
    4) Reduce power to about "**2200**" **[2400]** RPM

"To help you also on your scan, I want you to nail the CDI needle in the centered position at all times when established on your track from any VOR station. Watch its drift, put in the proper correction, and then when the needle is centered, take out half the correction. Now don't get so concentrated on the OBI that you drop the attitude indicator, or airspeed indicator, or VSI, or anything else out of the loop of your scan pattern. The key to smooth instrument flying is very minor corrections caught right at the start when they're needed. You are flying superbly - don't get disheartened by any mistakes made!"

South to Seattle:

    1) When the **NAV 2 CDI** is "**centered**", turn **RIGHT** to a heading of "**126**"

**   2) When wings are level, press "**P**" to pause the simulation
    3) Record your:
        NAV 1 DME DIST_____(35 pts)
        NAV 2 DME DIST_____(35 pts)
        AIRSPEED_____(30 pts)
        PROBLEM IN FRONT OF YOU!_____(30 pts)
        NEEDED COURSE OF ACTION_____(25 pts)
        COM FREQUENCY_____(15 pts)
        NAME OF INTERSECTION JUST PASSED
        _____(15 pts)
    4) Press "**P**" to continue the simulation

"By gumbo! That was more exciting than a trick some friends and I played on cows in Sicily! They were asleep on their feet on a downward sloping hill at night, and we snuck up on them quietly! [Is there any other way to sneak up on something, but quietly?] Then with awesome coordination, we all pushed our designated cows and they woke up off balance, rolling down the hill, and mooing like nobody's business! Well, that was youth amok!"

    5) Track inbound on the **SEATTLE VOR 306** radial
    6) Set the **DME** to "**NAV 2**"

Port Angeles to Seattle   143

7) Tune **NAV 1** to "**114.2**" [**110.6**] (PAE)
8) Set the **NAV 1 OBS** to "**236**"

"I like it! Could you identify the next intersection without using Paine VOR? Certainly! But you are thinking again, just in case Seattle VOR has a problem. Seattle's navaid signal should always be available to us because we're above the minimum enroute altitude that's shown for this segment on the low altitude enroute chart, right? So why the redundancy? Simple! The VOR station itself could fail."

**

9) When the NAV 2 DME DIST reads "**30.5**", record your:
   NAV 1 CDI POSITION_____(40 pts)
   HEADING for centered NAV 2 CDI_____(35 pts)
10) When the **NAV 1 CDI** is 1 dot **LEFT** of center, turn **RIGHT** to a heading of "**170**"

"And isn't it amazing how close the NAV 2 CDI is to being centered! Technology, you can't beat it!"

11) When wings are level, press "**P**" to pause the simulation

**

12) Record your:
    NAV 2 DME DIST_____(25 pts)
    ALTITUDE_____(20 pts)
    AIRSPEED_____(20 pts)
    NAME OF INTERSECTION JUST PASSED
    _____(15 pts)
    VSI_____(15 pts)
13) Press "**P**" to continue the simulation

Seattle Center:

"CESSNA 13MIKE, SEATTLE CENTER, DESCEND AND MAINTAIN SEVEN THOUSAND."

You:

"CESSNA 13MIKE, LEAVING NINER FOR SEVEN THOUSAND."

5

144 IFR Flights of "13MIKE"

14) Begin a descent to **"7000"** feet and maintain **"2200" [2400]** RPM

"This is prolifically a navaid switching drill when you're staying ahead of the airplane and switching from one Victor airway to another as you're doing! Olympia is important to us, and guess what's next to become important? You bet your bippy, baby! Seattle again!"

15) Tune **NAV 2** to **"113.4"** (OLM)
16) Set the **NAV 2 OBS** to **"170"**
17) Track inbound on the **OLYMPIA VOR 350** radial

"Before getting too close to SEATAC, you'll need to get ATIS information. You have thirty four miles until reaching CARRO intersection, so take advantage of the distance and time involved, and ask Seattle Center for permission to get ATIS."

You:

"SEATTLE CENTER, CESSNA 9413MIKE, REQUEST PERMISSION TO SWITCH OFF THE FREQUENCY FOR A MOMENT."

Seattle Center:

"CESSNA 13MIKE, APPROVED AS REQUESTED. REPORT BACK ON."

18) Tune **COM** to **"118.0"** (SEATAC ATIS)

"SEATTLE TACOMA INTERNATIONAL AIRPORT, INFORMATION NOVEMBER, TWO TWO FIVE FIVE ZULU WEATHER, ESTIMATED CEILING THREE THOUSAND FIVE HUNDRED OVERCAST, VISIBILITY TWO ZERO. TEMPERATURE SIX THREE, DEWPOINT FOUR EIGHT. WIND THREE ONE ZERO AT ONE ZERO, ALTIMETER TWO NINER NINER ZERO. LANDING RUNWAY THREE FOUR RIGHT, DEPARTING RUNWAY THREE FOUR LEFT. IF FIELD IN SIGHT, REQUEST A VISUAL. ADVISE ON INITIAL CONTACT YOU HAVE INFORMATION NOVEMBER."

Port Angeles to Seattle

19) Set **ALTIMETER**, set **HI**, check **FUEL**
20) Tune **COM** to "**120.3**" (Seattle Center)

"That just verifies what we thought! The weather is getting better down here quickly, and somewhere in some part of our final descent, we'll see the wonders of SEATAC and the Puget Sound. I used to live in Bremerton for two years. Yeah! I was on the USS Enterprise while it was in overhaul back in '79 to '81 as the Assistant Fuels Officer. The Fuels Officer was the neatest guy I ever worked for, but for the life of me, I can't remember his name."

You:

"SEATTLE CENTER, CESSNA 9413MIKE IS BACK WITH YOU."

Seattle Center:

"CESSNA 13MIKE, CONTACT SEATTLE APPROACH ONE TWO THREE POINT NINER."

You:

"CESSNA 13MIKE, SWITCHING SEATTLE APPROACH, ONE TWO THREE POINT NINER."

21) Tune **COM** to "**123.9**" (Seattle Approach)

You:

"SEATTLE APPROACH, CESSNA 9413MIKE IS WITH YOU."

Seattle Approach:

"CESSNA 13MIKE, SEATTLE APPROACH, RADAR CONTACT."

22) Tune **NAV 1** to "**116.8**" (SEA)
23) Set the **NAV 1 OBS** to "**048**"

146   IFR Flights of "13MIKE"

Off-airway tracking:

**   1) When the **NAV 2 DME DIST** reads "**42.5**", what heading will hold the **NAV 2 CDI centered**?_____(30 pts)

**   2) When the **NAV 2 DME DIST** reads "**36.0**", record your:
         NAV 2 CDI POSITION_____(35 pts)
         ALTITUDE_____(25 pts)
         GROUND SPEED_____(25 pts)
         COM FREQUENCY_____(15 pts)

     3) Press "**P**" to continue the simulation

     4) When the **NAV 2 DME DIST** reads "**34.0**":

Seattle Approach:

"CESSNA 13MIKE, TURN LEFT HEADING ZERO EIGHT ZERO, DIRECT SEATTLE VORTAC, DESCEND AND MAINTAIN THREE THOUSAND. EXPECT VISUAL APPROACH RUNWAY THREE FOUR RIGHT. REPORT FIELD IN SIGHT."

You:

"CESSNA 13MIKE, TURN LEFT HEADING ZERO EIGHT ZERO, DIRECT SEATTLE VORTAC, DESCEND AND MAINTAIN THREE THOUSAND. EXPECT VISUAL APPROACH RUNWAY THREE FOUR RIGHT. REPORT FIELD IN SIGHT."

     5) Turn **LEFT** to a heading of "**080**"
     6) Center the **NAV 1 CDI** and fly direct to **SEATTLE VOR** on that inbound course

"Well, this certainly saves us some time, not having to go all the way down to CARRO intersection! I'm coming sooner than you think, New York Knicks, thanks to Seattle Center!"

Port Angeles to Seattle

Weather:

Clouds
1) Set Bottom Level - **TOPS** to "**5000**"
2) Set Bottom Level - **BASE** to "**4000**"

Setup for visual approach:

1) Descend to and maintain "**3000**" feet expeditiously
2) Reduce power to about "**1900**" [**2100**] RPM

"What's one of the things you expect to see when you pop out of the clouds? Water! Lots of water! Start pre-briefing yourself on the Mall Visual Approach Runway three four Right. The fingers at the end of Commencement Bay are scenically noteworthy! Just a personal note. When descending in clouds, my personal limit is about fifteen hundred feet per minute rate of descent at the most! That's where my individual loss of control bubble extends to. I'm telling you this because it is very important for you to determine what your personal limits are. Food for thought!"

Visual approach:

1) When breaking out of the clouds:

You:

"SEATTLE APPROACH, CESSNA 9413MIKE, FIELD IN SIGHT."

Seattle Approach:

"CESSNA 9413MIKE, CLEARED FOR MALL VISUAL APPROACH RUNWAY THREE FOUR RIGHT."

You:

"CESSNA 13MIKE, CLEARED MALL VISUAL APPROACH RUNWAY THREE FOUR RIGHT."

2) Fly to and along **COLVOS PASSAGE**

148   IFR Flights of "13MIKE"

    3) When at "**3000**" feet, maintain about "**1900**" [**2100**] RPM

"Nicely done! Colvos Passage is the first water lane you see in front of you. The airport is just a glimpse due to the visibility, but we've got lots of visual aids to steer us properly. So that we can incorporate all kinds of scan practice for you, set up your number one OBS to the inbound VOR track and use that initially to ensure you're lined up on the visual final approach. I thought I saw a shark down there! Tough passage!"

    4) Set the **NAV 1 OBS** to "**338**"

**   5) What is the name of the airport off your right wing?

    _____(20 pts)

    6) Prior to the **BRIDGE**, and **NORTH** of **COMMENCEMENT BAY**, turn **LEFT** to follow the water passage

"Well, at least I think that's the bridge! Maybe it's Narrows Airport. Meanwhile, hold that three thousand feet. You're visual, but stay hawked on scanning the six pack of attitude indicator, airspeed, heading, VSI, turn coordinator, and power. I swear Jaws is following us!"

    7) Set DME to "**NAV 1**"
    8) At the end of the water passage, turn **LEFT** on a gradual curve until the **NAV 1 CDI** is 2 dots **RIGHT** of center
    9) Turn **LEFT** to a heading of "**338**"
    10) Visually line up on runway **34R**

"Just so you don't get confused - visual approaches are not all charted like this one is. As a matter of fact, most visual approaches are just the kind where they say, 'Do you see the airport or traffic in front of you? Go for it, or follow him!' You'll be doing more of these kind of approaches to your destinations as a professional pilot than you will of instrument approach procedures. Do you understand why this procedure is not authorized at night? Can't see the water, or heaven forbid, the mall after closing hours!"

Port Angeles to Seattle 149

Seattle Approach:

> "CESSNA 13MIKE, SEATTLE APPROACH, CONTACT SEATTLE TOWER ONE ONE NINER POINT NINER."

You:

> "CESSNA 13MIKE, SWITCHING TOWER ONE ONE NINER POINT NINER. THANKS!"

11) Tune **COM** to "**119.9**" (Seattle Tower)

You:

> "SEATTLE TOWER, CESSNA 9413MIKE AT NINER DME INBOUND, MALL VISUAL APPROACH RUNWAY THREE FOUR RIGHT. I HAVE INFORMATION NOVEMBER."

Seattle Tower:

> "CESSNA 9413MIKE, SEATTLE TOWER, REPORT FOUR MILE FINAL."

You:

> "CESSNA 13MIKE WILL REPORT FOUR MILE FINAL."

12) When the **NAV 1 DME DIST** reads "**7.5**", reduce power to about "**1500**" [**1800**] RPM

"We're still pretty far out, so no rush in descending. Flaps will take judgment - nothing mechanical about predetermined checkpoints here, is there? It's a visual thing. But our power is set back because we do need to slow down so that we're close to a feasible approach speed. Now don't be a martyr! You have DME - use it! If a resource is there, use it. But take a picture in your mind of the airport when four DME occurs so you know what a four mile final is pictured as."

13) Begin a gradual descent for a visual landing
14) When the **NAV 1 DME DIST** reads "**4.0**":

150   IFR Flights of "13MIKE"

You:

> "SEATTLE TOWER, CESSNA 13MIKE AT FOUR."

Seattle Tower:

> "CESSNA 13MIKE, RUNWAY THREE FOUR RIGHT, CLEARED TO LAND."

You:

> "CESSNA 13MIKE, THREE FOUR RIGHT, CLEARED TO LAND."

15) When the **NAV 1 DME DIST** reads "**2.5**", select **GEAR** "**DOWN**"

**
"Another logical point is this:
1) What's the airport elevation?_____(5 pts)
2) So about what altitude would you be at normally in a visual landing pattern when you are three quarters to a mile on final?_____(5 pts)
So control your descent so that you don't arrive at that altitude or below before you see one DME!"

16) Set **CARB HEAT "ON"**
17) Reduce power to about "**1300**" [**1700**] **RPM** so as to attain **90 knots**
18) When the **NAV 1 DME DIST** reads "**2.2**", set **FLAPS** to **first notch** (10 degrees)
19) When the **NAV 1 DME DIST** reads "**1.8**", set **FLAPS** to **second notch** (20 degrees)
20) When the **NAV 1 DME DIST** reads "**0.9**", set **FLAPS** to **third notch** (30 degrees)
21) Airspeed should be **70 knots**

Port Angeles to Seattle

**
      22) Press "**P**" to pause the simulation
      23) Record your:
           ALTITUDE_____(25 pts)
           VSI_____(25 pts)
           AIRSPEED_____(20 pts)
           GEAR_____(15 pts)
           FLAPS_____(15 pts)
           STROBES_____(10 pts)
           COM FREQUENCY_____(10 pts)
           NAME OF PARALLEL RUNWAY!_____(5 pts)
      24) Press "**P**" to continue the simulation

Seattle Tower:

    "CESSNA 13MIKE, WIND THREE ONE ZERO AT ONE THREE."

      25) When you are 10 to 20 feet off the runway, reduce power to about "**1000**" RPM and start to slowly pitch the nose of the aircraft up to slow your descent and establish a touchdown attitude
      26) When you are five feet off the runway, hold the nose of the aircraft up and allow the airspeed to **SLOWLY** bleed off. Your aircraft will <u>settle</u> onto the runway while you follow the centerline
      27) After touchdown, reduce power to **600 RPM**
      28) Apply the brakes

Seattle Tower:

    "CESSNA 13MIKE, TURN RIGHT ON THE FIRST AVAILABLE TURNOFF. CONTACT GROUND POINT SEVEN EXITING THE RUNWAY."

You:

    "CESSNA 13MIKE, ROGER. GROUND POINT SEVEN."

      29) Taxi the aircraft off the active runway to the **RIGHT**

152   IFR Flights of "13MIKE"

      30) When the aircraft has stopped, set **CARB HEAT** to "**OFF**"
      31) Set **FLAPS** to "**0**"

"Wasn't that a thrill and a half?! Another cross country to a new airport for you! Another style of arriving at your destination! Another opportunity to get to know me better! If I remember right, Seattle has some of the best tasting smoked salmon I have ever had! It's expensive, but when it melts in your mouth, who cares?! I bought the hot chocolate for you back in Fairchild, so you get the salmon! Let's wrap this up. High grades for you in your performance this flight! I like flying with you."

      32) Tune **COM** to "**121.7**" (Seattle Ground)

You:

    "SEATTLE GROUND, CESSNA 9413MIKE ON BRAVO ELEVEN FOR TAXI."

Seattle Ground:

    "CESSNA 9413MIKE, SEATTLE GROUND, TURN LEFT AND PROCEED TO THE NORTH SATELLITE RAMP."

You:

    "CESSNA 13MIKE, THANKS A LOT! NORTH SATELLITE RAMP."

  **   33) Record the **TIME**_____(5 pts)

          TOTAL POINTS POSSIBLE FOR THIS FLIGHT___**1005**___

Flight Scenario Six

Oceanside to Van Nuys

(Southern California Area - estimated flying time 65 minutes)

Here we are back in Southern California! I was looking forward to lying on the beach and catching some rays, but it looks overcast and rather crudy! So I guess we can go flying. It's a great day for practicing your instrument flying inside a very busy airspace like Los Angeles' class B. Even though you are IMC (I can't see a thing!), you still need to stay alert for other aircraft and cumulus granite (mountains). It is totally beyond me, but some pilots will fly into places where they have no business flying, like clouds - and no one knows that they are there until it's too late. So stay alert.

This flight looks exciting. You'll leave Oceanside Airport, that's north of San Diego and south of Los Angeles, and transition through the Los Angeles busy class B airspace to shoot the ILS approach into Van Nuys. Let's look over the flight plan so you and Professor Calfior can get your weather brief. You and I will then setup some real derelict weather that you and Professor Calfior can practice in. Professor Calfior will love, just love, this flight! He will probably talk the entire flight!

Stay alert and listen to Professor Calfior. His wisdom could save your life someday.

IFR Flights of "13MIKE"

FLIGHT PLAN -

This route of flight follows well established departure, climb, cruise, descent, and landing procedures. At 0430 Zulu, you will depart Oceanside Municipal (**Airport diagram and Departure procedures in Appendix C6**) on runway 6. You are going to follow its IFR departure procedure which is a climbing right turn to a heading of 235 until reaching 1500 feet. You will initiate contact with San Diego Departure Control. Once past 1500 feet, then you need to turn further right and go direct to Oceanside VOR. True airspeed at your cruise altitude of 6000 feet is 140 knots.

Look at the low altitude enroute chart L-3 in **Appendix B2**. Upon reaching station passage at Oceanside VOR, you will proceed outbound on Victor 23, which is the 300 radial. Los Angeles Center will be controlling you at this point. At the halfway point between Oceanside VOR and Seal Beach VOR, you will transition to the Seal Beach VOR 120 radial inbound. Since you have a clearance only to Seal Beach VOR at this time, you will have to hold at Seal Beach until further clearance is received.

The holding pattern at Seal Beach is left hand turns off of the airway, so you can enter it direct. Once your further clearance is received, continue on Victor 23 off of the Seal Beach VOR 272 radial to HERMO intersection, which is 16 DME. Then fly on the Los Angeles VOR 124 radial inbound.

Once you have station passage at Los Angeles VOR, head direct to Van Nuys VOR. Los Angeles Center will hand you off to Burbank Approach Control who will probably clear you for the ILS RWY 16R approach (**Appendix C6**). Van Nuys VOR is the initial approach fix for this approach, and you proceed outbound on the 324 radial, maintaining 6000 feet.

Almost 15 miles out, you'll turn right on the Fillmore VOR 054 radial for 4.3 miles, so that you will intercept the Van Nuys localizer 340 radial inbound. Once you pass UMBER intersection, you can descend to the minimum glideslope altitude of 4300 feet, where you will then intercept the glideslope. Decision height for straight in to runway 16R is 1040 feet, which with the field in sight, you will land. Van Nuys airport diagram is in **Appendix C6**. If the field is not in sight at decision height, you will execute the published missed approach procedure and proceed to Oxnard Airport. Your 5 hours and 50 minutes of fuel on board is plentiful enough for this 65 minute trip.

Oceanside to Van Nuys

FILLING OUT THE FLIGHT PLAN -

Fill out the following Fight Plan completely, carefully paying attention to your route of flight. Trace out your route using the IFR low altitude enroute chart L-3 given to you in **Appendix B2**.

FLIGHT PLAN							

1. TYPE
  IFR
  VFR
  DVFR
	2. AIRCRAFT IDENTIFICATION	3. AIRCRAFT TYPE/ SPECIAL EQUIPMENT	4. TRUE AIRSPEED
			
			KNOTS
				5. DEPARTURE POINT	6. DEPARTURE TIME
					PROPOSED (Z) / ACTUAL (Z)
							7. CRUISING ALTITUDE

8. ROUTE OF FLIGHT							
9. DESTINATION (Name of airport and city)		10. EST. TIME ENROUTE HOURS / MINUTES		11. REMARKS			
12. FUEL ON BOARD HOURS / MINUTES		13. ALTERNATE AIRPORT(S)		14. PILOT'S NAME, ADDRESS, TELEPHONE NO. AND AIRCRAFT HOME BASE			15. NO. ABOARD
16. COLOR OF AIRCRAFT			CLOSE FLIGHT PLAN WITH_____FSS				

Now answer these questions from your flight plan and enroute chart.

** a) What is in block 8, Route of flight, of your flight plan?
_____(10 pts)

** b) There are four intersections along Victor 23 from Oceanside VOR. What are they and who are they referenced from?
  1. _____
  2. _____
  3. _____
  4. _____
  Referenced from_____(10 pts)

** c) What kind of a navigational aid does John Wayne-Orange County Airport have that's shown on the enroute chart?
_____(10 pts)

** d) The airfield east of Van Nuys Airport is named what?
_____(10 pts)

** e) Los Angeles International Airport can accept special VFR traffic.
  True   or   False_____(10 pts)

156 IFR Flights of "13MIKE"

"Something a pilot should do often is to give pilot reports on current weather. Those become so invaluable to any pilot about to fly, and they are so easy to make. There is a format to giving these PIREPS, but don't let that deter you from giving them. When all is said and done, it's what you're saying or reporting that's newsworthy, not how you say it. But so you have an understanding of a complete PIREP, here are its parts:

1) Some 3 letter station identifier nearest you
2) Whether the PIREP is routine or urgent
3) Your location in relationship to a VOR
4) Time
5) Altitude
6) Your aircraft type
7) Sky cover - in other words, cloud coverage and height
8) The kind of weather you're encountering
9) Temperature
10) Wind
11) Turbulence
12) Icing

And any other remarks which you feel are important. On some future flights which we'll fly together, we'll work on giving some PIREPS. But I want you to see that they are fairly easy to give and to understand.

Well, it's time for another brief. You'll have to call San Diego this time, since Oceanside obviously doesn't have its own FSS! See you in about fifteen, twenty minutes, Okay?"

WEATHER BRIEF

You:
"San Diego! It looks like another gorgeous southern California day to fly in your neck of the woods! Have you ever heard of a book called **Flights of '13MIKE'**?"

San Diego FSS:

"Yeah! Everybody out here has been talking about it as the greatest procedural tool for flight training that has come out since the American Revolution! Why do you ask?"

You:

"Well, I'm interested in obtaining a weather brief for an IFR cross country. Tail number is November 9413MIKE, a Cessna 182 RG. I'd like to depart Oceanside Municipal at zero four three zero Zulu, one hour from now. Cruising at six thousand feet and going north to Van Nuys Airport. Time enroute will be one hour, and I'm a commercial pilot, instrument rated."

San Diego FSS:

"WOW! What a coincidence! Your tail number is just like the book's! That's pretty terrific! That's really something that you're also a Cessna 182 RG!"

You:

"Yes! And not only that, but this is the very same 13MIKE that all of California is talking about! And you are going to be in the second book, which is part of what this flight is all about! Congratulations!"

San Diego FSS:

"Gee, wait till I tell my husband! I'm honored to hear from you! As far as I'm concerned, you take the place of Superman, who kept on busting regulations whenever he flew! Never respected Victor airways, didn't bother to get any takeoff clearances, and certainly kept passing up his preflight checklists! 13MIKE is my hero now!

Okay, I better get serious now!

There is a flight precaution in southern California for widely scattered thunderstorms.

There is a low pressure center over southern California with a cold front extending north from San Diego.

> Currently at Oceanside, measured ceiling one thousand one hundred overcast, five thousand overcast, visibility four in light rain showers, temperature five six, wind one one zero at one zero, with rain having begun two five minutes past the hour. Altimeter two niner niner niner.
> Enroute ceilings are generally one thousand five hundred broken with scattered thunderstorms.
> Van Nuys is reporting estimated ceiling three hundred overcast, visibility one and a half miles in haze, temperature five zero, wind one four zero at one two, and altimeter two niner niner eight.
> No PIREPs.
> Oceanside is forecast ceiling one thousand overcast, visibility three, wind one zero zero at one zero.
> Enroute, ceiling is forecast generally two thousand five hundred overcast.
> Van Nuy's terminal forecast beginning zero five zero zero Zulu is ceiling five hundred overcast, visibility two, wind one three zero at one five.
> At six thousand, winds aloft one four zero at two four.
> There are no local or distant NOTAMs.
> Now this is interesting! An FDC NOTAM is in effect from two three zero zero to zero seven zero zero this week. Temporary flight restrictions are in effect due to a tethered balloon operation on both VFR and IFR weather in the airspace at and below five thousand feet MSL, one nautical mile radius of Paradise VORTAC (PDZ) two niner zero degree radial at twenty seven nautical miles.
> Now make sure you make me sound real good in your book, okay?!"

FILING THE FLIGHT PLAN -

You:

> "Don't worry! You've charmed me by your mannerisms already! If you're ready, I can go ahead and give you my flight plan for this trip. Thank you for the spectacular weather brief - it's as complete a picture as I'll ever need."

San Diego FSS:

"You're more than welcome! I'm alive with happy fingers!"

You:

"IFR, November 9413MIKE, Cessna 182 RG - slash A, one forty true, Departure - Oceanside Municipal, zero four three zero Zulu, six thousand feet, Route - direct OCN VORTAC, Victor 23 LAX, direct to VNY Destination. ETE is one plus zero five. Fuel on board is five plus five zero. Alternate - Oxnard. [YOUR NAME - CONTACT PHONE NUMBER - HOME BASE], request an ILS approach runway one six Right for practice and landing. Two on board, Red over white."

San Diego FSS:

"Let me get on the line with Los Angeles Center and if you hang on, I'll get you a clearance."

You:

"I'll be right here!"

San Diego FSS:

"All right! I have your clearance. Are you ready to copy?"

You:

"I'm set! Go ahead."

San Diego:

"ATC clears Cessna 9413MIKE to Seal Beach VOR. Expect further clearance zero five one five Zulu. Maintain six thousand. San Diego Departure frequency will be one two seven point three, squawk four three three three. Clearance Void Time will be zero four four five. Time now zero three three zero."

You:

"Cessna 9413MIKE is cleared to Seal Beach VOR. EFC zero five one five Zulu. Maintain six thousand. Departure one two seven point three, squawk four three three three. Void zero four four five."

IFR Flights of "13MIKE"

San Diego FSS:

"Readback correct! Have a safe one, and keep writing your 13MIKE books!"

You:

"You're a swell fan! I'll send you a free copy of the newest upcoming release! Thank you!"

SETUP

Aircraft:
  1) Choose **"Cessna Skylane RG"**

Weather:

Winds
  1) Set Surface winds **"DEPTH"** to **"1000"**
  2) Set Surface winds **"DIR"** to **"110"**
  3) Set Surface winds **"SPEED"** to **"10"**
  4) Set Level 1 **"TOPS"** to **"4000"**
  5) Set Level 1 **"BASE"** to **"1050"**
  6) Set Level 1 **"DIR"** to **"130"**
  7) Set Level 1 **"SPEED"** to **"16"**
  8) Set Level 2 **"TOPS"** to **"7000"**
  9) Set Level 2 **"BASE"** to **"4000"**
  10) Set Level 2 **"DIR"** to **"140"**
  11) Set Level 2 **"SPEED"** to **"24"**

Clouds
  1) Set Bottom Level - **TOPS** to **"4000"**
  2) Set Bottom Level - **BASE** to **"1200"**
  3) Set Bottom Level - **COVER** to **"overcast"**
  4) Set Top Level - **TOPS** to **"8500"**
  5) Set Top Level - **BASE** to **"5100"**
  6) Set Top Level - **COVER** to **"overcast"**
  7) Set Thunderstorms - **TOPS** to **"8500"**

Oceanside to Van Nuys

8) Set Thunderstorms - **BASE** to "**3000**"
9) Set Thunderstorms - **COVERAGE** to "**scattered**"

Aircraft Position:
1) "**NORTH**" to "**14974.2071**" [N033° 13' 05.5455]
2) "**EAST**" to "**6095.0017**" [W117° 21' 08.1480]
3) "**ALTITUDE**" to "**36**" [0]
4) "**HEADING**" to "**150**"

note: At this point you may wish to save this setup for future use

PREFLIGHT

note: Set **ZOOM** to "**1.0**"
Set **TIME** to "**21:30**"

"All righty-O! We've got our clearance, and this time rather than having it all the way to the destination at Van Nuys, they've given us a clearance limit to Seal Beach VOR. A clearance limit is always accompanied by an expect further clearance (EFC) time, so that if you lose radio communications at the clearance limit, you can depart that limit at the EFC time, rather than waiting until the ETA to your destination. Beautiful Oceanside! It'll be sad to leave. The Mission San Louis Rey, plus the pier and harbor were peaceful to visit. But a pilot must do what a pilot must do, so let's UNICOM it!"

Instruments:

1) Tune **COM** to "**123.0**" (UNICOM)

You:

"OCEANSIDE UNICOM, CESSNA 9413MIKE IS AT THE RAMP. WOULD YOU PLEASE GIVE ME YOUR ADVISORIES ON WIND, RUNWAY IN USE, AND ALTIMETER SETTING PLEASE?"

Oceanside UNICOM:

"CESSNA 9413MIKE, WIND ZERO NINER ZERO AT NINER, YOU'LL TAKEOFF ON RUNWAY SIX. ALTIMETER TWO NINER NINER NINER."

You:

"THANKS UNICOM. I'LL LET YOU KNOW WHEN I'M TAXIING."

"Because we're taking off from an uncontrolled airport, we again have a clearance void time to work with. We'll easily make its window, but if for instance, we ate too many burgers and realized we'd be late, then it's important to call up the FSS and revise the clearance void time. They expect to hear from us airborne by that time. I'll continue this dialog, [or is it a monologue?], after you've set up your instruments."

2) Set "**Altimeter**" and "**Heading Indicator**"
3) Set **XPDR** to "**4333**" (assigned IFR code)
4) Tune **NAV 1** to "**115.3**" (OCN)
5) Set **NAV 1 OBS** to a **centered** "**TO**" needle
6) Tune **NAV 2** to "**115.7**" (SLI)
7) Set **NAV 2 OBS** to "**300**"
8) Set the **DME** to "**NAV 1**" and "**DIST**"
9) Check **CARB HEAT** is "**OFF**"
10) Check **GEAR** "**DOWN**"
11) Turn **STROBE** "**ON**"
12) Turn **LIGHTS** "**ON**"

"Takeoff plans become rather simple in this case, don't they? No SID, no vectors - oh, they could give us some vectors once we talk to them, but most likely you'll just be flying the IFR departure procedure listed for this airport. Runway six is the active, so you're looking at a climbing right turn to a heading of two three five, and then eventually pointing your nose to Oceanside VOR. Piece of cake!"

You:

"OCEANSIDE UNICOM, CESSNA 13MIKE TAXIING TO RUNWAY SIX FOR DEPARTURE, IFR."

Oceanside UNICOM:

"CESSNA 13MIKE, TAKE CARE!"

TAXI -

"It's a right turn and taxi straight towards those shadowy night silhouetted little mountains until you're at the hold short for runway six. There are two basic requirements to flying in instrument meteorological conditions (IMC) within controlled airspace. One is that you must have a filed flight plan. Two is that you receive a clearance from that flight plan. Do you know what situation we would be in if we took off late, like past the clearance void time, and then checked in with departure control? We'd be in violation because once the void time was past, our clearance would have been canceled! That's why you've got to watch your time management under this situation."

RUN UP -

        1) Set brake (hold down to prevent aircraft from moving)
        2) Advance power to about "**1800**" RPM
**   3) Select **CARB HEAT "ON"**, record RPM drop_____(5 pts)
        4) Select **CARB HEAT "OFF"**
**   5) Select "**LEFT**" Mag, record RPM drop_____(5 pts)
        6) Select "**BOTH**" Mags
**   7) Select "**RIGHT**" Mag, record RPM drop_____(5 pts)
        8) Select "**BOTH**" Mags
        9) Reduce power to **idle**

"Let's do a no flap takeoff this time. It's good to vary things once in a while. 13MIKE can handle the pressure, I'm sure!"

        10) Check **FLAPS** are up

"Just to wrap up this clearance void time stuff, you do have a thirty minute window past the void time to call FSS and advise of the change in your plans. What's hard on the airspace system is that for the thirty minutes after your void time, all IFR traffic is suspended for Oceanside, in order to ensure no potential conflict with you. After thirty minutes, ATC sends the dogs out after you to sniff and hunt you out! What I mean is, they start making phone calls, which is the beginning of search and rescue initiation procedures taking place on your behalf. Anyway, we haven't goofed on this one, so talk to traffic and let's have some more fun in the sky!"

164   IFR Flights of "13MIKE"

You:
        "OCEANSIDE TRAFFIC, CESSNA 13MIKE IS TAKING THE ACTIVE, RUNWAY SIX, IFR. RIGHT TURNOUT."

FLIGHT

Takeoff:

"Turning onto an open runway is life in the fast lane! Who in his or her right mind wouldn't want to be a pilot, if they knew what this was all about? You know, at the Naval Academy, I had a very similar feeling when cruising with the Yard Patrol craft in Santee Basin and the Chesapeake Bay. Open those throttles up and smell the diesel, watch the water rush by under the bow, and see the other YP craft somewhere within the formation pattern. The freedom of the seas is much the same as the freedom of the skies. I love it! Yeah, yeah, okay! Sentimental fool that I am! Only joshing! Check fuel, flaps are up - remember, no flap takeoff - oil temperature and pressure green, and trimmed for takeoff. Lined up beautifully - go!"

1) Record TIME_____
2) Release brakes and taxi onto runway 6
3) Advance power to "**FULL**"
4) Maintain centerline of runway
5) At **50 knots** airspeed, lift nose wheel off runway
6) At **70 knots,** ease back on the yoke to establish a 10 degree pitch up attitude
7) Maintain a climb **AIRSPEED** of **80 knots**
8) Raise **Gear** when there is no more runway to land on
9) Reset **NAV 1 OBS** to a **centered** needle
10) At "**600**" feet above the ground, turn **RIGHT** to a heading of "**235**"
11) Tune **COM** to "**127.3**"

"Perfect! Very nicely flown! You jumped on that like a bug on a pork chop, or however that saying goes in Texas!"

Oceanside to Van Nuys 165

You:

> "SAN DIEGO DEPARTURE, CESSNA 9413MIKE IS WITH YOU, PASSING NINER HUNDRED FOR SIX THOUSAND."

San Diego Departure:

> "CESSNA 9413MIKE, SAN DIEGO DEPARTURE, IDENT."

12) Reduce power to about "**2300**" RPM at "**1000**" feet above the ground (AGL)
13) Press the IDENT button (simulate)
14) Reset **NAV 1 OBS** to a **centered** needle

"Wonderful! Now don't forget about the fifteen hundred foot move. You're a smoothie on this departure!"

15) When the altimeter reads "**1500**" feet, turn **RIGHT** to a **centered** needle
16) Track inbound on the **OCEANSIDE VOR** direct radial displayed

** 17) What is the NAV 1 OBS **centered** needle **HEADING**? _____ (25 pts)

San Diego Departure:

> "CESSNA 9413MIKE, SAN DIEGO DEPARTURE, RADAR CONTACT."

You:

> "CESSNA 13MIKE, ROGER."

"Well, well! No vectors, just a 'Be on your way' kind of salutation! Next comes station passage over Oceanside VOR, then a straight shot to Seal Beach VOR with either a clearance to continue or else we'll have some holding practice. Boy, is that ever a Pandora's Box full of treasures and techniques when talking about holding! I'll introduce some of those concepts for you during this flight."

6

IFR Flights of "13MIKE"

Instrument Departure:

1) When the **DME** on **NAV 1** reads "**0.4**" **[0.5]**, turn right to a heading of "**300**"
2) Set **NAV 1 OBS** to "**300**"
3) Track outbound on the **OCEANSIDE VOR 300** radial

4) When passing "**5000**" feet, press "**P**" to pause the simulation

** 5) Record your:

    NAV 1 CDI POSITION_____(40 pts)
    AIRSPEED_____(35 pts)
    HEADING_____(30 pts)
    NAV 1 DME DIST_____(25 pts)
    RPM_____(25 pts)
    LIGHTS_____(15 pts)

6) Press "**P**" to continue the simulation

**

"Atten-hut! Parade right! Salute the Marines at Camp Pendleton off our right wing! HWWRRAHHH! You know, I used to associate those sounds with the Marine Corps, but now it seems more normal to consider them of Klingon origin! What are the names of the three intersections we'll fly over on this Victor airway?

    1)_____
    2)_____
    3)_____(10 pts)

How many miles is it from Oceanside VOR to Seal Beach VOR?
_____(5 pts)

Southwest of Van Nuys is the home of the world's greatest Buffalo Burgers imaginable! What airport am I talking about?
_____(5 pts)

[If you miss this one, get 13MIKE's first book!]

What is the outbound course of the enroute holding pattern at Seal Beach?_____(5 pts)

And you can see it's left hand turns, not right hands turn, right? That makes it a nonstandard holding pattern, since right hand turns are standard."

Level off:

    1) Begin to level off when the altimeter reads "**5900**" feet
    2) Maintain "**6000**" feet
    3) Reduce power to about "**2200**" [**2400**] RPM

San Diego Departure:

    "CESSNA 13MIKE, CONTACT LOS ANGELES CENTER ONE TWO SIX POINT THREE FIVE."

You:

    "CESSNA 13MIKE, SWITCHING ONE TWO SIX POINT THREE FIVE. SO LONG!"

    4) Tune **COM** to "**126.35**" (Los Angeles Center)

You:

    "LOS ANGELES CENTER, CESSNA 9413MIKE WITH YOU SIX THOUSAND."

Los Angeles Center:

    "CESSNA 9413MIKE, LOS ANGELES CENTER, RADAR CONTACT."

Enroute Hold:

**   1) When the **NAV 1 DME DIST** reads "**18.0**", record your:
       GROUND SPEED_____(25 pts)
       DISTANCE REMAINING TO SEAL BEACH VOR
       _____(15 pts)
    2) When the **NAV 1 DME DIST** reads "**23.0**", transition to **NAV 2 OBI**
    3) Set **DME** to "**NAV 2**"
    4) Track inbound on the **SEAL BEACH VOR 120** radial

168 IFR Flights of "13MIKE"

"Do you know why we switched to Seal Beach at twenty three DME from Oceanside? Because that's what is called the changeover point for this specific leg of the Victor airway we're on. There are three ways to identify a changeover point. And by the way, a changeover point, or COP, is where you switch a navaid frequency to where you're going instead of where you came from. Anyway a COP occurs either:
  1. *where it's designated by what I call a half a swastika symbol*
  2. *where a definite course change occurs*
     or
  3. *at the halfway point, if reasons one or two don't happen*

In our case, it's halfway, so that's why we did the switcheroo!"

**   5) When the **NAV 2 DME DIST** reads "**13.5**", record your:
       NAV 2 CDI POSITION_____(30 pts)
       ALTITUDE_____(20 pts)
**   6) How many seconds does it take for the **NAV 2 DME DIST**
       to go from "**11.0**" to "**10.1**"?_____(20 pts)
**   7) Based on this data, what is your GROUND SPEED?
       _____(20 pts)

"What you have just accomplished is called an airborne ground speed check. DME pretty much gets rid of that procedure, unless you're off airway not tracking a VOR, but you still want to know the basics of IFR navigation, and that's one of them. We're about three minutes away from Seal Beach, so let's give Center a jingle to see whether we can boost a clearance out of them, or else maintain the original game plan until the EFC time arrives."

You:
> **"LOS ANGELES CENTER, CESSNA 9413MIKE WOULD LIKE FURTHER CLEARANCE FROM SEAL BEACH TO VAN NUYS IF POSSIBLE."**

Los Angeles Center:
> **"CESSNA 9413MIKE, LOS ANGELES CENTER, EXPECT FURTHER CLEARANCE IN ONE FIVE MINUTES. HOLD SOUTHEAST AS PUBLISHED."**

Oceanside to Van Nuys

You:

> "CESSNA 13MIKE, HOLD SOUTHEAST SEAL BEACH AS PUBLISHED."

"Two important factors about holding are the control of a one minute inbound leg, and whatever necessary crab correction you'll need to fly a good holding pattern. One rule of thumb to remember is that if you have a certain crab angle needed to maintain the inbound holding pattern track, then make sure you double that angle on the outbound one. In our case, winds are from one four zero degrees, so it'll be a little bit of a left correction on the inbound leg. Whatever the correction is, double it to the right on the outbound leg."

8) When the **NAV 2 DME DIST** reads "**7.5**", reduce power to about "**1600**" [**2050**] RPM (100 knot holding speed)
9) When the **NAV 2 DME DIST** reads "**0.4**" [**0.9**], turn **LEFT** to a heading of "**120**" (standard rate)
10) Maintain "**120**" course for **1½** minutes

You:

> "LOS ANGELES CENTER, CESSNA 13MIKE HAS ENTERED HOLDING."

Los Angeles Center:

> "CESSNA 13MIKE, ROGER."

"We're going outbound for a minute and a half because it's a headwind you're flying into, twenty degrees off your right nose. So to get that one minute inbound leg, where the ground speed will be greater than the outbound leg, we must extend the time on the outbound leg."

11) Turn **LEFT** towards a heading of "**300**" (standard rate)

"I believe we'll overshoot our inbound course because of the wind, so don't forget to turn past the three zero zero heading to get back on the inbound track."

12) When wings are level, note TIME_____
13) Track inbound on the **SEAL BEACH VOR 120** radial
14) When the **NAV 2 DME DIST** reads "**0.4**" [**0.9**], note TIME, and turn **LEFT** to a heading of "**125**"_____

** 15) TOTAL INBOUND TIME IS_____(20 pts)
16) Maintain "**125**" course for **1 3/4** minutes

"This is a slight correction to the right to compensate for overshooting the inbound course the first time. And we needed more outbound time to get the one minute inbound time, so we'll see how this works!"

17) Turn **LEFT** towards a heading of "**300**"
18) Track inbound on the **SEAL BEACH VOR 120** radial

Los Angeles Center:

"CESSNA 13MIKE, CLEARED TO VAN NUYS AIRPORT."

You:

"CESSNA 13MIKE IS CLEARED VAN NUYS."

"Okay! They cleared us a little bit earlier than our EFC time. I was getting dizzy anyway! Now we head towards Los Angeles and begin our next major consideration of an instrument approach into Van Nuys. Always think ahead. Otherwise the AHEAD will become the PAST NOW! Got that? And that's when all of a sudden you've switched activities from flying to playing pool - because you got yourself behind the eight ball!"

19) When the **NAV 2 DME DIST** reads "**0.4**" [**0.9**], turn **LEFT** to a heading of "**272**"
20) Set **NAV 2 OBS** to "**272**"
21) Increase power to about "**2200**" [**2400**] RPM
22) Track outbound on the **SEAL BEACH VOR 272** radial

"Now is as good a time as any, while you're reporting to Center anyway, to get a frequency change approved so you can receive Van Nuy's ATIS information."

Oceanside to Van Nuys

You:

> "LOS ANGELES CENTER, CESSNA 13MIKE IS LEAVING HOLDING. REQUEST PERMISSION TO SWITCH OFF FREQUENCY FOR A MOMENT."

Los Angeles Center:

> "CESSNA 13MIKE, APPROVED AS REQUESTED. REPORT BACK ON."

Enroute Cruise:

1) Tune **NAV 1** to "**113.6**" (LAX)
2) Set **NAV 1 OBS** to "**304**"
3) Tune **COM** to "**118.45**" (Van Nuys ATIS)

> "VAN NUYS AIRPORT, INFORMATION ALPHA, ZERO FOUR FIVE FIVE ZULU WEATHER, ESTIMATED CEILING FOUR HUNDRED OVERCAST, VISIBILITY TWO AND ONE HALF IN HAZE, TEMPERATURE FIVE THREE, DEWPOINT FOUR ONE. WIND ONE FOUR ZERO AT ONE TWO, ALTIMETER TWO NINER NINER SIX. ILS RUNWAY ONE SIX RIGHT IN USE. LANDING RUNWAY ONE SIX RIGHT. ADVISE ON INITIAL CONTACT YOU HAVE INFORMATION ALPHA."

4) Set **ALTIMETER**, set **HI**, and check **FUEL**
5) Tune **COM** to "**126.35**" (Los Angeles Center)

You:

> "LOS ANGELES CENTER, CESSNA 9413MIKE IS BACK WITH YOU."

Los Angeles Center:

> "CESSNA 9413MIKE, LOS ANGELES CENTER. ROGER."

172   IFR Flights of "13MIKE"

    6) When the **NAV 2 DME DIST** reads "**10.0**", press "**P**" to pause the simulation

**   7) Record your:

        HEADING to keep NAV 2 CDI centered_____(35 pts)
        ALTITUDE_____(25 pts)
        AIRSPEED_____(20 pts)
        RPM_____(15 pts)
        COM FREQUENCY_____(10 pts)
        LOS ANGELES VOR IDENT
        _____(5 pts)

    8) Press "**P**" to continue the simulation

** "Your next checkpoint of interest is what?_____(5 pts)
Do you see the comment 'V-25 2700 SE' associated with that fix? That's a minimum crossing altitude, and it pertains to you only if you are heading southeast bound from the intersection along Victor twenty five. In other words, if you were coming from Los Angeles VOR southeast bound along Victor twenty five, some time before reaching this intersection, you would have to scoot up two hundred feet from the shown two thousand five hundred MEA to at least the required two thousand seven hundred right at the intersection, and continue the climb to three thousand two hundred which is the following MEA."

    9) When the **NAV 2 DME DIST** reads "**16.0**", turn **RIGHT** to a heading of "**304**"
   10) Track inbound on the **LOS ANGELES VOR 124** radial that your **NAV 1 OBI** is displaying
   11) Tune **NAV 2** to "**113.1**" (VNY)
   12) Set **DME** to "**NAV 1**"
   13) When the **NAV 1 DME DIST** reads "**0.7**" **[1.2]**, set **NAV 2 OBS** to a **centered** "**TO**" needle
   14) When the **NAV 1 DME DIST** reads "**0.4**" **[0.9]**, turn to the heading of the centered needle
   15) Track inbound on that direct radial to **VAN NUYS VOR**
   16) Set **DME** to "**NAV 2**"

** 17) What radial are you tracking inbound on?_____(40 pts)

Oceanside to Van Nuys   173

"You notice there is no Victor Airway from this point on? That's why on the flight plan, it's filed as Los Angeles VOR direct to Van Nuys, which then happens to be the initial approach fix for the ILS into runway one six, which ATIS told us was in use. This stuff is easy, ain't it?"

Los Angeles Center:

> **"CESSNA 13MIKE, CONTACT BURBANK APPROACH ONE THREE FOUR POINT TWO."**

You:

> **"CESSNA 13MIKE, SWITCHING ONE THREE FOUR POINT TWO. ENJOYED IT!"**

    18) Tune **COM** to "**134.2**" (Burbank Approach)

You:

> **"BURBANK APPROACH, CESSNA 9413MIKE IS WITH YOU."**

Burbank Approach:

> **"CESSNA 9413MIKE, BURBANK APPROACH, RADAR CONTACT. CLEARED ILS RUNWAY ONE SIX RIGHT APPROACH INTO VAN NUYS. REPORT UMBER INBOUND."**

You:

> **"CESSNA 13MIKE CLEARED ILS RUNWAY ONE SIX RIGHT. WILL REPORT UMBER INBOUND."**

    19) Press "**P**" to pause the simulation

**

"While I've got your attention, turn to your approach plate for the ILS runway one six right into Van Nuys.
    1. What is your initial heading once crossing Van Nuys VOR?
        _____(5 pts)
    *2. If glideslope fails, this approach could continue as a localizer approach. TRUE or FALSE*_____(5 pts)

6

IFR Flights of "13MIKE"

3. How many miles is it from Van Nuys VOR to the displaced threshold of runway 16R?_____(5 pts)

4. You can go no lower than what altitude before intercepting glideslope?_____(5 pts)

5. A straight in landing to runway 16R has for a decision height an altitude of_____(5 pts)

6. The first altitude of concern in the missed approach procedure is to be at or below_____(5 pts)

Oh boy! It's almost time to do an ILS! These are great experiences, especially with the localizer being as sensitive as it is. Also, note that you will have to use both the localizer and the VOR for this approach. Well, you don't have to, but if you want to know your DME, you will have to!"

    20) Press "**P**" to continue the simulation

    21) Tune **NAV 1** to "**112.5**" (FIM)
    22) Set **NAV 1 OBS** to "**054**"
    23) When the **NAV 2 DME DIST** reads "**0.4**" **[0.8]**, turn **LEFT** to a heading of "**324**"

"Now begins the initial segment of this instrument approach procedure. You're looking cool!"

    24) Set **NAV 2 OBS** to "**324**"
    25) Track outbound on the **VAN NUYS VOR 324** radial

Weather:

    <u>**Clouds**</u>

    1) Set Thunderstorm - **COVERAGE** to "**widely scattered**"

Initial approach segment:

    1) When the **NAV 2 DME DIST** reads "**11.5**", press "**P**" to pause the simulation

**
2) Record your:
   NAV 2 CDI POSITION_____(35 pts)
   HEADING to keep NAV 2 CDI centered
   _____(30 pts)
   VSI_____(25 pts)
3) Press "**P**" to continue the simulation

4) When the **NAV 2 DME DIST** reads "**12.0**", reduce power to about "**2000**" **[2300]** RPM (120 knots)
5) When the **NAV 1 CDI** is 2 dots **LEFT** of center, turn **RIGHT** to a heading of "**054**"
6) Track outbound on the **FILLMORE VOR 054** radial
7) Set **NAV 2 OBS** to "**334**"
8) Reduce power to about "**1800**" **[2150]** RPM (110 knots)
9) When the **NAV 2 CDI** is **centered**, turn a very gradual **RIGHT** to a heading of "**160**" (half standard rate turn)
10) Tune **NAV 1** to "**111.3**" (IVNY)
11) Set **NAV 1 OBS** to "**160**"
12) Track inbound on the **IVNY LOCALIZER 340** radial

"Now begins your intermediate segment of the instrument approach procedure. Remember to report UMBER inbound. You're looking neat!"

Final approach:

1) Descend to and maintain "**4300**" feet at **110 knots**

You:

"**BURBANK APPROACH, CESSNA 9413MIKE, UMBER INBOUND.**"

Burbank Approach:

"**CESSNA 13MIKE, BURBANK APPROACH, CONTACT VAN NUYS TOWER ONE ONE NINER POINT THREE.**"

You:

"**CESSNA 13MIKE, SWITCHING TOWER ONE ONE NINER POINT THREE.**"

IFR Flights of "13MIKE"

       2) Tune **COM** to "**119.3**" (Van Nuys Tower)

You:

"VAN NUYS TOWER, CESSNA 9413MIKE, LOCALIZER INBOUND RUNWAY ONE SIX RIGHT APPROACH WITH ALPHA."

Van Nuys Tower:

"CESSNA 9413MIKE, VAN NUYS TOWER, RUNWAY ONE SIX RIGHT, CLEARED TO LAND. WIND ONE FIVE ZERO AT ONE ONE. REPORT FIELD IN SIGHT."

You:

"CESSNA 13MIKE, CLEARED TO LAND. WILL REPORT FIELD."

       3) When at "**4300**" feet, adjust airspeed to **100 knots**
       4) When the **NAV 2 DME DIST** reads "**7.6**", glideslope needle should be centered
       5) Begin descent on glideslope
       6) Select **GEAR** "**DOWN**"
       7) Set **CARB HEAT** "**ON**"

"Keep scanning that glideslope needle and CDI, but don't chase. Set a rate of descent, set a heading, and then analyze if they are right. If not, set a different rate of descent, a different heading, and analyze again. Over and over. You're looking suave!"

       8) When the **NAV 2 DME DIST** reads "**4.0**", press "**P**" to pause the simulation

**   9) Record your:
           NAV 1 GLIDESLOPE INDICATOR POSITION
           _____(40 pts)
           ALTITUDE_____(35 pts)
           AIRSPEED_____(30 pts)
           VSI_____(25 pts)
           STROBES_____(20 pts)

Oceanside to Van Nuys

                GEAR_____(20 pts)
                RPM_____(15 pts)
                DECISION HEIGHT_____(10 pts)
                COM FREQUENCY_____(10 pts)
                CARB HEAT_____(10 pts)

   10) Press "**P**" to continue the simulation

   11) When runway 16R is in sight, slow to **90 knots**

You:

   "VAN NUYS TOWER, CESSNA 13MIKE HAS THE FIELD."

Van Nuys Tower:

   "CESSNA 13MIKE, ROGER."

   12) Set **FLAPS** to **first notch** (10 degrees)
   13) Set **FLAPS** to **second notch** (20 degrees)
   14) Airspeed should be **75 knots**
   15) When you are 10 to 20 feet off the runway, reduce power to about "**1000**" RPM and start to slowly pitch the nose of the aircraft up to slow your descent and establish a touchdown attitude
   16) When you are five feet off the runway, hold the nose of the aircraft up and allow the airspeed to **SLOWLY** bleed off. Your aircraft will <u>settle</u> onto the runway while you follow the centerline
   17) After touchdown, reduce power to **600 RPM**
   18) Apply the brakes

Van Nuys Tower:

   "CESSNA 13MIKE, TURN RIGHT FOURTH INTERSECTION, ONE ZERO GOLF. CONTACT GROUND POINT SEVEN EXITING THE RUNWAY."

You:

   "CESSNA 13MIKE, ONE ZERO GOLF."

178 IFR Flights of "13MIKE"

"WOW! That was pretty seeing the field pop visible like it did! And you absolutely stunned me with your control of that approach! What a pilot! Wrap things up for us, and we'll close another exciting adventure with a successful check mark of fun!"

    19) Taxi the aircraft off the active runway to the **RIGHT**
    20) When the aircraft has stopped, set **CARB HEAT** to "**OFF**"
    21) Set **FLAPS** to "**0**"
    22) Tune **COM** to "**121.7**" (Van Nuys Ground)

You:

    "VAN NUYS GROUND, CESSNA 9413MIKE ON ONE ZERO GOLF FOR TAXI."

Van Nuys Ground:

    "CESSNA 9413MIKE, VAN NUYS GROUND, TURN LEFT AND PROCEED TO PARKING BY THE TOWER."

You:

    "CESSNA 13MIKE, ROGER."

**   23) Record the **TIME**_____(5 pts)

    TOTAL POINTS POSSIBLE FOR THIS FLIGHT___**930**___

Flight Scenario Seven

Watsonville to Oakland

(San Francisco Area - estimated flying time 70 minutes)

Watsonville! Watsonville! Where is Watsonville? Who was Watson anyway? Okay! Okay! I found Watsonville. It's south of San Jose on the coast. Pretty little place. Okay, now that I have found Watsonville, let's see where you will be going. Looks like you will be going to Oakland International Airport. You may have to do some fancy flying to get into this place, with the weather the way it is. They will probably make you fly some STAR and make you jump through hoops, and roll over or something like that! Well, let's look over the flight plan, and get a weather brief so Professor Calfior can get you airborne. He is trying to find Watsonville! I will try and give him directions, but you know Professor Calfior. You can lead him to water but he still can't find Watsonville! I'm sure he will arrive before departure time. He has never let a student down yet. Be kind to him when he does arrive. It's not easy trying to drive and read a low altitude enroute chart. It doesn't have any roads on it!

Read Professor Calfior's lips. He can help you nail these numbers and procedures. Even if he can't find Watsonville!

Don't bark when they have you roll over! It's not polite!

FLIGHT PLAN -

This route of flight follows well established departure, climb, cruise, descent, and landing procedures. You will depart Watsonville Municipal (**Airport diagram and Departure procedures in Appendix C7**) on runway 26, following the prescribed IFR departure procedures. Time to takeoff will be 1200 Zulu.

Upon getting airborne and safely established, you will commence a climbing left turn direct to PAJAR NDB, contact Monterey Departure Control, then proceed outbound on the 212 degree magnetic bearing to MOVER intersection on Victor 25. This is shown both on the Departure procedures and the IFR low altitude enroute chart L-2, of which the chart is in **Appendix B4**. You will climb up to and maintain 8000 feet cruise, where you'll reach a true airspeed of 125 knots. There is an 1800 foot restriction at MOVER intersection, but you will be well above that then, so you immediately can go outbound on the Salinas VOR 292 radial.

You'll be switched soon to Oakland Center. Upon arriving at SANTY intersection, try to get a radar vector to EUGEN intersection on Victor 27, which is on the Big Sur VOR 310 radial at 67 DME. It is now that you will begin the HADLY ONE ARRIVAL (**Appendix C7**) into Oakland International Airport.

From EUGEN intersection, track inbound on the Point Reyes VOR 144 radial inbound, through TAILS intersection and then to HADLY intersection. A descent into Oakland International Airport may commence at this point, after you turn right and go inbound on the Sausalito VOR 168 radial. You will be given to Bay Approach Control.

From the weather, runway 27 will be the active runway for ILS approaches, so you might find Bay Approach desiring you to arc around to the east, in order to set up for the ILS RWY 27R instrument approach. (**Appendix C7**) You will descend to some intermediate altitude, and either be vectored to the final approach course, or as stated previously, fly an arc.

Once established on the final approach course, minimum glideslope altitude will be 3500 feet, but can be dropped down to 3000 feet at ATC's discretion. This approach becomes interesting because you are tracking inbound on the localizer, but relying upon DME information from Oakland VOR. Decision height for this approach is 254 feet, and there's a good chance, because of the low cloud deck, that you might have to go missed approach. That means onward to San Jose International! But if the runway does pop into sight, then land straight ahead on runway 27R. Oakland's airport diagram is in **Appendix C7**. This should take you 70 minutes, which is a drop in the bathtub of your 5 hours and 45 minutes of fuel on board!

FILLING OUT THE FLIGHT PLAN -

Fill out the following Flight Plan completely, carefully paying attention to your route of flight. Trace out your route using the IFR low altitude enroute chart L-2 (**Appendix B4**).

FLIGHT PLAN

1. TYPE	2. AIRCRAFT IDENTIFICATION	3. AIRCRAFT TYPE/ SPECIAL EQUIPMENT	4. TRUE AIRSPEED	5. DEPARTURE POINT	6. DEPARTURE TIME		7. CRUISING ALTITUDE
IFR VFR DVFR			KNOTS		PROPOSED (Z)	ACTUAL (Z)	

8. ROUTE OF FLIGHT

9. DESTINATION (Name of airport and city)	10. EST. TIME ENROUTE HOURS MINUTES	11. REMARKS

12. FUEL ON BOARD HOURS MINUTES	13. ALTERNATE AIRPORT(S)	14. PILOT'S NAME, ADDRESS, TELEPHONE NO. AND AIRCRAFT HOME BASE	15. NO. ABOARD

16. COLOR OF AIRCRAFT

CLOSE FLIGHT PLAN WITH_____ FSS

Now answer these questions from your flight plan and enroute chart.
** a) What is in block 8, Route of Flight, of your flight plan?
_____(10 pts)
** b) What is the minimum obstruction clearance altitude for the leg on Victor 25 between MOVER and SANTY intersections?____(10 pts)
** c) Off of what VOR does EUGEN intersection's minimum reception altitude pertain to? _____(10 pts)
** d) How many miles is it from EUGEN to HADLY intersection, and then direct to Oakland VOR?_____(10 pts)
** e) How many different Victor airway radials extend outward from Oakland VOR?_____(10 pts)

"By casting my eyeballs in the direction of the skies, I can safely say there's a fairly low cloud deck. No thunderstorms, as far as I can see or hear. Just a pretty day to go flying all in all.

Did I ever tell you that I flew into a thunderstorm once? Daggondest thing! All the dumb things I've done were while I was in the military, but the thing was embedded and poof! I was in it! It's a whole new world inside a thunderstorm cell! An adjective befitting the interior is violent. Updrafts, down drafts, side rides, you name it - they're there! According to the AIM, the best thing to do is to hold your attitude and make a one hundred and eighty degree turn to fly back out where you flew in.

I stress the word '*attitude*', because your airplane is dancing to heavy metal rock and roll music inside. To try to hold an altitude will over stress your airplane. And to maintain an airspeed is impossible because you are literally at the mercy of the storm cell. By holding an attitude, your airplane is being bounced around, but you're not fighting it, so you are not inducing any stress yourself on the airplane.

So I simply worked on a standard rate turn for sixty seconds, rolled out, and almost immediately, I was out! Now that I think about it, this would be a good visual simulator drill for every pilot to experience. It sure opens your eyes to the power of a thunderstorm, and why you don't play with them, or even try to get close.

Go ahead and get our weather if you would. The phone is right over there, under the sign that reads, '**Tony the Terminator ate lead here, may he rest in peace!**' There're still pockmarks on the wall, too! I'll tell you what, use the other phone over there! I can't afford to lose a customer!"

WEATHER BRIEF

You:

"Salinas FSS, good early morning to you! I'm off to a dawn start on an IFR cross country in aircraft tail number November 9413MIKE, which is a Cessna 182 RG. Departure from Watsonville Municipal in about forty five minutes, and I'll cruise at eight thousand feet. This will be a coastal route up to the north, west of Woodside to Oakland International. ETE will be seventy minutes."

Salinas FSS:

"There are no flight precautions for your flight.
A strengthening low pressure system is over central California.
Watsonville's weather currently is reported as a measured ceiling two hundred overcast, visibility one in heavy rain, temperature seven two, wind two niner zero at six, altimeter two niner eight six.
Enroute ceilings are generally one thousand broken, six thousand overcast.
Oakland currently is reporting estimated ceiling four hundred broken, two thousand five hundred overcast, visibility one and a half miles in light rain and fog. Temperature six niner, dewpoint six five, wind two eight zero at one zero, altimeter two niner eight four.
About one half hour ago, a King Air reported flying through seven thousand feet in a climb, fifteen miles south of Woodside VOR, and encountering light turbulence.
Terminal forecast for Watsonville is ceiling three hundred overcast, visibility two.
Enroute ceilings are forecast one thousand overcast.
Oakland's terminal forecast for your time of arrival is ceiling five hundred broken, three thousand overcast, visibility one and a half miles, wind two seven zero at one one.
Winds at niner thousand, which are good for eight thousand, expect two five zero at two niner.
No NOTAMs, either local or distant.
Is there anything else I can do for you?"

FILING THE FLIGHT PLAN -

You:

"Can you slip some of that coffee through the telephone lines?!! I think I'll go ahead and file. It all sounds good to me."

IFR Flights of "13MIKE"

Salinas FSS:

"Go ahead!"

You:

"IFR, November 9413MIKE, Cessna 182 RG - slash A, one two five true airspeed, Departure - WVI, one two zero zero Zulu, eight thousand feet, Route - AY NDB, direct MOVER intersection, Victor twenty five to SANTY intersection, direct EUGEN intersection, HADLY ONE ARRIVAL to destination Oakland. ETE is zero plus seven zero. Fuel on board five plus four five. Alternate - San Jose International, [YOUR NAME - CONTACT PHONE NUMBER - HOME BASE], two on board, Red over white."

Salinas FSS:

"Okay! Let me verify this somewhat. You want to fly direct from AY NDB to MOVER, right? Then also direct from SANTY to EUGEN?"

You:

"Yeah! Let's work with that, and I'll probably get vectors once I'm flailing around up there anyway! No problem from my point of view. Is it okay?"

Salinas FSS:

"Oh sure! I just wanted to make sure you weren't planning on Victor airway-ing it all the way through. Give me a moment to contact Oakland Center, and I'll have your clearance for you."

You:

"Thank you."

Salinas FSS:

"If you're ready to copy, I have your clearance."

You:

"I'm ready to copy."

Salinas FSS:

"ATC clears Cessna 9413MIKE to Oakland International Airport as filed. Maintain eight thousand. Monterey Departure frequency will be one two seven point one five. Squawk five six one six. Clearance Void Time will be one two one five Zulu."

You:

"Cleared to Oakland as filed, eight thousand, Monterey Departure one two seven point one five. Five six one six is the squawk, and void time of one two one five."

Salinas FSS:

"Readback correct. Have a great flight!"

You:

"Thanks, and have the best day all day!"

SETUP

Aircraft:
   1) Choose "**Cessna Skylane RG**"

Weather:

   <u>**Winds**</u>
   1) Set Surface winds "**DEPTH**" to "**1000**"
   2) Set Surface winds "**DIR**" to "**290**"
   3) Set Surface winds "**SPEED**" to "**6**"
   4) Set Level 1 "**TOPS**" to "**5000**"
   5) Set Level 1 "**BASE**" to "**1170**"
   6) Set Level 1 "**DIR**" to "**280**"
   7) Set Level 1 "**SPEED**" to "**20**"
   8) Set Level 2 "**TOPS**" to "**8500**"
   9) Set Level 2 "**BASE**" to "**5000**"
   10) Set Level 2 "**DIR**" to "**270**"
   11) Set Level 2 "**SPEED**" to "**25**"

Clouds

1) Set Bottom Level - **TOPS** to "5500"
2) Set Bottom Level - **BASE** to "260"
3) Set Bottom Level - **COVER** to "overcast"
4) Set Top Level - **TOPS** to "9000"
5) Set Top Level - **BASE** to "6000"
6) Set Top Level - **COVER** to "overcast"

Aircraft Position:

1) "**NORTH**" to "16995.7636" [N036° 56' 13.8493]
2) "**EAST**" to "5137.7624" [W121° 47' 19.3886]
3) "**ALTITUDE**" to "167" [0]
4) "**HEADING**" to "350"

note: At this point you may wish to save this setup for future use.

PREFLIGHT

note: Set **ZOOM** to "1.0"
Set **TIME** to "05:00"

"I love these early morning starts! And this one in particular will be exciting because you get to do some work using an NDB for departure! With all these stars above, it promises to be a sweet sunrise also. Have you ever gone fishing? I took my daughter out for her first time yesterday! She's five years old, and it was very enjoyable to see her excitement. All day, we didn't catch one fish, but each time we threw out the line, it was exciting to anticipate the tug of a fish grabbing the bait! Flying is like that! You keep on going up for more, and each flight is rewarding in itself. Okay, do your stuff!"

Instruments:

1) Tune **COM** to "122.8" (UNICOM)

You:

> "WATSONVILLE UNICOM, GOOD MORNING! CESSNA 9413MIKE. WOULD YOU GIVE ME SOME OF YOUR NUMBERS, PLEASE?"

Watsonville UNICOM:

> "CESSNA 9413MIKE, WE'LL USE RUNWAY TWO SIX AS THE ACTIVE, SINCE WIND IS TWO NINER ZERO AT SIX. ALTIMETER TWO NINER EIGHT SIX."

You:

> "I'M GOING TO DO SOME CHECKS HERE, AND THEN I'LL CALL AGAIN TO LET YOU KNOW WHEN I'M TAXIING."

"It's so quiet out here on the ramp! Even the props seem quiet. Let's get our instruments set up, with the ADF having a frequency of three two seven. Salinas and Big Sur are the first two VORs that you'll be using, right?"

2) Set "**Altimeter**" and "**Heading Indicator**"
3) Set **XPDR** to "**5616**" (assigned IFR code)
4) Tune **NAV 1** to "**117.3**" (SNS)
5) Set **NAV 1 OBS** to "**292**"
6) Set **ADF** to "**327**" (AY NDB - PAJAR)
7) Activate "**ADF**"
8) Tune **NAV 2** to "**114.0**" (BSR)
9) Set the **DME** to "**NAV 1**" and "**DIST**"
10) Check **CARB HEAT** is "**OFF**"
11) Check **GEAR** "**DOWN**"
12) Turn **STROBE** "**ON**"
13) Turn **LIGHTS** "**ON**"

"We really ought to do more night time or early morning flying. Those flashing lights of red and green on the wings kind of lull me into a mellow mood! I know it's tempting to crank up the instrument panel lights so you can see better, but keep them at a low setting. You don't want to destroy the night vision you have. Are you ready to taxi to two six? Call UNICOM then."

188 IFR Flights of "13MIKE"

You:
>"WATSONVILLE UNICOM, CESSNA 13MIKE TAXIING RUNWAY TWO SIX, IFR DEPARTURE."

Watsonville UNICOM:
>"CESSNA 13MIKE, SEE YOU!"

TAXI -

"Okay! Just turn right and taxi down to the approach end of runway two six. And be thinking about the departure procedure, as we've discussed in the brief. From seeing your past flying skills, I have not a worry in the world that you'll do as well throughout this flight."

RUN UP -

        1) Set brake (hold down to prevent aircraft from moving)
        2) Advance power to about "**1900**" RPM
**   3) Select **CARB HEAT "ON"**, record RPM drop_____(5 pts)
        4) Select **CARB HEAT "OFF"**
**   5) Select "**LEFT**" Mag, record RPM drop_____(5 pts)
        6) Select "**BOTH**" Mags
**   7) Select "**RIGHT**" Mag, record RPM drop_____(5 pts)
        8) Select "**BOTH**" Mags
        9) Reduce power to **idle**
        10) Set **FLAPS** to **first notch** (10 degrees takeoff configuration)

**
"Let's look at the departure procedure. It says that aircraft departing MOVER intersection three zero zero degrees clockwise to one zero zero degrees climb on course. All other aircraft climb in MOVER intersection holding pattern (hold northeast, right turns, two one two degrees inbound) to cross MOVER intersection at or above eighteen hundred feet, then climb on course. What is our heading out of MOVER? _____(5 pts)

*So we fit in the category of potentially holding, if we're not at eighteen hundred feet at MOVER, right? We'll see where you're at when the time arrives. But think of your holding entry. Would it be direct, teardrop, or parallel?*_____*(5 pts)*
*You know, this airport has available to it a localizer approach, a VOR approach, and an NDB approach. Can it be used as an alternate when a destination gets weathered in?*_____*(5 pts)*
*Runway eight has what kind of visual path indicator?*_____*(5 pts)*
Runway two six is narrower than runway two by how many feet?
_____*(5 pts)*
I'm ready to takeoff when you are!"

You:

"WATSONVILLE TRAFFIC, CESSNA 13MIKE IS TAKING THE ACTIVE, RUNWAY TWO SIX, IFR. LEFT TURNOUT."

FLIGHT

Takeoff:

"We're going! We're going! All right! We're taxiing, then we're going! Do your checks. Another commandment to safe flying is **'Ignoreth not thy checklists, for many are the switches, handles, gauges, and other devils awaiting to take cruel vengeance upon thee.'** *Don't ever shirk your duty to safety! Right! Fuel full, flaps are at ten, your trim is hep for takeoff, and the oil temperature/pressure is groovy. Lights are on. Now we're going!"*

1) Record TIME_____
2) Release brakes and taxi onto runway 26
3) Advance power to "**FULL**"
4) Maintain centerline of runway
5) At **50 knots** airspeed, lift nose wheel off runway
6) At **70 knots**, ease back on the yoke to establish a 10 degree pitch up attitude
7) Maintain a climb **AIRSPEED** of **80 knots**
8) Raise **Gear** when there is no more runway to land on

IFR Flights of "13MIKE"

    9) At "**500**" feet above the ground, raise the **FLAPS** to "**0**"
    10) Tune **COM** to "**127.15**" (Monterey Departure)

You:

    "MONTEREY DEPARTURE, CESSNA 9413MIKE IS WITH YOU, PASSING NINER HUNDRED FOR EIGHT THOUSAND."

Monterey Departure:

    "CESSNA 9413MIKE, MONTEREY DEPARTURE, IDENT."

    11) Press the IDENT button (simulate)
    12) Reduce power to about "**2300**" RPM at "**1000**" feet above the ground (AGL)

    13) Press "**P**" to pause the simulation
**   14) Record your:
        AIRSPEED_____(30 pts)
        HEADING_____(25 pts)
        CARD COURSE which the ADF needle is pointing to
        _____(25 pts)
        ANTICIPATED LEFT TURN ROLLOUT HEADING
        _____(20 pts)
        ALTITUDE_____(15 pts)
        COM FREQUENCY_____(15 pts)
        XPDR_____(10 pts)
        GEAR_____(10 pts)
        FLAPS_____(10 pts)
        RPM_____(5 pts)
    15) Press "**P**" to continue the simulation

    16) Turn **LEFT** and proceed direct to AY NDB (PAJAR) on the **ADF**

Monterey Departure:

    "CESSNA 9413MIKE, MONTEREY DEPARTURE, RADAR CONTACT."

You:

> "CESSNA 13MIKE."

"Superimposing the head of the ADF on your heading indicator will tell you what course to turn to, in order to put the ADF needle on the nose. Another method is to add your magnetic course to the card course on the head of the ADF needle, and if necessary, subtract three hundred and sixty degrees to get the proper course to turn to. That's with a fixed ADF card. If you can rotate the ADF card, then simply put your magnetic course on the top and read what the head of the ADF needle says. Or another method is to just guess! Of the choices offered, which one would you throw out?!"

IFR Departure Procedure:

1) When the **ADF** needle falls left or right **90 degrees**, turn **RIGHT** to a heading of "**212**"
2) Track outbound on the **AY NDB 212** magnetic bearing
3) Climb up to and maintain "**8000**" feet

"To know an ADF is to love an ADF! Do you remember what your forecast winds are from the weather briefing? They're just about straight off your right side at two seven or two eight zero, twenty-ish or so knots. Being blown to the left, you'll need a right correction to hold the two one two magnetic bearing. So take a correction to the right, and the goal is for the ADF to remain fixed on that equal correction to the right. Then you're tracking outbound."

Monterey Approach:

> **"CESSNA 9413MIKE, CONTACT OAKLAND CENTER ONE TWO FIVE POINT FOUR FIVE."**

You:

> **"CESSNA 9413MIKE, SWITCHING OAKLAND CENTER, ONE TWO FIVE POINT FOUR FIVE. GOOD DAY!"**

4) Tune **COM** to "**125.45**" (Oakland Center)

IFR Flights of "13MIKE"

You:

"OAKLAND CENTER, CESSNA 9413MIKE IS WITH YOU."

Oakland Center:

"CESSNA 9413MIKE, OAKLAND CENTER, RADAR CONTACT."

** 5) When the **NAV 1 CDI** is ½ dot **LEFT** of center, record the wind correction angle you needed to track outbound _____(45 pts)

6) Turn **RIGHT** to a heading of "**292**"

7) When wings are level, press "**P**" to pause the simulation

** 8) Record your:
NAV 1 DME DIST_____(35 pts)
ALTITUDE_____(30 pts)
AIRSPEED_____(25 pts)
RPM_____(20 pts)
COM FREQUENCY_____(15 pts)
IS **MOVER** intersection BEHIND or IN FRONT OF you?_____(15 pts)

9) Press "**P**" to continue the simulation

10) Track outbound on the **SALINAS VOR 292** radial
11) When level, reduce power to about "**2200**" [**2400**] RPM

"Outstanding job! I think that's enough ADF work for you, until I get you back to Block Island! We'll go up to SANTY intersection now. Do you see that note on 'MRA 7000' at SANTY? That's called a minimum reception altitude. It refers to an off airway aid to help identify SANTY. You see, being at or above the minimum enroute altitude of five thousand feet on our Victor twenty five, we will have either Salinas VOR or Woodside VOR to be always in touch. But in case one fails, SANTY intersection can also be found by way of the one seven niner degree radial from San Jose VOR. To get that signal, you must be at or above the minimum reception altitude given of seven thousand feet. Neat, huh?"

Enroute - Victor 25 to Victor 27:

1) Deactivate the **ADF**
2) Set **NAV 2 OBS** to "**310**"

"Now that's a good prep on your part! Three one zero is the radial you should be on once you're established on Victor twenty seven! I'm going to have to give you some emergencies like a puppy peeing on the wing, or something, in order to rile you up!"

**   3) When the **NAV 1 DME DIST** reads "**26.0**", record your:
         NAV 1 CDI POSITION_____(30 pts)
         HEADING_____(25 pts)
         RPM_____(20 pts)
4) When the **NAV 1 DME DIST** reads "**28.5**":

"See if you can get a vector from Center to side slip us over to Victor twenty seven."

You:

    "OAKLAND CENTER, CESSNA 13MIKE, REQUEST RADAR VECTOR TO INTERCEPT VICTOR TWENTY SEVEN SOUTH OF EUGEN INTERSECTION."

Oakland Center:

    "CESSNA 13MIKE, ROGER. TURN LEFT HEADING TWO FIVE ZERO, INTERCEPT VICTOR TWO SEVEN, BIG SUR THREE ONE ZERO DEGREE RADIAL, SOUTH OF EUGEN INTERSECTION, THEN PROCEED ON COURSE."

You:

    "CESSNA 13MIKE, LEFT TWO FIVE ZERO. THANKS!"

5) When the **NAV 1 DME DIST** reads "**29.0**", turn **LEFT** to a heading of "**250**"

**   6) What intersection did you just reach?_____(15 pts)
7) Set "**DME**" to "**NAV 2**"

8) Tune **NAV 1** to "**114.1**" (SJC)
9) Set **NAV 1 OBS** to "**220**"

"That again is excellent forethought! You've recognized that on Victor twenty seven, it's a long way from Big Sur, about sixty seven nautical miles, to EUGEN intersection. It's also a long way to Point Reyes VOR, about sixty two nautical miles. So using San Jose's two two zero degree radial is a great insurance policy, just in case Big Sur or Point Reye's DME or radial information poof out on us!"

10) When the **NAV 2 CDI** is centered, turn **RIGHT** to a heading of "**310**"
11) Track outbound on the **BIG SUR VOR 310** radial
12) If the **NAV 2 DME** becomes lost, maintain track and reference the **NAV 1 OBI**

** 13) What heading will you fly to maintain track?_____(30 pts)
14) When the **NAV 1 CDI** is **centered**, turn **RIGHT** to a heading of "**319**" (wind correction heading)
15) Tune **NAV 1** to "**113.7**" (PYE)
16) Set **NAV 1 OBS** to "**324**"
17) Set **DME** to "**NAV 1**"

18) Press "**P**" to pause the simulation
** 19) Record your:
    NAV 1 DME DIST_____(35 pts)
    NAV 1 CDI POSITION_____(30 pts)
    AIRSPEED_____(20 pts)
    ALTITUDE_____(20 pts)
    POINT REYES VOR IDENT
    _____(10 pts)
    What intersection was just passed?_____(5 pts)
20) Press "**P**" to continue the simulation

21) Track inbound on the **POINT REYES VOR 144** radial

Watsonville to Oakland

"If you notice from your HADLY ONE arrival plate, we kind of fell into this arrival route from midway in. Because it actually starts at Big Sur VOR, but you didn't want to fly south that far just to start it proper! Many times, to intersect an arrival route at midstream is no problem at all. Sometimes, it's disapproved, but few and far between in frequency. Now you can put down your sectional, and fly your STAR."

To HADLY Intersection:

**

1) Tune **NAV 2** to "**113.9**" (OSI)
2) Set **NAV 2 OBS** to "**222**"
3) After the **NAV 2 CDI** is **centered**, record the:
   NAV 1 DME DIST_____(25 pts)
   NAV 1 CDI POSITION_____(25 pts)
   What intersection did you just pass?_____(10 pts)
4) Tune **NAV 2** to "**116.2**" (SAU)
5) Set **NAV 2 OBS** to "**348**"

"This is smart to keep working off of the NAV 2 VOR, because first of all, you're still flying off of Point Reyes from your track. Secondly, reserve the NAV 1 for Oakland's VOR, where most of your work will concentrate. I'm clueless as to what's happening in Oakland, so what should YOU do? ATIS it is!"

You:

"OAKLAND CENTER, CESSNA 13MIKE, REQUEST PERMISSION TO SWITCH OFF FREQUENCY FOR A SHORT TIME."

Oakland Center:

"CESSNA 13MIKE, APPROVED AS REQUESTED. REPORT BACK ON BAY APPROACH ONE THREE FIVE POINT SIX FIVE."

You:

"CESSNA 13MIKE, BAY APPROACH ONE THREE FIVE POINT SIX FIVE."

IFR Flights of "13MIKE"

      6) Tune **COM** to "**128.5**" (Oakland ATIS)

"OAKLAND INTERNATIONAL AIRPORT, INFORMATION DELTA, ONE ONE FIVE FIVE ZULU WEATHER, ESTIMATED CEILING THREE HUNDRED OVERCAST, VISIBILITY ONE AND A HALF, LIGHT RAIN AND FOG. TEMPERATURE SEVEN ZERO, DEWPOINT SIX SEVEN. WIND TWO EIGHT ZERO AT ONE THREE. ALTIMETER TWO NINER EIGHT FOUR. ILS RUNWAYS TWO NINER AND TWO SEVEN RIGHT IN USE. LANDING AND DEPARTING RUNWAYS TWO NINER AND TWO SEVEN RIGHT AND LEFT. ADVISE ON INITIAL CONTACT YOU HAVE INFORMATION DELTA."

      7) Set **ALTIMETER**, set **HI**, check **FUEL**
      8) Tune **COM** to "**135.65**" (Bay Approach)

You:

"BAY APPROACH, CESSNA 9413MIKE, SOUTH OF HADLY AT EIGHT THOUSAND."

Bay Approach:

"CESSNA 9413MIKE, BAY APPROACH, SQUAWK TWO SEVEN THREE FOUR, AND IDENT."

You:

"CESSNA 13MIKE, SQUAWK TWO SEVEN THREE FOUR, AND IDENT."

      9) Set **XPDR** to "**2734**" (new assigned IFR code)
      10) Press the IDENT button (simulate)

Bay Approach:

"**CESSNA 13MIKE, RADAR CONTACT.**"

"Now we wait for HADLY intersection, and then the fun will really begin. I think I know what Bay Approach has in store for you, and it'll be brand new to your experience. I've done it a couple of times here, and it's great exercise! Someone once told me that whenever he felt like exercising, he just went to lay down in bed until the feeling went away! Well, you're not that way! Prepare to exercise!"

    11) When the **NAV 2 CDI** is **centered**, turn **RIGHT** to a heading of "**348**"
    12) Track inbound on the **SAUSALITO VOR 168** radial

Enroute Descent:

Bay Approach:

    "CESSNA 13MIKE, BAY APPROACH, DESCEND AND MAINTAIN FOUR THOUSAND. CIRCLE NORTHEASTWARD ONE FIVE NAUTICAL MILE ARC OFF OAKLAND VOR UNTIL ESTABLISHED ON THE LOCALIZER FOR ILS RUNWAY TWO SEVEN RIGHT APPROACH. REPORT LOCALIZER INBOUND."

You:

    "CESSNA 13MIKE, LEAVING EIGHT FOR FOUR. ONE FIVE MILE ARC NORTHEASTWARD OFF OAKLAND VOR FOR LOCALIZER INBOUND ILS RUNWAY TWO SEVEN RIGHT. REPORT LOCALIZER INBOUND."

"Yup! They did done it, they dood! This is what I was talking about - arcing to the localizer! Challenging, but I know you love challenges! Priority is get down fast, like now! As that's happening, set up NAV 1 for your arcing work with Oakland VOR."

    1) Establish a "**1500**" **FPM** rate of descent
    2) Reduce power to about "**1900**" [**2200**] RPM
    3) Track inbound on the **SAUSALITO VOR 168** radial
    4) Descend to and maintain "**4000**" feet
    5) While in the descent, tune **NAV 1** to "**116.8**" (OAK)
    6) When at "**4000**", keep power at about "**1900**" [**2200**] RPM

IFR Flights of "13MIKE"

South Arc to the Localizer:

1) Set **NAV 1 OBS** to a **centered** needle
2) Keep the **NAV 1 CDI** needle **centered** periodically with a **TO** indication

"You do that so you know which heading to turn to when you turn right ninety degrees from the radial track you're on. A DME arc means DME is definitely hyped in your scan."

3) When the **NAV 1 DME DIST** reads "**16.0**", the **NAV 1 CDI** should be centered with around **050 TO**

4) Press "**P**" to pause the simulation

** 5) Record your:
   NAV 2 CDI POSITION_____(35 pts)
   ALTITUDE_____(30 pts)
   AIRSPEED_____(25 pts)
   RPM_____(20 pts)
   NAV 1 OBS with centered needle "TO"_____(15 pts)
6) Press "**P**" to continue the simulation

7) Turn **RIGHT** to a heading of "**140**"

*"See? You're leading the turn to the arc by about one nautical mile. The goal is to stay at fifteen DME all throughout the arc. For every **point one** nautical mile inside the arc, correct to the right by five degrees. For every **point one** nautical mile outside the arc, correct to the left by ten degrees. Once established here, reset your NAV 1 OBS to the next ten degree radial heading **TO**, which is zero four zero, since we started with zero five zero."*

8) Hold onto "**15.0**" on the **NAV 1 DME DIST**
9) Set **NAV 1 OBS** to "**040**"
10) Turn **LEFT** to a heading of "**130**"
11) When **NAV 1 CDI** is **centered**, set **NAV 1 OBS** to "**030**"
12) Turn **LEFT** to a heading of "**120**"

13) When **NAV 1 CDI** is **centered**, set **NAV 1 OBS** to "**020**"
14) Turn **LEFT** to a heading of "**110**"
15) When **NAV 1 CDI** is **centered**, set **NAV 1 OBS** to "**010**"
16) Turn **LEFT** to a heading of "**100**"

17) When the **NAV 1 CDI** is **centered**, press "**P**" to pause the simulation

** 18) Record your:
   NAV 1 DME DIST_____(40 pts)
   ALTITUDE_____(35 pts)
   XPDR_____(25 pts)
   COM FREQUENCY_____(25 pts)
   RPM_____(15 pts)
19) Press "**P**" to continue the simulation

20) Set **NAV 1 OBS** to "**000**"
21) Turn **LEFT** to a heading of "**090**"

"Because you'll be on the ILS to Oakland, you better set up your NAV 1 to the localizer. Just get Oakland VOR into your NAV 2 now, and it'll be much easier towards the end. I'm impressed with how you're arcing! Stay with it."

22) Tune **NAV 2** to "**116.8**" (OAK)
23) Set the **NAV 2 OBS** to "**000**", transition to **NAV 2 OBI** for the remaining arc
24) Set **DME** to "**NAV 2**"
25) Tune **NAV 1** to "**109.9**" (IOAK Localizer)
26) Set **NAV 1 OBS** to "**276**"
27) When **NAV 2 CDI** is **centered**, set **NAV 2 OBS** to "**350**"
28) Turn **LEFT** to a heading of "**080**"
29) When **NAV 2 CDI** is **centered**, set **NAV 2 OBS** to "**340**"
30) Turn **LEFT** to a heading of "**070**"
31) When **NAV 2 CDI** is **centered**, set **NAV 2 OBS** to "**330**"
32) Turn **LEFT** to a heading of "**060**"
33) When **NAV 2 CDI** is **centered**, set **NAV 2 OBS** to "**320**"
34) Turn **LEFT** to a heading of "**050**"

IFR Flights of "13MIKE"

    35) When **NAV 2 CDI** is **centered**, set **NAV 2 OBS** to "310"
    36) Turn **LEFT** to a heading of "040"

"Stupendous! Keep up the good work! Now somewhere close by, you'll get a false localizer signal where the CDI will start to go through the center. Don't get fooled by it! From the approach plate, you know that you have to be east of the localizer, so our heading before turning inbound must be about three six zero or so, east of Oakland's airport."

    37) When **NAV 2 CDI** is **centered**, set **NAV 2 OBS** to "300"
    38) Turn **LEFT** to a heading of "030"
    39) When **NAV 2 CDI** is **centered**, set **NAV 2 OBS** to "290"
    40) Turn **LEFT** to a heading of "020"
    41) When **NAV 2 CDI** is **centered**, set **NAV 2 OBS** to "280"
    42) Turn **LEFT** to a heading of "010"
    43) When **NAV 2 CDI** is **centered**, set **NAV 2 OBS** to "270"
    44) Turn **LEFT** to a heading of "000"

"Pretty soon now, that localizer will start moving. Keep your scan fluid, but check more regularly the NAV 1 CDI, because once it moves, it MOVES! At fifteen miles out, four dots is a good lead in to the turn, which equates to eight degrees localizer."

Off the arc to the localizer:

    1) When the **NAV 1 CDI** is moving inside 4 dots **RIGHT** of center, turn **LEFT** to a heading of "276"

    2) When wings are level, press "**P**" to pause the simulation
**   3) Record your:
        ALTITUDE_____(30 pts)
        NAV 2 DME DIST_____(25 pts)
        Are you BELOW or ABOVE glideslope?_____(15 pts)
        NAME OF NEXT CHECKPOINT ON ILS
        _____(10 pts)
        NAME OF CHECKPOINT FOLLOWING THAT
        _____(10 pts)

Watsonville to Oakland

GLIDESLOPE INTERCEPTION ALTITUDE
_____(10 pts)
NAME OF AIRPORT on the south side of the
LOCALIZER TRACK_____(10 pts)
OAKLAND LOCALIZER IDENT
_____(10 pts)

4) Press "**P**" to continue the simulation

You:

> "BAY APPROACH, CESSNA 13MIKE, LOCALIZER INBOUND."

Bay Approach:

> "CESSNA 13MIKE, ROGER. CLEARED FOR ILS RUNWAY TWO SEVEN RIGHT APPROACH. DESCEND AND MAINTAIN THREE THOUSAND. REPORT HAYZE INBOUND."

You:

> "CESSNA 13MIKE, ILS RUNWAY TWO SEVEN RIGHT. REPORT HAYZE INBOUND."

"What's important now is to slow the airspeed down to one hundred knots, and lose one thousand feet so we can be at minimum glideslope altitude. A note on the approach does say that ATC can bring us down to three thousand if they desire, in case you're wondering. But sweat usually shows there are other things on your mind!"

5) Reduce power to about "**1600**" [**2000**] RPM
6) Descend to and maintain "**3000**" feet
7) Track inbound on the **OAKLAND LOCALIZER**

"Keep that RPM where it's at! It's tempting to want to scoot it back up, but you're now in approach territory, which calls for ninety to a hundred knots thereabouts. Also, remember that your DME information on this approach is coming from Oakland VOR, not the localizer."

8) When the **NAV 2 DME DIST** reads "**11.7**", reduce power to about "**1500**" **[1800]** RPM
9) When the glideslope needle centers, select **GEAR "DOWN"**
10) Set **CARB HEAT "ON"**
11) Set **FLAPS** to **first notch** (10 degrees)
12) Maintain glideslope with a "**400 - 500**" **FPM** rate of descent
13) Reduce power to about "**1400**" **[1950]** RPM
14) When **NAV 2 DME** reads "**9.0**":

You:

"BAY APPROACH, CESSNA 13MIKE, HAYZE INBOUND."

Bay Approach:

"CESSNA 13MIKE, CONTACT OAKLAND TOWER ONE ONE EIGHT POINT THREE."

You:

"CESSNA 13MIKE, SWITCHING TOWER ONE ONE EIGHT POINT THREE. THANKS FOR THE ARC PRACTICE!"

"Did you really mean that thanks?!!! Don't forget to put your strobes back on."

15) Tune **COM** to "**118.3**" (Oakland Tower)

You:

"OAKLAND TOWER, CESSNA 9413MIKE, EIGHT MILES INBOUND FOR LANDING, ILS RUNWAY TWO SEVEN RIGHT. I HAVE INFORMATION DELTA."

Oakland Tower:

"CESSNA 9413MIKE, OAKLAND TOWER, RUNWAY TWO SEVEN RIGHT, CLEARED TO LAND."

16) When **NAV 2 DME DIST** reads "**6.0**", press "**P**" to pause the simulation

** 17) Record your:
  GLIDESLOPE NEEDLE POSITION_____(45 pts)
  NAV 1 CDI NEEDLE POSITION_____(45 pts)
  ALTITUDE_____(35 pts)
  VSI_____(30 pts)
  AIRSPEED_____(20 pts)
  DECISION HEIGHT_____(20 pts)
  GEAR_____(15 pts)
  FLAPS_____(15 pts)
  STROBES_____(10 pts)

18) Press "**P**" to continue the simulation

Missed Approach Point:

1) When field is in sight at "**254**" feet, set **FLAPS** to **second notch** (20 degrees)

"Right on the money! Get thirty degrees of flaps in! This is great!"

2) When stabilized, set **FLAPS** to **third notch** (30 degrees)
3) Airspeed should be **70 knots**
4) When you are 10 to 20 feet off the runway, reduce power to about "**1000**" RPM and start to slowly pitch the nose of the aircraft up to slow your descent and establish a touchdown attitude
5) When you are five feet off the runway, hold the nose of the aircraft up and allow the airspeed to **SLOWLY** bleed off. Your aircraft will <u>**settle**</u> onto the runway while you follow the centerline
6) After touchdown, reduce power to **600 RPM**
7) Apply the brakes

IFR Flights of "13MIKE"

Oakland Tower:

> "CESSNA 13MIKE, WELCOME TO OAKLAND! TURN RIGHT FIRST INTERSECTION. CONTACT GROUND POINT NINER EXITING THE RUNWAY."

You:

> "CESSNA 13MIKE, FIRST INTERSECTION. GROUND POINT NINER."

"What are you sweating so much for? You made it look so easy! I'll tell you what! I'll buy you a rum and coke, with no rum! To the right, it looks like a regular metropolis. Don't be in a rush. Relax a little, and then contact Ground. You're quite disciplined to fly as well as you have!"

    8) Taxi the aircraft off the active runway to the **RIGHT**
    9) When the aircraft has stopped, set **CARB HEAT** to "**OFF**"
    10) Set **FLAPS** to "**0**"
    11) Tune **COM** to "**121.9**" (Oakland North Complex Ground)

You:

> "OAKLAND GROUND, CESSNA 9413MIKE ON ECHO FOR TAXI."

Oakland Ground:

> "CESSNA 9413MIKE, OAKLAND GROUND, TURN LEFT AND TAXI TO THE EXECUTIVE TERMINAL ABOUT YOUR ELEVEN O'CLOCK POSITION."

You:

> "CESSNA 13MIKE, EXECUTIVE TERMINAL. THANKS!"

**   12) Record the **TIME**_____(5 pts)

    TOTAL POINTS POSSIBLE FOR THIS FLIGHT__**1365**__

Flight Scenario Eight

Block Island to Marthas Vineyard

(New York Area - estimated flying time 45 minutes)

It looks like Professor Calfior found Watsonville after all. I gave him directions that Wrong Way Corrigan could have followed! It seems just a short time ago we were on scenario one and here it is scenario eight. They have been exciting flights and I hate to see this all come to an end. But wait! I have a great idea! I'll talk Professor Calfior into helping me write another book, and we can continue our adventures with 13MIKE. I think we'll call it **Airienteering with "13MIKE"**. What is Airienteering, you say? Well, Airienteering is the art of pilotage by way of clues. These clues come in the form of puzzles of various sorts, brain teasers, consulting your local aviation books, or fellow flyers. Most of, but not all, the answers to the puzzles will be provided. I get excited just talking about it! Before we forget, you have a flight to go on. So let's get cracking! You depart Block Island, Rhode Island and shoot the ILS into Marthas Vineyard, Massachusetts. The ceilings are going to be rather low, so be ready for anything. You will go over the flight plan, get the weather, file your flight plan, setup the aircraft, pick up Professor Calfior and have an exciting flight.

See you in the next book. Professor Miller signing off.

FLIGHT PLAN -

This route of flight follows well established departure, climb, cruise, descent, and landing procedures. It is a nice short 45 minute flight, and you have lots of fuel on board. You have computed 6 hours. You will depart Block Island State Airport (**Airport diagram in Appendix C8**) at 2345 Zulu on runway 28. Upon takeoff, maintain runway heading until 1500 feet, then reverse your course with a turn to the left and go direct to Block Island NDB. Climb up to 5000 feet as cruise altitude. Your true airspeed at cruise will be 120 knots.

You will contact Ocean Departure as soon as possible so they know you're airborne. Now follow the IFR low altitude enroute chart L-25 in **Appendix B6**. At station passage over Block Island NDB, you will proceed outbound on Victor 268 which is the Sandy Point VOR 046 radial to MINNK intersection. If Sandy Point VOR continues to be out of service, then you can expect radar vectors and a flip over to Boston Center.

Eventually, you'll intercept Victor 374, which is flown via the Marthas Vineyard 282 radial inbound. You might want to descend to 3000 feet on Victor 374 since that is its minimum enroute altitude. As you near Marthas Vineyard, you will be switched to Cape Approach Control, where you will be cleared for the ILS RWY 24 instrument approach procedure into Marthas Vineyard. From 3000 feet, you'd descend when cleared, to 1500 feet.

The ILS RWY 24 instrument approach plate (**Appendix C8**) shows that BORST intersection is the initial approach fix. So from Marthas Vineyard VOR, you'd turn left to track outbound on the Marthas Vineyard 058 radial for 4.2 miles until intercepting BORST intersection at 5.0 DME on the Marthas Vineyard localizer.

Now, you need to reverse course so that you can proceed inbound on the final approach course. To do that, it's a holding pattern turn as depicted, so you must shoot for the outside corner of the holding pattern shown. That takes a 30 degree cut, called a teardrop entry, to a heading of 086 for 1 minute, then a standard rate turn to the left in order to intercept the Marthas Vineyard localizer for a 236 degree inbound course.

When glideslope is intercepted, descend on glideslope to your decision height of 263 feet for a straight in landing to runway 24. Again, the cloud deck is fairly low, so be prepared to execute missed approach procedures to New Bedford Regional, if the field is not in sight. Marthas Vineyard airport diagram is in **Appendix C8**.

Block Island to Marthas Vineyard

FILLING OUT THE FLIGHT PLAN -

Fill out the following Flight Plan completely, carefully paying attention to your route of flight. Trace out your route using the IFR low altitude enroute chart L-25.

FLIGHT PLAN

1. TYPE	2. AIRCRAFT IDENTIFICATION	3. AIRCRAFT TYPE/ SPECIAL EQUIPMENT	4. TRUE AIRSPEED	5. DEPARTURE POINT	6. DEPARTURE TIME		7. CRUISING ALTITUDE
IFR VFR DVFR			KNOTS		PROPOSED (Z)	ACTUAL (Z)	

8. ROUTE OF FLIGHT

9. DESTINATION (Name of airport and city)	10. EST. TIME ENROUTE		11. REMARKS
	HOURS	MINUTES	

12. FUEL ON BOARD		13. ALTERNATE AIRPORT(S)	14. PILOT'S NAME, ADDRESS, TELEPHONE NO. AND AIRCRAFT HOME BASE	15. NO. ABOARD
HOURS	MINUTES			

16. COLOR OF AIRCRAFT

CLOSE FLIGHT PLAN WITH_____FSS

Now answer these questions from your flight plan and enroute chart.

** a) What is in block 8, Route of Flight, of your flight plan?
_____(10 pts)

** b) With a runway 28 departure from Block Island, and a left turn back to the NDB, what navaid, radial and DME would be most appropriate to also help define the NDB as a backup?
_____(10 pts)

** c) What is the airport elevation at Marthas Vineyard Airport?
_____(10 pts)

** d) What is the TACAN (Tactical Air Navigation used by the military) station frequency at Marthas Vineyard?_____(10 pts)

** e) MINNK intersection is what DME:
from Norwich VOR_____
from Marthas Vineyard VOR_____
from Sandy Point VOR_____
from Groton VOR _____(10 pts)

"Another beautiful evening in the Caribbean with floating banana boats, and a Bartles and Jaymes Pina Colada wine cooler to ease our blanched and pallid brows from the balmy sweat induced eighty plus degrees of muggy temperature! It's my fantasy, so shut up ... please! Reggae music is playing in the background, and I can just hear the giggling laughter of children playing on the beach. All of a sudden, in a whirlwind, a NOTAR helicopter signals to land on our verandah, and one of those fancy hotel doormen steps down, snaps me a salute, hands me a message in a bottle, gets back in the cockpit, and disappears into the evening twilight!

Pretty dumb to send a message in a bottle, because most of the time, one has to break the dumb bottle to get it! I do! It's addressed to me in a painful script, an urgent appeal, call it a plea if you want, to put an end to the second book in the series of CalMil's flying adventures! There are tear stains on the cracked paper, no doubt due to the personage's sadness over the book again coming to an end.

Well, fear not, oh troubled heart! For there is much more to the instrument environment than one book can detail. We shall return with a following more advanced set of flight scenarios for the fourth book in the series! With a wave of my hand, an SR-71 Blackbird Stealth aircraft lands on my verandah, and at Mach some secret number, I gladly dedicate myself to Block Island, Rhode Island, to fly this last scenario with a very astute, well deserving, and emotionally relieved instrument pilot!

Weather brief, if you will.

It'll take a call in to Bridgeport, since Block Island is kind of a floating paradise of isolation in the Atlantic."

WEATHER BRIEF

You:

"Hello! I would like to request a weather brief for an IFR cross country. The tail number of the aircraft I'll be flying is November 9413MIKE, a Cessna 182 RG. From Block Island Airport, I'll be leaving in one half hour. Cruise altitude is five thousand feet, and

I'll be flying Victor three seventy four to Marthas Vineyard Airport. ETE will be fifty minutes and this is the checkride for my instrument rating!"

Bridgeport FSS:

"There's a flight precaution of an intense line of thunderstorms one five miles wide moving northeastward at thirty five knots, south and east of Hampton with tops at two five thousand.

Your entire area is dominated by a low pressure system.

Okay! Let me see here. Block Island is currently reporting an estimated ceiling two hundred overcast, visibility two, rain and fog, temperature eight three, wind two seven zero at one five.

Altimeter is two niner seven eight.

Enroute, ceilings are generally one thousand broken, four thousand five hundred overcast with widely scattered thunderstorms.

Weather at Marthas Vineyard is measured ceiling one hundred overcast, visibility one half mile in fog, temperature eight zero, dewpoint seven eight, wind two six zero at one zero, and altimeter two niner seven seven.

No PIREPS.

The forecast for Block Island is ceiling two hundred overcast, visibility one and a half mile, rain showers and fog, wind two seven zero at one eight.

Enroute, ceilings are forecast eight hundred broken, four thousand overcast, with widely scattered thunderstorms. Cumulonimbus tops are forecast at two seven thousand.

Terminal forecast for Marthas Vineyard is one hundred overcast, visibility one half mile in thunderstorms, rain showers and fog, wind two five zero at one three.

Winds aloft for six thousand feet, which will work for your cruise altitude, are forecast two eight zero at three two.

No NOTAMs L or D in effect for you, and that completes the brief."

FILING THE FLIGHT PLAN -

You:

    "Let me file, then, and receive a clearance from ATC."

Bridgeport FSS:

    "All right, I'll get oriented here on the terminal - yeah, that's it! Okay, give me what you got!"

You:

    "IFR, November 9413MIKE, Cessna 182 RG - slash A, one twenty true, Departure - BID, two three four five Zulu, five thousand feet, Route - BID NDB, Victor two sixty eight MINNK, Victor three seventy four MVY, BORST - Destination - MVY. ETE one plus zero zero. Six plus one zero fuel on board, Alternate - New Bedford Regional, [YOUR NAME - CONTACT PHONE NUMBER - HOME BASE], two on board, Red over white."

Bridgeport FSS:

    "All right! I've got it! Let me get with Boston and I'll get right back to you for your clearance.
    You there? I've got your clearance.
    ATC clears Cessna 9413MIKE to Marthas Vineyard Airport as filed. Maintain five thousand feet. Contact Ocean Departure frequency one one niner point four five. Squawk three one one six. Clearance Void at zero zero zero zero Zulu. Time now two three one five."

You:

    "Okay! I'm cleared to Marthas Vineyard Airport as filed, five thousand feet, Ocean Departure on one one niner point four five, squawk three one one six. Clearance Void at zero zero zero zero Zulu. Thanks for your brief! It was great talking to you!"

Bridgeport FSS:

    "Readback correct. You're welcome! Have yourself a safe and enjoyable flight."

Block Island to Marthas Vineyard

SETUP

Aircraft:

1) Choose **"Cessna Skylane RG"**

Weather:

Winds

1) Set Surface winds **"DEPTH"** to **"1400"**
2) Set Surface winds **"DIR"** to **"260"**
3) Set Surface winds **"SPEED"** to **"12"**
4) Set Level 1 **"TOPS"** to **"3000"**
5) Set Level 1 **"BASE"** to **"1510"**
6) Set Level 1 **"DIR"** to **"285"**
7) Set Level 1 **"SPEED"** to **"23"**
8) Set Level 2 **"TOPS"** to **"6500"**
9) Set Level 2 **"BASE"** to **"3000"**
10) Set Level 2 **"DIR"** to **"295"**
11) Set Level 2 **"SPEED"** to **"37"**

Clouds

1) Set Bottom Level - **TOPS** to **"3800"**
2) Set Bottom Level - **BASE** to **"265"**
3) Set Bottom Level - **COVER** to **"overcast"**
4) Set Top Level - **TOPS** to **"7500"**
5) Set Top Level - **BASE** to **"4700"**
6) Set Top Level - **COVER** to **"overcast"**
7) Set Thunderstorms - **TOPS** to **"24000"**
8) Set Thunderstorms - **BASE** to **"4500"**
9) Set Thunderstorms - **COVERAGE** to **"widely scattered"**

212 IFR Flights of "13MIKE"

Aircraft Position:

1) **"NORTH"** to **"17351.8919"** [N041° 10' 06.8790]
2) **"EAST"** to **"21749.4873"** [W071° 34' 41.5834]
3) **"ALTITUDE"** to **"111"** [0]
4) **"HEADING"** to **"145"**

note: At this point you may wish to save this setup for future use.

PREFLIGHT

note: Set **ZOOM** to **"1.0"**
Set **TIME** to **"19:45"**

"As I've promised you, there is one more exercise in the use of ADF tracking, or in this case, it'll be homing. That plus Sandy Point VOR are the two navaids here on Block Island. From the ground, this place looks gorgeous! From the air, it'll be even more gorgeous as we fly in and out of clouds and check out some thunderstorms from a safe distance. I believe it is time to call Block Island UNICOM."

Instruments:

1) Tune **COM** to **"123.0"** (UNICOM)

You:

"BLOCK ISLAND UNICOM, CESSNA 9413MIKE. PLEASE GIVE ME WINDS, ALTIMETER SETTING, AND WHATEVER ELSE IS NEEDED. I'M ABOUT READY TO DEPART TO MARTHAS VINEYARD."

Block Island UNICOM:

"CESSNA 9413MIKE, WIND TWO SEVEN ZERO AT ELEVEN, ALTIMETER TWO NINER SEVEN EIGHT, AND RUNWAY TWO EIGHT IS THE ACTIVE RUNWAY."

You:

    "THANKS BLOCK ISLAND."

    "Ooh! Did you see that lightning? It's a good thing they're scattered about. It's a good thing my chest is covered with Kevlar anti-static lightning chain mail! Of course, if it zaps my head, I'm a toasted bagel! ADF frequency is two one six, and you know the rest of the routine."

        2) Set **"Altimeter"** and **"Heading Indicator"**
        3) Set **XPDR** to **"3116"** (assigned IFR code)
        4) Tune **NAV 1** to **"113.6"** (HTO)
        5) Set **NAV 1 OBS** to **"080"**
        6) Set **ADF** to **"216"** (BID)
        7) Activate **"ADF"**
        8) Tune **NAV 2** to **"115.6"** (PVD)
        9) Set the **DME** to **"NAV 1"** and **"DIST"**
        10) Check **CARB HEAT** is **"OFF"**
        11) Check **GEAR "DOWN"**
        12) Turn **STROBE "ON"**
        13) Turn **LIGHTS "ON"**

    "Man, when you get schooled, you pick up on it good! Even though we'll use the NDB facility, Hampton VOR's zero eight zero degree radial is an excellent backup! By the way, this whole flight is flown over water until we arrive over Marthas Vineyard. Not that we'll be able to see anything, but just to know you're island hopping gives us an adventurous feeling deep down in the ankle! Tell UNICOM we're taxiing to runway two eight with unrelented passion in your voice!"

You:

    "BLOCK ISLAND UNICOM, CESSNA 13MIKE IS TAXIING TO RUNWAY TWO EIGHT FOR IFR DEPARTURE."

Block Island UNICOM:

    "ROGER, CESSNA 13MIKE."

IFR Flights of "13MIKE"

TAXI -

"Well, you just taxi down this pad, turn left and keep going until you reach the approach end of runway two eight. This is probably the shortest runway we've taken off from, but '13MIKE' can handle it. I see a thunderstorm cell moving in, so let's hot foot it, get our runup complete, and skedaddle out of here. It might not be any better at Marthas Vineyard, but there's a celebrity who lives there, if I'm not mistaken!"

RUN UP -

1) Set brake (hold down to prevent aircraft from moving)
2) Advance power to about "**2000**" RPM
** 3) Select **CARB HEAT "ON"**, record RPM drop_____(5 pts)
4) Select **CARB HEAT "OFF"**
** 5) Select "**LEFT**" Mag, record RPM drop_____(5 pts)
6) Select "**BOTH**" Mags
** 7) Select "**RIGHT**" Mag, record RPM drop_____(5 pts)
8) Select "**BOTH**" Mags
9) Reduce power to **idle**
10) Set **FLAPS** to **first notch** (10 degrees takeoff configuration)

"Carly Simon is the one who lives there, and she writes children's books - real good ones, at that! She will always be unforgettable to me because at the Naval Academy, I think around 1973 or 1974, James Taylor was to put on a concert for us midshipmen. It was rumored that Carly Simon would be there also to sing with him - and the newest release was the Mockingbird Song. Well, he did his whole concert, and Carly didn't show until the very last song. Backstage, we all heard Carly start the song, and we went nuts! Thunderous applause and total awe at her graciousness and ability to sing! Oops! That storm's not going away, is it? Tell everybody we're out of here!"

You:

"**BLOCK ISLAND TRAFFIC, CESSNA 13MIKE IS TAKING OFF, RUNWAY TWO EIGHT, IFR.**"

Block Island to Marthas Vineyard

FLIGHT

Takeoff:

"I can hear the Rawhide song now! 'Roll 'em, roll 'em, roll 'em. Keep them doggies rollin'. Roll 'em, roll 'em, roll 'em, RAWHIDE!' We better do that for it's right on our tail. Yippee! Fuel - good. Trim - takeoff. Oil - both pressure and temperature, no trouble. Lights on. Flaps at ten. We're off - or on - or up - or going - or going to be up!"

1) Record TIME_____
2) Release brakes and taxi onto runway 28
3) Advance power to "**FULL**"
4) Maintain centerline of runway
5) At **50 knots** airspeed, lift nose wheel off runway
6) At **70 knots,** ease back on the yoke to establish a 10 degree pitch up attitude
7) Maintain a climb **AIRSPEED** of **80 knots**
8) Raise **Gear** when there is no more runway to land on
9) At "**500**" feet above the ground, raise the **FLAPS** to "**0**"

"That's right! Call up Departure Control now, but meanwhile, keep that runway heading until given further instructions. Scan, scan, scan!"

10) Tune **COM** to "**119.45**" (Ocean Departure)

You:

"OCEAN DEPARTURE, CESSNA 9413MIKE IS WITH YOU, PASSING EIGHT HUNDRED FOR FIVE THOUSAND."

Ocean Departure:

"CESSNA 9413MIKE, OCEAN DEPARTURE, IDENT."

You:

"CESSNA 13MIKE, IDENT."

216   IFR Flights of "13MIKE"

    11) Press the IDENT button (simulate)
    12) Reduce power to about **"2300"** RPM at **"1000"** feet above the ground (AGL)

Ocean Departure:

    "CESSNA 13MIKE, OCEAN DEPARTURE, RADAR CONTACT."

You:

    "CESSNA 13MIKE."

"It's not necessary for them to tell us anything, so don't look so surprised! Remember, we already have our clearance to five thousand, and it's overflying the NDB, so now's as good a time as any to course reverse and home in to the NDB facility."

Departure:

    1) When the altimeter reads **"1500"** feet, turn **LEFT** and home in directly to the **BLOCK ISLAND NDB**

    2) When wings are level, press **"P"** to pause the simulation

**   3) Record your:
        HOMING HEADING to BLOCK ISLAND NDB
        _____(40 pts)
        ALTITUDE_____(30 pts)
        AIRSPEED_____(30 pts)
        NAV 1 DME DIST_____(25 pts)
        GEAR_____(20 pts)
        FLAPS_____(15 pts)
        XPDR_____(10 pts)
        COM FREQUENCY_____(10 pts)
        LIGHTS_____(5 pts)

    4) Press **"P"** to continue the simulation

Block Island to Marthas Vineyard

"You don't have to hold a set in cement magnetic course to the NDB. That's the pure joy of homing to an NDB. Simply keep the needle on the top of the indicator at all times, until it falls off to the left or to the right. If the needle falls slowly to the left or right at station passage, that means you're offset right or left of the station. If the ADF falls rapidly, then you passed directly overhead."

Ocean Departure:

"CESSNA 13MIKE, OCEAN DEPARTURE, OVER BLOCK ISLAND NDB, TURN LEFT HEADING ZERO FOUR ZERO UNTIL INTERCEPTING VICTOR THREE SEVEN FOUR."

You:

"CESSNA 13MIKE, AT BLOCK ISLAND NDB, TURN LEFT HEADING ZERO FOUR ZERO TO INTERCEPT VICTOR THREE SEVEN FOUR."

"Well, that's good! We could have taken a zero four six magnetic bearing from the NDB, but I think we've both had enough work in that area! And Sandy Point VOR is under maintenance because you can't get an ident off of it, so this vector is quite helpful."

5) When the **ADF** needle falls left or right **90 degrees**, turn **LEFT** to a heading of "**040**"
6) Begin to level off when the altimeter reads "**4900**" feet
7) Maintain "**5000**" feet
8) Reduce power to about "**2250**" [**2450**] RPM

"Yeah! Let's keep the power up because it's no use dragging our way to Marthas Vineyard. It might prove to save us from messing around with any thunderstorms that are broodingly moving in to the airport."

9) Tune **NAV 1** to "**108.2**" [**114.5**] (MVY)
10) Set the **NAV 1 OBS** to "**102**"
11) Deactivate the **ADF**
12) Set the **NAV 2 OBS** to "**166**"

"I like it! Providence VOR is going to be used to verify you've passed the checkpoint or intersection on our airway to Marthas Vineyard. Jolly good show! And the '102' you've set into the OBS of number one is the inbound heading to Marthas Vineyard, rather than the '100' from Groton VOR. Keep those sound decisions coming!"

Ocean Departure:

"CESSNA 13MIKE, CONTACT BOSTON CENTER ONE THREE TWO POINT NINER."

You:

"CESSNA 13MIKE, SWITCHING ONE THREE TWO POINT NINER. GOOD DAY!"

    13) Tune **COM** to "**132.9**" (Boston Center)

You:

"BOSTON CENTER, CESSNA 9413MIKE WITH YOU AT FIVE THOUSAND."

Boston Center:

"CESSNA 13MIKE, RADAR CONTACT."

"It'd be fascinating to visit one of these Center facilities one day! I'd ask them to let me say one thing over the radios! 'RADAR CONTACT'. There's a certain amount of power behind those words! You know, such as, 'I see you, but you can't see me!' Well, all joking aside, Center has always been nothing but help to us pilots. And they love us too!"

Victor Airway enroute:

    1) When the **NAV 1 DME DIST** reads "**37.0**":

Boston Center:

"CESSNA 13MIKE, BOSTON CENTER, TURN LEFT HEADING ZERO THREE ZERO, VECTOR FOR TRAFFIC."

Block Island to Marthas Vineyard

You:

> "CESSNA 13MIKE, LEFT ZERO THREE ZERO."

"There's a prime example of why Center is so vital. Someone is close to us. He's not referring to barge traffic on the water, that's for sure! I see your eyes roving erratically! Don't drop the NAV 1 CDI out of your scan because it'll be moving soon and that's our cue to press straight on to Marthas Vineyard."

2) Turn **LEFT** to a heading of "**030**"
3) When the **NAV 1 CDI** is ½ dot **LEFT** of center, turn **RIGHT** to a heading of "**102**"

4) When wings are level, press "**P**" to pause the simulation

**

5) Record your:
   - NAV 1 DME DIST_____(35 pts)
   - IS MINNK INTERSECTION BEHIND OR IN FRONT OF YOU?_____(30 pts)
   - ALTITUDE_____(25 pts)
   - RPM_____(20 pts)
   - VSI_____(20 pts)
   - AIRSPEED_____(15 pts)
   - MARTHAS VINEYARD VOR IDENT _____(10 pts)

6) Press "**P**" to continue the simulation

7) Track inbound on the **MARTHAS VINEYARD 282** radial

"How about we get below the reported base of those thunderstorms by descending to three thousand feet. That's the MEA along this Victor airway we're on anyway, so navigation signal loss won't be a concern. No, we don't want to be below cumulonimbus clouds, but no use accidentally flying into one either!"

You:

> "BOSTON CENTER, CESSNA 13MIKE, REQUEST DESCENT TO THREE THOUSAND."

IFR Flights of "13MIKE"

Boston Center:

"CESSNA 13MIKE, DESCEND AND MAINTAIN THREE THOUSAND."

8) When the **NAV 2 CDI** is **centered**, establish a "**500**" feet per minute rate of descent to "**3000**" feet

"Now don't get mechanical on me! Just because you're starting a descent doesn't mean that power always has to come off! As long as we don't exceed the maximum RPM's for the altitude we're at, let's see how close to the Blackbird's top speed we can get! Would you believe a Cessna Citation VI? How about a duck in the jet stream?!"

9) Maintain power at about "**2250**" [**2450**] RPM

** 10) What intersection did you just pass?_____(30 pts)
** 11) What HEADING keeps the NAV 1 CDI needle centered?
_____(25 pts)
** 12) When passing through "**4000**" feet, record your:
GROUND SPEED_____(25 pts)
VSI_____(25 pts)
AIRSPEED_____(20 pts)

"We need ATIS information from Marthas Vineyard - you're absolutely on the mark! You have the honors!"

You:

"BOSTON CENTER, CESSNA 13MIKE, WOULD LIKE TO SWITCH OFF THE FREQUENCY FOR A MOMENT."

Boston Center:

"CESSNA 13MIKE, APPROVED AS REQUESTED. WHEN ABLE, CONTACT CAPE APPROACH ONE TWO FOUR POINT SEVEN."

You:

> "CESSNA 13MIKE, CAPE APPROACH ONE TWO FOUR POINT SEVEN. THANK YOU FOR YOUR SERVICE."

    13) Tune **COM** to "**126.25**" (Marthas Vineyard ATIS)

> "MARTHAS VINEYARD AIRPORT, INFORMATION ZULU, TWO THREE FIVE FIVE ZULU WEATHER, ESTIMATED CEILING FIVE HUNDRED OVERCAST, VISIBILITY ONE, FOG, TEMPERATURE SEVEN SEVEN, DEWPOINT SEVEN FIVE. WIND TWO FIVE ZERO AT ONE FOUR. ALTIMETER TWO NINER SEVEN SIX. ILS RUNWAY TWO FOUR IN USE. LANDING RUNWAY TWO FOUR. ALL INBOUNDS CONTACT CAPE APPROACH ON ONE TWO FOUR POINT SEVEN. ADVISE ON INITIAL CONTACT YOU HAVE INFORMATION ZULU."

    14) Set **ALTIMETER**, set **HI**, check **FUEL**
    15) Tune **COM** to "**124.7**" (Cape Approach)

You:

> "CAPE APPROACH, CESSNA 9413MIKE IS WITH YOU AT THREE THOUSAND."

Cape Approach:

> "CESSNA 9413MIKE, CAPE APPROACH, SQUAWK FIVE FIVE THREE THREE, AND IDENT."

You:

> "CESSNA 13MIKE, SQUAWK FIVE FIVE THREE THREE, AND IDENT."

    16) Set **XPDR** to "**5533**" (new assigned IFR code)
    17) Press the IDENT button (simulate)

Cape Approach:

> "CESSNA 13MIKE, RADAR CONTACT."

"From the looks of things, I'd say we're going to go to BORST intersection as the initial approach fix for the ILS, through Marthas Vineyard VOR. To do a course reversal for this approach into runway two four, you have to do a holding pattern turn, as depicted on the approach chart. Look it over and I'll quiz you on it as we go!"

18) When the **NAV 1 DME DIST** reads "**10.0**":

Cape Approach:

> "CESSNA 13MIKE, CLEARED FOR ILS RUNWAY TWO FOUR APPROACH. DESCEND AND MAINTAIN ONE THOUSAND FIVE HUNDRED."

You:

> "CESSNA 13MIKE, ILS RUNWAY TWO FOUR, DESCEND AND MAINTAIN ONE THOUSAND FIVE HUNDRED."

19) Reduce power to about "**1700**" [**2100**] RPM
20) Descend to and maintain "**1500**" feet at a "**1200**" feet per minute rate of descent
21) When level, add power to about "**1900**" [**2200**] RPM

22) Press "**P**" to pause the simulation

"Now since the localizer is most important for you to navigate during this approach, set the localizer frequency on the top VOR indicator. When doing all this preliminary stuff, you'll just have to work it out with the lower indicator. But you've been doing that so often with me throughout our flights, that I know you have no problems using NAV 1 or NAV 2, huh?

Now take a look at your approach plate for the ILS runway two four approach into Marthas Vineyard.

Block Island to Marthas Vineyard

**
    A. What is the outbound course of the holding pattern depicted?
    _____(5 pts)
    B. How many miles is it from Marthas Vineyard VOR to the initial approach fix?_____(5 pts)
    C. What is the minimum glideslope altitude?_____(5 pts)
    D. At what altitude will you cross BORST if you're on glideslope?_____(5 pts)
    E. If the glideslope becomes out of service, how much higher is the minimum descent altitude (MDA) than the decision height (DH)?_____(5 pts)
    F. What is the touchdown zone elevation?_____(5 pts)

Okay! That's enough to round out your education as far as this flight is concerned! Now, let's fly this with a smiling brain!"

23) Press **"P"** to continue the simulation

To the initial approach fix:

1) Tune **NAV 2** to **"108.2"** **[114.5]** (MVY)
2) Set the **NAV 2 OBS** to **"058"**

3) When the **NAV 1 DME DIST** reads **"3.0"**, press **"P"** to pause the simulation

**
4) Record your:
    NAV 1 CDI POSITION_____(40 pts)
    RPM_____(30 pts)
    AIRSPEED_____(25 pts)
    VSI_____(20 pts)
    DISTANCE to ILS RWY 24 Initial Approach Fix
    _____(15 pts)
    XPDR_____(10 pts)

5) Press **"P"** to continue the simulation

6) When the **NAV 1 DME DIST** reads **"0.4"**, turn **LEFT** to a heading of **"058"**
7) Track outbound on the **MARTHAS VINEYARD VOR 058** radial which your **NAV 2 OBI** indicates

8) Tune **NAV 1** to "**108.7**" (IMVY localizer)
9) Set the **NAV 1 OBS** to "**236**"
10) Set the **DME** to "**NAV 2**" and "**DIST**"

"You somehow want to go to the far right corner of the holding pattern, so that you can execute a simple standard rate turn to the left, correct? To do that from BORST, it's a thirty degree cut from the zero five six outbound holding pattern heading, which makes it zero eight six, doesn't it? And you want to be about one hundred knots in any holding pattern."

Teardrop course reversal:

1) When the **NAV 2 DME DIST** reads "**4.2**", turn **RIGHT** to a heading of "**086**"
2) Maintain a heading of "**086**" for one minute
3) Set the **DME** to "**NAV 1**"
4) Reduce power to about "**1600**" [**2000**] RPM
5) Turn **LEFT** towards a heading which will intercept the localizer inbound

6) When wings are level, press "**P**" to pause the simulation

** 7) Record your:
    NAV 1 DME DIST_____(40 pts)
    INTERCEPT HEADING_____(40 pts)
    AIRSPEED_____(25 pts)
    ANTICIPATED DME FOR GLIDESLOPE
        INTERCEPTION_____(20 pts)
    ALTITUDE_____(15 pts)
    DESIRED INBOUND LOCALIZER COURSE
    _____(10 pts)
    DECISION HEIGHT_____(10 pts)
    RPM_____(10 pts)
    STROBES_____(5 pts)
8) Press "**P**" to continue the simulation

Block Island to Marthas Vineyard

    9) Track inbound on the **MARTHAS VINEYARD LOCALIZER 056** radial off of the **NAV 1 OBI**
    10) Maintain an airspeed of about **100 knots**

"It's all yours! You know the deck is low, so be particularly sharp on being on glideslope and on course. Don't forget how sensitive the CDI needle becomes in close, so don't fly with bacon in your hands! Get it? Don't be ham-fisted!"

ILS inbound:

    1) When the glideslope needle is **centered**, select **GEAR "DOWN"**
    2) Set **CARB HEAT "ON"**
    3) Set **FLAPS** to **first notch** (10 degrees)
    4) Maintain glideslope with a **"500-600" FPM** rate of descent
    5) Reduce power to about **"1500" [1900]** RPM

Cape Approach:

    "CESSNA 13MIKE, CONTACT MARTHAS VINEYARD TOWER ONE TWO ONE POINT FOUR."

You:

    "CESSNA 13MIKE, SWITCHING TOWER ONE TWO ONE POINT FOUR. IT'S BEEN GREAT!"

    6) Tune **COM** to **"121.4"** (Vineyard Tower)

You:

    "VINEYARD TOWER, CESSNA 9413MIKE FOUR MILES INBOUND, ILS RUNWAY TWO FOUR APPROACH, WITH INFORMATION ZULU."

Vineyard Tower:

    "CESSNA 9413MIKE, VINEYARD TOWER, RUNWAY TWO FOUR, CLEARED TO LAND. REPORT FIELD IN SIGHT."

IFR Flights of "13MIKE"

You:
> "CESSNA 13MIKE, CLEARED TO LAND, WILL REPORT FIELD IN SIGHT."

"Be thinking of your missed approach instructions. You'll be needing to use the NAV 2 for it, if the field doesn't pop into sight. Keep thinking ahead!"

Missed Approach Point:

1) When the **NAV 1 DME DIST** reads "**2.5**", press "**P**" to pause the simulation

** 2) Record your:
   NAV 1 GLIDESLOPE NEEDLE POSITION
   _____(45 pts)
   NAV 1 CDI POSITION_____(45 pts)
   HEADING_____(35 pts)
   VSI_____(30 pts)
   ALTITUDE_____(25 pts)
   GEAR_____(15 pts)
   FLAPS_____(15 pts)
   COM FREQUENCY_____(15 pts)

3) Press "**P**" to continue the simulation

4) When the altimeter reads "**265**" feet, the field should suddenly pop into sight

"You can't get much closer to missing the field than that! But what a beautiful sight right down the runway! Take '13MIKE' in, Skymaster!"

5) Set **FLAPS** to **second notch** (20 degrees)

You:
> **"VINEYARD TOWER, CESSNA 13MIKE HAS FIELD."**

Vineyard Tower:

"CESSNA 13MIKE, ROGER! WINDS ARE TWO SIX ZERO AT ONE TWO."

6) When the altimeter reads "**150**" feet, set **FLAPS** to **third notch** (30 degrees)
7) Airspeed should be **70 knots**
8) When you are 10 to 20 feet off the runway, reduce power to about "**1000**" RPM and start to slowly pitch the nose of the aircraft up to slow your descent and establish a touchdown attitude
9) When you are five feet off the runway, hold the nose of the aircraft up and allow the airspeed to **SLOWLY** bleed off. Your aircraft will <u>settle</u> onto the runway while you follow the centerline
10) After touchdown, reduce power to **600 RPM**
11) Apply the brakes

Vineyard Tower:

"CESSNA 13MIKE, CROSS RUNWAY ONE FIVE - THREE THREE, AND TURN LEFT ON FOLLOWING INTERSECTION. CONTACT GROUND POINT EIGHT EXITING THE RUNWAY."

You:

"CESSNA 13MIKE, ROGER. GROUND POINT EIGHT."

"There's the control tower, and I believe they're pretty close to shutting operations down. Hey, look at that deer that crossed in front of us! They're probably drawn by the taxi lights. Let's park this phenomenally fine-tuned aircraft, and we'll debrief the flight."

12) Taxi the aircraft off the active runway to the **LEFT**
13) When the aircraft has stopped, set **CARB HEAT** to "**OFF**"
14) Set **FLAPS** to "**0**"
15) Tune **COM** to "**121.8**" (Marthas Vineyard Ground)

228 IFR Flights of "13MIKE"

You:

"VINEYARD GROUND, CESSNA 9413MIKE FOR TAXI."

Vineyard Ground:

"CESSNA 9413MIKE, VINEYARD GROUND, TAXI STRAIGHT AHEAD TO THE BASE OF THE CONTROL TOWER."

You:

"CESSNA 13MIKE, TO THE TOWER. THANKS!"

"This flight was one of your best ones! Thank you for paying such undivided attention to my instructions, but you have reaped the gratifying rewards of a job excellently well done. As a prize, Professor Miller has a stuffed '13MIKE' model waiting for you on the ramp! See it? Its prop even glows in the dark!"

**   16) Record the **TIME**_____(5 pts)

         TOTAL POINTS POSSIBLE FOR THIS FLIGHT __1105__

Answers

Flight Scenario One

FILLING OUT THE FLIGHT PLAN -
- ** a) What is in block 8, Route of Flight, of your flight plan?
       CCC BOUNO (10 pts)
- ** b) The leg from Bridgeport to RYMES intersection crosses what Victor Airway? **V99** (10 pts)
- ** c) From Long Island MacArthur to Calverton, what NDB do you pass to the right of you? **PECONIC** (10 pts)
- ** d) What is the minimum reception altitude at RYMES intersection?
       5000 (10 pts)
- ** e) List the Victor airways that RYMES intersection is on.
       V123   V483 (10 pts)

TAXI -
- ** 1. What is the standard takeoff minimums for runway 6?
       1 SM (5 pts)
- ** 2. How much of runway 6's length is usable for landing?
       6000 (5 pts)
- ** 3. Which runway is only 75 feet wide? **15L - 33R** (5 pts)
- ** 4. What is the field elevation? **99** (5 pts)
- ** 5. To the nearest whole number, what is the variation at Islip?
       14 degrees W (5 pts)
- ** 6. Does runway 6 have an upslope, downslope, or no slope to it?
       NO SLOPE (5 pts)

RUN UP -
- ** 3) Select **CARB HEAT "ON"**, record RPM drop **80 [50]** (5 pts)

IFR Flights of "13MIKE"

    **   5) Select "**LEFT**" Mag, record RPM drop __**150 [120]**__ (5 pts)
    **   7) Select "**RIGHT**" Mag, record RPM drop __**150 [120]**__ (5 pts)

Takeoff:
    **   10) At what MSL altitude were you when **FLAPS** were raised?
                                   __**600**__   (25 pts)

Climb out:
    **   7) Record your:

AIRSPEED	**97 - 102**	(30 pts)
RPM	**2292 - 2308**	(25 pts)
HEADING	**076 - 080**	(25 pts)
VSI	**+900 - +1100**	(20 pts)
NAV 1 DME DIST	**12.3 - 12.7 [13.2 - 13.6]**	(20 pts)
GEAR	**UP**	(15 pts)
FLAPS	**UP**	(15 pts)
COM FREQUENCY	**118.00**	(10 pts)

Level off:
    **   5) Record your:

NAV 1 CDI POSITION	**CENTERED**	(30 pts)
HEADING for centered NAV 1 CDI	**081 - 084**	(30 pts)
NAV 1 DME DIST	**6.6 - 6.2 [6.1 - 5.7]**	(25 pts)
CALVERTON VOR's IDENT	**-·-· -·-· -·-·**	(5 pts)

All that the IDENT button does is supply some vitamins to our radar image on the controller's scope, so that they know we are we! Pretty soon, we should have station passage, which means we've passed overhead of Calverton VOR. Station passage occurs when the '**TO**' flips to '**FROM**' on the OBI. How many miles will we go outbound on our new radial? __**14**__ (5 pts)
See? You just keep thinking ahead, just like in a chess game.

Course change 1:
    **   5) Record your:

NAV 1 CDI POSITION	**CENTERED**	(40 pts)
HEADING	**009 - 012**	(35 pts)
ALTITUDE	**4950 - 5050**	(25 pts)
AIRSPEED	**127 - 132**	(15 pts)
COM FREQUENCY	**124.50**	(10 pts)

Answers

NAME OF INTERSECTION YOU'RE ALMOST
AT _____**ZAHNN**_____ (5 pts)

**   What is the name of the next intersection off of this Calverton radial?
_____**EILEN**_____ (5 pts)

Course change 2:
**   4) Record your:
NAV 1 DME DIST_____**13.5 - 13.9**_____ (30 pts)
VSI_____**-50 to +50**_____ (25 pts)
ALTITUDE_____**4950 - 5050**_____ (20 pts)
BRIDGEPORT VOR's IDENT
_____ - · · ·   - · ·   · - · _____ (15 pts)

What is the name of the remote site which is in this sector of Boston Center? (mistakenly labeled 'New York')
_____***DOUGLASTON***_____ (5 pts)

How many miles is it from this latest turnoff to Bridgeport VOR?
_____**12**_____ (5 pts)

Based on your cruise winds and a computed true airspeed of about one hundred and thirty knots, how long will it take to arrive at Bridgeport from the turnoff? _____**4.5 - 5.0 minutes**_____ (5 pts)

Enroute Descent:
**   13) What heading is an established **LEFT BASE**? **250** (30 pts)

Approach:
**   16) Record the **TIME**_____**11:12 - 11:17**_____ (5 pts)

You are in the same league as:

Jack Knight	576 to 645 pts
Jimmy Doolittle	496 to 575 pts
Charles Lindbergh	386 to 495 pts
Amelia Earhart	266 to 385 pts
Wrong Way Corrigan	141 to 265 pts
TAKE THE BUS	000 to 140 pts

Flight Scenario Two

FILLING OUT THE FLIGHT PLAN -
** a) What is in block 8, Route of Flight, of your flight plan?
             HARBR2.SLI   (10 pts)
** b) What restricted airspaces are to the right of you about 40 miles out
     from San Diego?   **R-2533   R-2503**   (10 pts)
** c) How many miles is it from Seal Beach VOR to Los Angeles VOR
     along Victor 23?   **22**   (10 pts)
** d) The name of the compass locator beacon southwest of Seal Beach
     VOR is what?   **BECCA**   (10 pts)
** e) The minimum enroute altitude from Seal Beach VOR along Victor 8
     to WILMA intersection is what?   **2300**   (10 pts)

Instruments:
*What's the first heading you are interested in once you get airborne?
Check your SID*   **290**   (5 pts)
And what is the first critical altitude you want to be aware of?
                          4000   (5 pts)

TAXI -
** 1. What is the variation around this geographic area to the nearest
     whole number?   **13 degrees East**   (5 pts)
   2. What is the length of runway 9-27?   **9400**   (5 pts)
   3. What is the elevation of the approach end of runway 27?
                          14   (5 pts)
   4. From where you're sitting here at the ramp, is the control tower in
      front of you and to the LEFT, or in front of you and to the RIGHT?
                          LEFT   (5 pts)
   5. What is the name of the north taxiway paralleling runway 9-27?
                          C   (5 pts)
   6. The alignment of runway 27 is actually what magnetic course?
                          272.6 degrees   (5 pts)

RUN UP -
** 3) Select **CARB HEAT "ON"**, record RPM drop **80 [55]** (5 pts)
** 5) Select **"LEFT"** Mag, record RPM drop **150 [125]** (5 pts)
** 7) Select **"RIGHT"** Mag, record RPM drop **150 [125]** (5 pts)

Course change 1:
** 3) Record your:

NAV 1 DME DIST	**23.6 - 24.4**	(25 pts)
ALTITUDE	**3950 - 4050**	(20 pts)
AIRSPEED	**127 - 133**	(15 pts)
RPM	**2242 - 2258**	(15 pts)
VSI	**-50 to +50**	(15 pts)
COM FREQUENCY	**134.50**	(15 pts)
XPDR	**6452**	(10 pts)

We're in no rush to get to seven thousand feet, since the departure calls for us to be at or above six thousand five hundred by what intersection?
                LNSAY   (5 pts)

From your present position, at CLSTR, how many miles is it to the above intersection?   **18**   (5 pts)

Course changes 2:

LNSAY intersection is identified by twelve DME from Mission Bay, right? TRUE or FALSE? **FALSE** (5 pts)

Darn right, it's wrong! How many miles is **LNSAY** intersection from Mission Bay VOR?   **25**   (5 pts)

** 6) What is the heading which is maintaining your 314 degree radial track?   **305 - 309**   (30 pts)

** 9) Record your:

NAV 2 DME DIST	**26.0 - 26.3**	(25 pts)
NAV 1 DME DIST	**47.5 - 47.8**	(20 pts)
ALTITUDE	**6950 - 7050**	(20 pts)

Course change 3:

** 3) Write out the 'dit-dah' Morse code for **SEAL BEACH VOR** as you identify it   **··· ·-·· ··**   (20 pts)

** 14) When the **NAV 2 DME DIST** reads "20.0", record:

HEADING for centered NAV 2 CDI	**316 - 319**	(30 pts)
GROUND SPEED	**122 - 128**	(25 pts)
XPDR	**5552**	(20 pts)
COM FREQUENCY	**124.50**	(20 pts)

IFR Flights of "13MIKE"

Initial Approach Fix inbound:
**   7) Record your:
- NAV 2 DME DIST   **7.6 - 8.0 [9.7 - 10.1]**   (25 pts)
- RPM   **1692 -1708 [1992 - 2008]**   (20 pts)
- AIRSPEED   **111 - 116**   (20 pts)
- HEADING   **310 - 315**   (20 pts)
- NAME of intersection you are heading to **FITON** (15 pts)

**   15) Answer the following questions by referencing the VOR or TACAN or GPS RWY 25L/R instrument approach plate:

A. What five airports can be found on the south side of your inbound track and north of Victor 64? (Use L-3)
1. **FULLERTON MUNICIPAL**
2. **LONG BEACH DAUGHERTY FIELD**
3. **COMPTON AIRPORT**
4. **HAWTHORNE MUNICIPAL**
5. **ZAMPERINI FIELD**   (25 pts)

B. What's the next altitude to descend to?   **2000**   (5 pts)

C. What is the altitude restriction prior to reaching NOELE intersection?   **620**   (5 pts)

D. If you didn't have DME or a second VOR, what would be your minimum descent altitude for this approach?   **620**   (5 pts)

E. How many miles is it from NOELE to the missed approach point?   **1.3**   (5 pts)

F. If you didn't have DME, how would you know when you've arrived at the missed approach point with a 90 knot ground speed?   **3:12 past FREBY**   (5 pts)

Final Approach to Landing:
**   5) Record your:
- COM FREQUENCY   **120.95**   (15 pts)
- CARB HEAT   **ON**   (10 pts)
- AIRSPEED   **95 - 105**   (10 pts)

**   12) Record your:
- AIRSPEED   **70 - 75**   (25 pts)
- VSI   **-350 to -450**   (25 pts)
- HEADING   **245 - 253**   (25 pts)

GEAR	**DOWN**	(15 pts)
FLAPS	**30 degrees DOWN**	(15 pts)
NAV 1 DME	**2.7 - 2.9**	(10 pts)
STROBE	**ON**	(10 pts)
** 23) Record the **TIME**	**15:08 - 15:13**	(5 pts)

You are in the same league as:
Jack Knight	701 to 765 pts
Jimmy Doolittle	601 to 700 pts
Charles Lindbergh	481 to 600 pts
Amelia Earhart	341 to 480 pts
Wrong Way Corrigan	201 to 340 pts
TAKE THE BUS	000 to 200 pts

Flight Scenario Three

FILLING OUT THE FLIGHT PLAN -
** a) What is in block 8, Route of Flight, of your flight plan?
          RBS   (10 pts)
** b) The length of Greater Kankakee Airport's longest runway is what?
          5979 - 6000   (10 pts)
** c) If intercepting NEWTT intersection to the west of Kankakee VOR, what is the remaining distance to Willard-Champaign Airport along Victor 191 and Victor 429?   **62**   (10 pts)
** d) Around Roberts VOR, what is Chicago Center's sector name and frequency?   **MILFORD   127.45**   (10 pts)
** e) What are the geographical coordinates of Champaign VOR?
          N040 02.07'   W088 16.56'   (10 pts)

TAXI -
   1. What is the elevation of the ground where you're parked?
          683   (5 pts)
   2. What is the width of runway 34?   **75 feet**   (5 pts)

IFR Flights of "13MIKE"

    3. Can Kankakee be used as an alternate airport in the IFR environment? (check notes below minimums section) __NO__ (5 pts)
    4. What are the intensity of the runway lights on 34? Low, Medium, or High? __MEDIUM__ (5 pts)
    5. What is the elevation at Greater Kankakee Airport? __629__ (5 pts)
    6. What is the runway length of 34? __4398__ (5 pts)

RUNUP -
- ** 5) Select **CARB HEAT "ON"**, record RPM drop __80 [60]__ (5 pts)
- ** 7) Select **"LEFT"** Mag, record RPM drop __150 [140]__ (5 pts)
- ** 9) Select **"RIGHT"** Mag, record RPM drop __150 [140]__ (5 pts)

Pattern Departure:
- ** 5) Record your:
  - HEADING __206 - 210__ (25 pts)
  - ALTITUDE __2900 - 3100__ (25 pts)
  - NAV 1 DME DIST __30.9 - 31.3 [31.5 - 31.9]__ (25 pts)
  - AIRSPEED __75 - 85__ (20 pts)
  - RPM __2292 - 2309__ (20 pts)
  - GEAR __UP__ (15 pts)
  - FLAPS __UP__ (15 pts)
  - XPDR __1200__ (10 pts)
  - COM FREQUENCY __123.0__ (10 pts)

Level off:
- ** 4) When the NAV 1 DME DIST reads "17.0", record your ground speed __149 -154 [140 - 145]__ (20 pts)
- ** 6) Record your:
  - HEADING with centered NAV 1 CDI __213 - 217__ (30 pts)
  - AIRSPEED __126 - 133__ (25 pts)
  - ALTITUDE __4450 - 4550__ (20 pts)
  - RPM __2292 - 2309__ (10 pts)

Enroute Intersection:
    Looking at the approach plate for the VOR DME runway two two Right approach, what potential initial approach fix did we just pass? __ROBERTS VOR__ (5 pts)
    How many other initial approach fixes does this approach have anyway? Look carefully, because it's pretty tricky! __4__ (5 pts)

Answers

    **   5) When NAV 1 DME DIST reads "**10.5**", record:
                HEADING for centered NAV 1 CDI __**186 - 188**__ (30 pts)

Enroute Descent:
    **   7) Answer the following from the VOR/DME RWY 22R approach plate:
          A. At what DME is the arcing part of the procedure?
                __**12**__ (5 pts)
          B. When can you leave 2400 feet? __**STADI**__ (5 pts)
          C. Where is the missed approach point at?
                __**CHAMPAIGN VOR**__ (5 pts)
          D. If you didn't sight the field until right at the missed approach point, would you turn **LEFT** or **RIGHT** to begin circling? __**LEFT**__ (5 pts)
          E. What is the airport elevation? __**754**__ (5 pts)
          F. At the 2.7 DME fix, what altitude should you be at if the altimeter setting you have is not Champaign's, but Decatur's? __**1540**__ (5 pts)
          G. If your approach speed is 90 knots, what is the minimum descent altitude for your circling approach with Champaign's altimeter setting? __**1160**__ (5 pts)

VOR Approach Inbound:
    **   5) Record your:
            HEADING for a centered NAV 2 CDI __**214 - 218**__ (30 pts)
            ALTITUDE __**2350 - 2450**__ (25 pts)
            AIRSPEED __**87 - 94**__ (20 pts)
            XPDR __**4562**__ (15 pts)
            GEAR __**DOWN**__ (15 pts)
            CARB HEAT __**ON**__ (15 pts)
            COM FREQUENCY __**121.35**__ (10 pts)
    **   10) Record your:
            VASI Lights color sequence __**RED**__ over __**WHITE**__ (40 pts)
            RPM __**1100 - 1300**__ (20 pts)
            HEADING __**315 - 325**__ (20 pts)
            VSI __**-600 to -800**__ (20 pts)
            FLAPS __**30 degrees DOWN**__ (15 pts)
            COM FREQUENCY __**120.4**__ (15 pts)

238 IFR Flights of "13MIKE"

        AIRSPEED   **65 - 75**   (10 pts)
**   19) Record the **TIME**   **08:43 - 08:48**   (5 pts)

You are in the same league as:
Jack Knight	666 to 715 pts
Jimmy Doolittle	541 to 665 pts
Charles Lindbergh	401 to 540 pts
Amelia Earhart	261 to 400 pts
Wrong Way Corrigan	121 to 260 pts
TAKE THE BUS	000 to 120 pts

Flight Scenario Four

FILLING OUT THE FLIGHT PLAN -
**   a) What is in block 8, Route of Flight, of your flight plan?
      SHOR9.LIN V28 RICHY LAZEE   (10 pts)
**   b) If going outbound on Victor 28 from Oakland VOR, and told to hold at ALTAM intersection, what kind of holding entry would be exercised?   **DIRECT**   (10 pts)
**   c) What is the minimum obstruction clearance altitude on the leg of Victor 28 from SPOOK intersection to RICHY intersection?
       12000   (10 pts)
**   d) Without using Linden VOR or Mustang VOR, what two other ways can SPOOK intersection be identified?
    1.   **HNW 086 / 23**
    2.   **INTERSECTION OF HNW 086 and SWR 164**   (10 pts)
**   e) What is the total mileage from Linden VOR along Victor 28 to Mustang VOR?   **109**   (10 pts)

RUN UP -
**   3) Select **CARB HEAT "ON"**, record RPM drop **80 [50]** (5 pts)
**   5) Select **"LEFT"** Mag, record RPM drop   **150   [120]** (5 pts)
**   7) Select **"RIGHT"** Mag, record RPM drop **150   [120]** (5 pts)

Takeoff:
** 15) Record your:
    ALTITUDE __**850 - 950**__ (30 pts)
    NAV 2 DME DIST __**9.1 - 9.3**__ (30 pts)
    NAV 2 CDI POSITION __**1/2 to 1 dot LEFT**__ (25 pts)
    AIRSPEED __**77 - 83**__ (20 pts)
    GEAR __**UP**__ (15 pts)
    FLAPS __**UP**__ (15 pts)
    COM FREQUENCY __**120.45**__ (10 pts)

Departure Track:
** 3) When the **NAV 2 DME DIST** reads "**3.0**", record:
    HEADING for centered NAV 2 CDI __**031 - 034**__ (35 pts)
    ALTITUDE __**3800 - 3950**__ (25 pts)
** 5) What altitude did you pass when the NAV 2 flag flipped to a **FROM** indication? __**4950 - 5150**__ (30 pts)
** 7) Record your **NAV 2 DME DIST** at "**6000**" feet __**2.5-2.8**__ (30 pts)

Transition:
** 3) What heading now is necessary to keep centered the **NAV 2 CDI**? __**034 - 036**__ (35 pts)
** 10) When reaching "**11000**" feet, what is the **NAV 1 DME DIST**? __**39.5 - 40.4**__ (25 pts)

Step by step, you are flying this enroute portion of the Shoreline Nine Departure with amazing accuracy. But a SID comes to an end, as all good things do, to be replaced by even gooder things! In this case, you need to think ahead by way of your enroute chart because from Linden, we're flying Victor twenty eight to what intersection? __**KATSO**__ *(5 pts)*
How many miles is it from Linden to this intersection? __**24**__ *(5 pts)*
What additional two navaids could help to identify this fix?
1. __**SACRAMENTO VOR**__
2. __**HANGTOWN VOR**__ *(10 pts)*
In case you ran into any '13MIKE' mechanical problems, what airport can you put down to that's west northwest of this fix?
    __**WESTOVER FIELD**__ *(5 pts)*
What is this airport's elevation and runway length?
    __**1690 / 3400**__ *(10 pts)*

IFR Flights of "13MIKE"

 **   13) When the **NAV 1 DME DIST** reads "**24.0**", record your
      Ground speed_____**158 - 165**_____ (25 pts)
 **   14) When the **NAV 1 DME DIST** reads "**10.0**", what is your
      NAV 1 CDI needle position?____**CENTERED**____ (30 pts)

Enroute climb:
 **   6) Record your:
      NAV 1 DME DIST_____**23.1 - 23.5**_____ (35 pts)
      HEADING_____**024 - 026**_____ (25 pts)
      VSI_____**+300 to +400**_____ (20 pts)
      NAV 2 DME DIST_____**42.4 - 42.8**_____ (20 pts)
      NAV 1 CDI POSITION____**CENTERED**____ (20 pts)
      AIRSPEED_____**87 - 93**_____ (15 pts)
      ALTITUDE_____**14300 - 14600**_____ (15 pts)
      COM FREQUENCY_____**125.45**_____ (10 pts)
 **   14) When established in cruise, record your:
      AIRSPEED_____**115 - 120 [125 - 130]**_____ (25 pts)
      GROUND SPEED__**155 - 160 [160 - 165]**__ (25 pts)

Pre-initial approach fix:
 **   2) Record your:
      NAV 1 CDI POSITION____**CENTERED**____ (35 pts)
      NAV 1 DME DIST_____**47.6 - 47.9**_____ (30 pts)
      NAV 2 DME DIST_____**32.7 - 33.1**_____ (30 pts)
      NUMBER of Thunderstorms in sight___**3 [1]**___ (20 pts)
      RPM_____**2292 - 2308**_____ (15 pts)
      COM FREQUENCY_____**126.85**_____ (10 pts)

Initial segment:
 **   2) Record your:
      ALTITUDE____**14200 - 14700**____ (25 pts)
      VSI_____**-900 to -1100**_____ (25 pts)
      AIRSPEED___**115 - 120**___ (20 pts)
      NAV 1 DME DIST_____**11.6 - 12.1**_____ (20 pts)
      NAV 1 CDI position____**CENTERED**____ (20 pts)
      COM FREQUENCY_____**128.80**_____ (15 pts)

There is a visual segment to this approach, so as you near eighteen DME, where should you look for the airport? ____**RIGHT**____ *(5 pts)*

Answers   241

And what is the distance from the missed approach point at eighteen to the approach end of runway one eight? _____**4.2**_____ *(5 pts)*

How much altitude do you need to lose on the visual segment in order to land at the approach end of runway 18? _____**1736**_____ *(5 pts)*

At what altitude is the highest peak shown on the instrument approach procedure? (From the plan view) _____**10881**_____ *(5 pts)*

If you never saw the field at South Lake Tahoe, a part of the missed approach procedure is to proceed inbound on what radial of what VOR? _____**SQUAW VALLEY 102**_____ *(5 pts)*

From the airport diagram, which runway has the displaced threshold? _____**36**_____ *(5 pts)*

**   19) Record the **TIME** _____**13:30 - 13:35**_____ (5 pts)

You are in the same league as:

Jack Knight	896 to 990 pts
Jimmy Doolittle	721 to 895 pts
Charles Lindbergh	536 to 720 pts
Amelia Earhart	346 to 535 pts
Wrong Way Corrigan	141 to 345 pts
TAKE THE BUS	000 to 140 pts

Flight Scenario Five

FILLING OUT THE FLIGHT PLAN -

**   a) What is in block 8, Route of Flight, of your flight plan?
_____**PORT 1 V4 LOFAL V287 CARRO V27**_____ (10 pts)

**   b) The NDB that is practically on Victor 4 to the west of Port Angeles is named what, and is on what frequency? _____**ELWHA 515**_____ (10 pts)

242   IFR Flights of "13MIKE"

**   c) What kind of altitude restrictions are found at LOFAL intersection? (Type and altitude)
     1. _____**MRA 6000**_____
     2. _____**MCA 7000 S**_____ (10 pts)

**   d) West of Seattle, Victor 287 has what two VORs at either end of its airway segment? _____**OLYMPIA and PAINE**_____ (10 pts)

**   e) What military operating area (MOA) is southwest of Seattle?
_____**RAINIER 1,2,3**_____ (10 pts)

Instruments:
1) After takeoff, how soon do we start a turn? _____**AS SOON AS PRACTICABLE**_____ (5 pts)
2) What's the first heading to turn to? _____**040**_____ (5 pts)
3) When will you leave your heading? When given a **VECTOR** (5 pts)

RUN UP -
**   3) Select **CARB HEAT "ON"**, record RPM drop **80 [50]** (5 pts)
**   5) Select **"LEFT"** Mag, record RPM drop **150 [120]** (5 pts)
**   7) Select **"RIGHT"** Mag, record RPM drop **150 [120]** (5 pts)

Climb out:
**   4) Record your:
     HEADING _____**078 - 082**_____ (30 pts)
     ALTITUDE _____**2900 - 3050**_____ (30 pts)
     AIRSPEED _____**87 - 93**_____ (30 pts)
     NAV 1 DME DIST _____**48.5 - 48.9**_____ (25 pts)
     NAV 1 CDI POSITION _____**CENTERED**_____ (20 pts)
     RPM _____**2292 - 2308**_____ (20 pts)
     GEAR _____**UP**_____ (15 pts)
     FLAPS _____**UP**_____ (15 pts)
     TATOOSH IDENT _____**- --- ...**_____ (10 pts)
     COM FREQUENCY. _____**118.25**_____ (10 pts)
     XPDR _____**2226**_____ (10 pts)

Level off:
**   1) When the **NAV 1 DME DIST** reads "60.0", record:
     HEADING for centered NAV 1 CDI _____**060 - 065**_____ (35 pts)
     AIRSPEED _____**87 - 93**_____ (30 pts)

Answers

South to Seattle:
**   3) Record your:
            NAV 1 DME DIST __**69.7 - 70.1 [70.5 - 70.9]**__ (35 pts)
            NAV 2 DME DIST __**44.5 - 44.8 [44.0 - 44.4]**__ (35 pts)
            AIRSPEED __**122 - 128**__ (30 pts)
            PROBLEM IN FRONT OF YOU!
                   __**THUNDERSTORM [NA]**__ (30 pts)
            NEEDED COURSE OF ACTION **Go Right [NA]** (25 pts)
            COM FREQUENCY __**120.3**__ (15 pts)
            NAME OF INTERSECTION JUST PASSED
                   __**JAWBN**__ (15 pts)

**   9) When the **NAV 2 DME DIST** reads "**30.5**", record your:
            NAV 1 CDI POSITION __**1 1/2 to 2 dots LEFT**__ (40 pts)
            HEADING for centered NAV 2 CDI __**115 - 120**__ (35 pts)

**   12) Record your:
            NAV 2 DME DIST __**28.1 - 28.5 [29.0 - 29.4]**__ (25 pts)
            ALTITUDE __**8950 - 9050**__ (20 pts)
            AIRSPEED __**122 - 128**__ (20 pts)
            NAME OF INTERSECTION JUST PASSED
                   __**LOFAL**__ (15 pts)
            VSI __**-100 to +100**__ (15 pts)

Off-airway tracking:
**   1) When the **NAV 2 DME DIST** reads "**44.5**", the heading used to hold the NAV 2 CDI **centered** is __**167 - 170**__ (30 pts)

**   2) When the **NAV 2 DME DIST** reads "**36.0**", record your:
            NAV 2 CDI POSITION __**CENTERED**__ (35 pts)
            ALTITUDE __**6950 - 7050**__ (25 pts)
            GROUND SPEED __**154 - 160**__ (25 pts)
            COM FREQUENCY __**123.9**__ (15 pts)

Visual approach:
**   5) What is the name of the airport off your right wing?
                   __**BREMERTON**__ (20 pts)

     Another logical point is this:
     1) What's the airport elevation? __*429*__ (*5 pts*)

244   IFR Flights of "13MIKE"

    2) So about what altitude would you be at normally in a visual landing pattern when you are three quarters to a mile on final? __850 - 1050__ (5 *pts*)

**   23) Record your:
- ALTITUDE __800 - 1000__ (25 pts)
- VSI __-400 to -600__ (25 pts)
- AIRSPEED __70 - 75__ (20 pts)
- GEAR __DOWN__ (15 pts)
- FLAPS __30 degrees DOWN__ (15 pts)
- STROBES __ON__ (10 pts)
- COM FREQUENCY __119.9__ (10 pts)
- NAME OF PARALLEL RUNWAY! __34L__ (5 pts)

**   33) Record the **TIME** __16:26 - 16:31__ (5 *pts*)

You are in the same league as:

Jack Knight	926 to 1005 pts
Jimmy Doolittle	761 to 925 pts
Charles Lindbergh	576 to 760 pts
Amelia Earhart	386 to 575 pts
Wrong Way Corrigan	191 to 385 pts
TAKE THE BUS	000 to 190 pts

Flight Scenario Six

FILLING OUT THE FLIGHT PLAN -

**   a) What is in block 8, Route of flight, of your flight plan? __OCN V23 LAX VNY__ (10 pts)

Answers 245

** b) There are four intersections along Victor 23 from Oceanside VOR. What are they and who are they referenced from?
   1. **DAMPS**
   2. **KRAUZ**
   3. **BALBO**
   4. **MIDDS**
   Referenced from **SANTA CATALINA VOR** (10 pts)

** c) What kind of a navigational aid does John Wayne-Orange County Airport have that's shown on the enroute chart?
   BACK COURSE LOCALIZER (10 pts)

** d) The airfield east of Van Nuys airport is named what?
   BURBANK - GLENDALE - PASADENA (10 pts)

** e) Los Angeles International Airport can accept special VFR traffic.
   True or False **FALSE** (10 pts)

RUN UP -
** 3) Select **CARB HEAT "ON"**, record RPM drop **80 [55]** (5 pts)
** 5) Select **"LEFT"** Mag, record RPM drop **150 [125]** (5 pts)
** 7) Select **"RIGHT"** Mag, record RPM drop **150 [125]** (5 pts)

Takeoff:
** 17) What is the NAV 1 OBS **centered** needle **HEADING**?
   288 - 290 [278 - 282] (25 pts)

Instrument Departure:
** 5) Record your:
   NAV 1 CDI POSITION **CENTERED** (40 pts)
   AIRSPEED **77 - 83** (35 pts)
   HEADING **296 - 299** (30 pts)
   NAV 1 DME DIST **3.4 - 3.7 [4.6 - 5.0]** (25 pts)
   RPM **2292 - 2309** (25 pts)
   LIGHTS **ON** (15 pts)

**
   What are the names of the three intersections we'll fly over on this Victor airway?
   1) **DAMPS**
   2) **KRAUZ**
   3) **BALBO** *(10 pts)*

246 IFR Flights of "13MIKE"

How many miles is it from Oceanside VOR to Seal Beach VOR?
_____**46**_____ *(5 pts)*
Southwest of Van Nuys is the home of the world's greatest Buffalo Burgers imaginable! What airport am I talking about?
_____**SANTA CATALINA - AVALON AIRPORT**_____ *(5 pts)*
*What is the outbound course of the enroute holding pattern at Seal Beach?*_____**120**_____ *(5 pts)*

Enroute Hold:

**   1) When the **NAV 1 DME DIST** reads "18.0", record your:
       GROUND SPEED_____**153 - 157**_____ (25 pts)
       DISTANCE REMAINING TO SEAL BEACH VOR
                             28_____ (15 pts)

**   5) When the **NAV 2 DME DIST** reads "13.5", record your:
       NAV 2 CDI POSITION____**CENTERED**____ (30 pts)
       ALTITUDE_____**5950 - 6050**_____ (20 pts)

**   6) How many seconds does it take for the **NAV 2 DME DIST** to go from "11.0" to "10.1"? **19 - 21** (20 pts)

**   7) Based on this data, what is your GROUND SPEED?
                            160 - 164_____ (20 pts)

**   15) TOTAL INBOUND TIME IS____**:35 - :40**____ (20 pts)

Enroute Cruise:

**   7) Record your:
       HEADING to keep NAV 2 CDI centered
        _____**264 - 266 [268 - 270]**_____ (35 pts)
       ALTITUDE_____**5950 - 6050**_____ (25 pts)
       AIRSPEED_____**127 - 133**_____ (20 pts)
       RPM_____**2192 - 2208**_____ (15 pts)
       COM FREQUENCY_____**126.35**_____ (10 pts)
       LOS ANGELES VOR IDENT
         · — · ·   · —   — · · · _____ (5 pts)

*Your next checkpoint of interest is what?*_____**HERMO**_____ *(5 pts)*

**   17) What radial are you tracking inbound on? **154 - 158** (40 pts)

1. What is your initial heading once crossing Van Nuys VOR?
_____**324 - 326**_____ *(5 pts)*
*2. If glideslope fails, this approach could continue as a localizer approach. TRUE or FALSE*_____**FALSE**_____ *(5 pts)*

Answers 247

    3. *How many miles is it from Van Nuys VOR to the displaced threshold of runway 16R?* _____**34.3**_____ *(5 pts)*
    4. *You can go no lower than what altitude before intercepting glideslope?* _____**4300**_____ *(5 pts)*
    5. *A straight in landing to runway 16R has for a decision height an altitude of* _____**1040**_____ *(5 pts)*
    6. *The first altitude of concern in the missed approach procedure is to be at or below* _____**1750**_____ *(5 pts)*

Initial approach segment:
   **   2) Record your:
                NAV 2 CDI POSITION____**CENTERED**____ (35 pts)
                HEADING to keep NAV 2 CDI centered
                ____**325 - 327   [326 - 329]**____ (30 pts)
                VSI____**-50 to +50**____ (25 pts)
   **   9) Record your:
                NAV 1 GLIDESLOPE INDICATOR POSITION
                ____**CENTERED**____ (40 pts)
                ALTITUDE____**2650 - 2750**____ (35 pts)
                AIRSPEED____**95 - 105**____ (30 pts)
                VSI____**-600 to -800**____ (25 pts)
                STROBES____**ON**____ (20 pts)
                GEAR____**DOWN**____ (20 pts)
                RPM____**1400 - 1500   [1750 - 1850]**____ (15 pts)
                DECISION HEIGHT____**1040**____ (10 pts)
                COM FREQUENCY____**119.30**____ (10 pts)
                CARB HEAT____**ON**____ (10 pts)
   **   23) Record the **TIME**____**22:41 - 22:46**____ (5 pts)

You are in the same league as:

Jack Knight .... 876 to 930 pts
Jimmy Doolittle .... 701 to 875 pts
Charles Lindbergh .... 521 to 700 pts
Amelia Earhart .... 331 to 520 pts
Wrong Way Corrigan .... 141 to 330 pts
TAKE THE BUS .... 000 to 140 pts

248 IFR Flights of "13MIKE"

Flight Scenario Seven

FILLING OUT THE FLIGHT PLAN -

** a) What is in block 8, Route of Flight, of your flight plan?
    AY MOVER V25 SANTY EUGEN HADLY 1 (10 pts)

** b) What is the minimum obstruction clearance altitude for the leg on Victor 25 between MOVER and SANTY intersections? **4000** (10 pts)

** c) Off of what VOR does EUGEN intersection's minimum reception altitude pertain to? **SAN JOSE** (10 pts)

** d) How many miles is it from EUGEN to HADLY intersection, and then direct to Oakland VOR? **44** (10 pts)

** e) How many different Victor airway radials extend outward from Oakland VOR? **6** (10 pts)

RUN UP -

**   3) Select **CARB HEAT "ON"**, record RPM drop **80 [55]** (5 pts)
**   5) Select **"LEFT"** Mag, record RPM drop **150 [130]** (5 pts)
**   7) Select **"RIGHT"** Mag, record RPM drop **150 [130]** (5 pts)

What is our heading out of MOVER? **292 - 294** *(5 pts)*
Would it be direct, teardrop, or parallel? **DIRECT** *(5 pts)*
You know, this airport has available to it a localizer approach, a VOR approach, and an NDB approach. Can it be used as an alternate when a destination gets weathered in? **NO** *(5 pts)*
Runway eight has what kind of visual path indicator? **PAPI** *(5 pts)*
Runway two six is narrower than runway two by how many feet? **50** *(5 pts)*

Takeoff:

**   14) Record your:
    AIRSPEED **78 - 82** (30 pts)
    HEADING **258 - 262** (25 pts)
    CARD COURSE which the ADF needle is pointing to
    215 - 225   [235 - 245] (25 pts)
    ANTICIPATED LEFT TURN ROLLOUT HEADING
    105 - 115   [125 - 135] (20 pts)

Answers 249

        ALTITUDE __1200 - 1300__ (15 pts)
        COM FREQUENCY __127.15__ (15 pts)
        XPDR __5616__ (10 pts)
        GEAR __UP__ (10 pts)
        FLAPS __UP__ (10 pts)
        RPM __2292 - 2308__ (5 pts)

IFR Departure Procedure:

**   5) When the **NAV 1 CDI** is ½ dot **LEFT** of center, record the wind correction angle you needed to track outbound
        __10 - 15 [18 - 22]__ (45 pts)

**   8) Record your:
        NAV 1 DME DIST __18.1 - 18.5 [18.3 - 18.7]__ (35 pts)
        ALTITUDE __6850 - 7150 [6050 - 6450]__ (30 pts)
        AIRSPEED __78 - 82__ (25 pts)
        RPM __2292 - 2308__ (20 pts)
        COM FREQUENCY __124.45__ (15 pts)
        IS **MOVER** intersection BEHIND or IN FRONT OF you? __BEHIND__ (15 pts)

Enroute - Victor 25 to Victor 27:

**   3) When the **NAV 1 DME DIST** reads "26.0", record your:
        NAV 1 CDI POSITION __CENTERED__ (30 pts)
        HEADING __282 - 286__ (25 pts)
        RPM __2195 - 2205 [2395 - 2405]__ (20 pts)

**   6) What intersection did you just reach? __SANTY__ (15 pts)

**   13) What heading will you fly to maintain track?
        __303 - 307 [298 - 302]__ (30 pts)

**   19) Record your:
        NAV 1 DME DIST __60.9 - 60.4 [60.7 - 60.2]__ (35 pts)
        NAV 1 CDI POSITION
                __CENTERED [1/2 to 1 dot LEFT]__ (30 pts)
        AIRSPEED __125 - 130__ (20 pts)
        ALTITUDE __7950 - 8050__ (20 pts)
        POINT REYES VOR IDENT · - - ·   · - · ·   · (10 pts)

What intersection was just passed? __EUGEN__ (5 pts)

250   IFR Flights of "13MIKE"

To HADLY Intersection:
* ** 3) After the **NAV 2 CDI** is **centered**, record the:
        NAV 1 DME DIST **51.1 - 51.4 [50.6 - 50.9]**   (25 pts)
        NAV 1 CDI POSITION   **CENTERED**   (25 pts)
        What intersection did you just pass? **TAILS**   (10 pts)

South Arc to the Localizer:
* ** 5) Record your:
        NAV 2 CDI POSITION   **CENTERED**   (35 pts)
        ALTITUDE   **3950 - 4050**   (30 pts)
        AIRSPEED   **114 - 119**   (25 pts)
        RPM   **1895 - 1907 [2195 - 2207]**   (20 pts)
        NAV 1 OBS with centered needle "**TO**"
                        050 [056]   (15 pts)

* ** 18) Record your:
        NAV 1 DME DIST   **14.9 - 15.1**   (40 pts)
        ALTITUDE   **3950 - 4050**   (35 pts)
        XPDR   **2734**   (25 pts)
        COM FREQUENCY   **135.65**   (25 pts)
        RPM   **1895 - 1907 [2195 - 2207]**   (15 pts)

Off the arc to the localizer:
* ** 3) Record your:
        ALTITUDE   **3950 - 4050**   (30 pts)
        NAV 2 DME DIST   **14.3 - 14.7**   (25 pts)
        Are you BELOW or ABOVE glideslope?
                        BELOW   (15 pts)
        NAME OF NEXT CHECKPOINT ON ILS
                        GROVE   (10 pts)
        NAME OF CHECKPOINT FOLLOWING THAT
                        HAYZE   (10 pts)
        GLIDESLOPE INTERCEPTION ALTITUDE
                        3500   (10 pts)
        NAME OF AIRPORT on the south side of the
        LOCALIZER TRACK   **HAYWARD**   (10 pts)
        OAKLAND LOCALIZER IDENT
                .. --- .. --.   (10 pts)

* ** 17) Record your:
        GLIDESLOPE NEEDLE POSITION**CENTERED**(45 pts)

NAV 1 CDI NEEDLE POSITION __CENTERED__ (45 pts)
ALTITUDE_____ __1800 - 1900 [1600 - 1700]__ (35 pts)
VSI_____ __-400 to -600_____ (30 pts)
AIRSPEED_____ __85 - 92_____ (20 pts)
DECISION HEIGHT_____ __254_____ (20 pts)
GEAR_____ __DOWN_____ (15 pts)
FLAPS_____ __10 degrees DOWN_____ (15 pts)
STROBES_____ __ON_____ (10 pts)

** 12) Record the **TIME**_____ __06:18 - 06:23_____ (5 pts)

You are in the same league as:

Jack Knight	1216 to 1365 pts
Jimmy Doolittle	971 to 1215 pts
Charles Lindbergh	716 to 970 pts
Amelia Earhart	461 to 715 pts
Wrong Way Corrigan	196 to 460 pts
TAKE THE BUS	000 to 195 pts

Flight Scenario Eight

FILLING OUT THE FLIGHT PLAN -

** a) What is in block 8, Route of Flight, of your flight plan?
_____**BID V268 MINNK V374 MVY BORST**_____ (10 pts)

** b) With a runway 28 departure from Block Island, and a left turn back to the NDB, what navaid, radial and DME would be most appropriate to also help define the NDB as a backup?
_____**HAMPTON   079 / 37**_____ (10 pts)

** c) What is the airport elevation at Marthas Vineyard Airport?
_____**68**_____ (10 pts)

** d) What is the TACAN (Tactical Air Navigation used by the military) station frequency at Marthas Vineyard?_____**92**_____ (10 pts)

IFR Flights of "13MIKE"

 **   e) MINNK intersection is what DME:
    from Norwich VOR   **28**
    from Marthas Vineyard VOR   **37**
    from Sandy Point VOR   **14**
    from Groton VOR   **28**   (10 pts)

RUN UP -
 **   3) Select **CARB HEAT "ON"**, record RPM drop **80 [60]** (5 pts)
 **   5) Select **"LEFT"** Mag, record RPM drop **150 [140]** (5 pts)
 **   7) Select **"RIGHT"** Mag, record RPM drop **150 [140]** (5 pts)

Departure:
 **   3) Record your:
    HOMING HEADING to BLOCK ISLAND NDB
     065 - 075   (40 pts)
    ALTITUDE   **2300 - 2500**   (30 pts)
    AIRSPEED   **75 - 85**   (30 pts)
    NAV 1 DME DIST   **32.8 - 33.3 [34.5 - 35.0]** (25 pts)
    GEAR   **UP**   (20 pts)
    FLAPS   **UP**   (15 pts)
    XPDR   **3116**   (10 pts)
    COM FREQUENCY   **119.45**   (10 pts)
    LIGHTS   **ON**   (5 pts)

Victor Airway enroute:
 **   5) Record your:
    NAV 1 DME DIST **30.7 - 31.2 [32.5 - 33.0]** (35 pts)
    IS MINNK INTERSECTION BEHIND OR IN FRONT
    OF YOU?   **BEHIND**   (30 pts)
    ALTITUDE   **4950 - 5050**   (25 pts)
    RPM **2242 - 2258 [2442 - 2458]**   (20 pts)
    VSI   **-50 to +50**   (20 pts)
    AIRSPEED   **127 - 133**   (15 pts)
    MARTHAS VINEYARD VOR IDENT
     -- .... -.-.   (10 pts)
 **   10) What intersection did you just pass? **FALMA** (30 pts)
 **   11) What HEADING keeps the NAV 1 CDI needle centered?
     090 - 093   (25 pts)
 **   12) When passing through **"4000"** feet, record your:
    GROUND SPEED   **172 - 178**   (25 pts)

VSI. _____-400 to -600_____	(25 pts)
AIRSPEED___136 - 143 [139 - 146]___	(20 pts)

** A. What is the outbound course of the holding pattern depicted?
_____056_____ (5 pts)

B. How many miles is it from Marthas Vineyard VOR to the initial approach fix?_____4.2_____ (5 pts)

C. What is the minimum glideslope altitude?___1500___ (5 pts)

D. At what altitude will you cross BORST if you're on glideslope?_____1407_____ (5 pts)

E. If the glideslope becomes out of service, how much higher is the minimum descent altitude (MDA) than the decision height (DH)?_____177_____ (5 pts)

F. What is the touchdown zone elevation?___63___ (5 pts)

To the initial approach fix:
** 4) Record your:
NAV 1 CDI POSITION___**CENTERED**___ (40 pts)
RPM___1890 - 1910 [2190 - 2210]___ (30 pts)
AIRSPEED___115 - 122___ (25 pts)
VSI___-50 to +50___ (20 pts)
DISTANCE to ILS RWY 24 Initial Approach Fix
_____7.2_____ (15 pts)
XPDR___5533___ (10 pts)

Teardrop course reversal:
** 7) Record your:
NAV 1 DME DIST___6.7 - 7.0___ (40 pts)
INTERCEPT HEADING___250 - 270___ (40 pts)
AIRSPEED___97 - 102___ (25 pts)
ANTICIPATED DME FOR GLIDESLOPE
INTERCEPTION___5.5 - 6.0___ (20 pts)
ALTITUDE___1450 - 1550___ (15 pts)
DESIRED INBOUND LOCALIZER COURSE
___236___ (10 pts)
DECISION HEIGHT___263___ (10 pts)
RPM___1592 - 1608 [1992 - 2008]___ (10 pts)
STROBES___**ON**___ (5 pts)

IFR Flights of "13MIKE"

Missed Approach Point:
**   2) Record your:
            NAV 1 GLIDESLOPE NEEDLE POSITION
                 CENTERED   (45 pts)
            NAV 1 CDI POSITION   **CENTERED**   (45 pts)
            HEADING   **238 - 242**   (35 pts)
            VSI   **-500 to -650**   (30 pts)
            ALTITUDE   **880 - 920 [550 - 650]**   (25 pts)
            GEAR   **DOWN**   (15 pts)
            FLAPS   **10 degrees DOWN**   (15 pts)
            COM FREQUENCY   **121.40**   (15 pts)
**   16) Record the TIME   **20:27 - 20:32**   (5 pts)

You are in the same league as:

Jack Knight	996 to 1105 pts
Jimmy Doolittle	811 to 995 pts
Charles Lindbergh	611 to 810 pts
Amelia Earhart	401 to 610 pts
Wrong Way Corrigan	181 to 400 pts
TAKE THE BUS	000 to 180 pts

APPENDIX A

Flight plan form

FLIGHT PLAN

1. TYPE	2. AIRCRAFT IDENTIFICATION	3. AIRCRAFT TYPE/ SPECIAL EQUIPMENT	4. TRUE AIRSPEED	5. DEPARTURE POINT	6. DEPARTURE TIME		7. CRUISING ALTITUDE
IFR					PROPOSED (Z)	ACTUAL (Z)	
VFR			KNOTS				
DVFR							

8. ROUTE OF FLIGHT

9. DESTINATION (Name of airport and city)	10. EST. TIME EN ROUTE		11. REMARKS
	HOURS	MINUTES	

12. FUEL ON BOARD		13. ALTERNATE AIRPORT(S)	14. PILOT'S NAME, ADDRESS, TELEPHONE NO. AND AIRCRAFT HOME BASE	15. NO. ABOARD
HOURS	MINUTES			

16. COLOR OF AIRCRAFT

CLOSE FLIGHT PLAN WITH _____ FSS

IFR Flights of "13MIKE"

Flight plan worksheet

NAVIGATION LOG

Aircraft Number N _____   Notes

Check Points (Fixed)	VOR Ident Freq.	Course (Route)	Altitude	Wind Dir / Vel Temp	CAS TAS	TC L R WCA	TH E W Var	MH Dev	CH	Dist Leg Rem	GS Est. Act.	Time off ETE ATE	GPH ETA ATA	Fuel Rem
Totals ▷														

Airport & ATIS Advisories

	Departure	Destination
ATIS Code		
Ceiling/Vis		
Winds		
Altimeter		
Approach		
Runway		
Time Check		

Airport Frequencies

	Departure	Destination
ATIS		ATIS
FSS		FSS
Grnd		Apch
Tower		Tower
Dep.		Grnd
UNICOM		UNICOM
Block In		Log Time
Block Out		

APPENDIX B

New York
Low Altitude Enroute Chart
L-28

B1

The Low Altitude Enroute Chart, for the New York flight scenario, is on the following page. The map scale is 1" = 8 NM. Study the chart, there is a wealth of information on it. The area that this section of the chart covers is illustrated in Figure B.1.

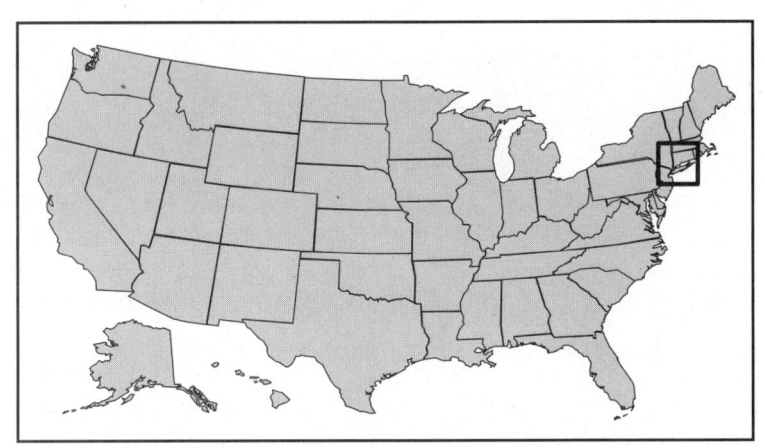

Figure B.1.

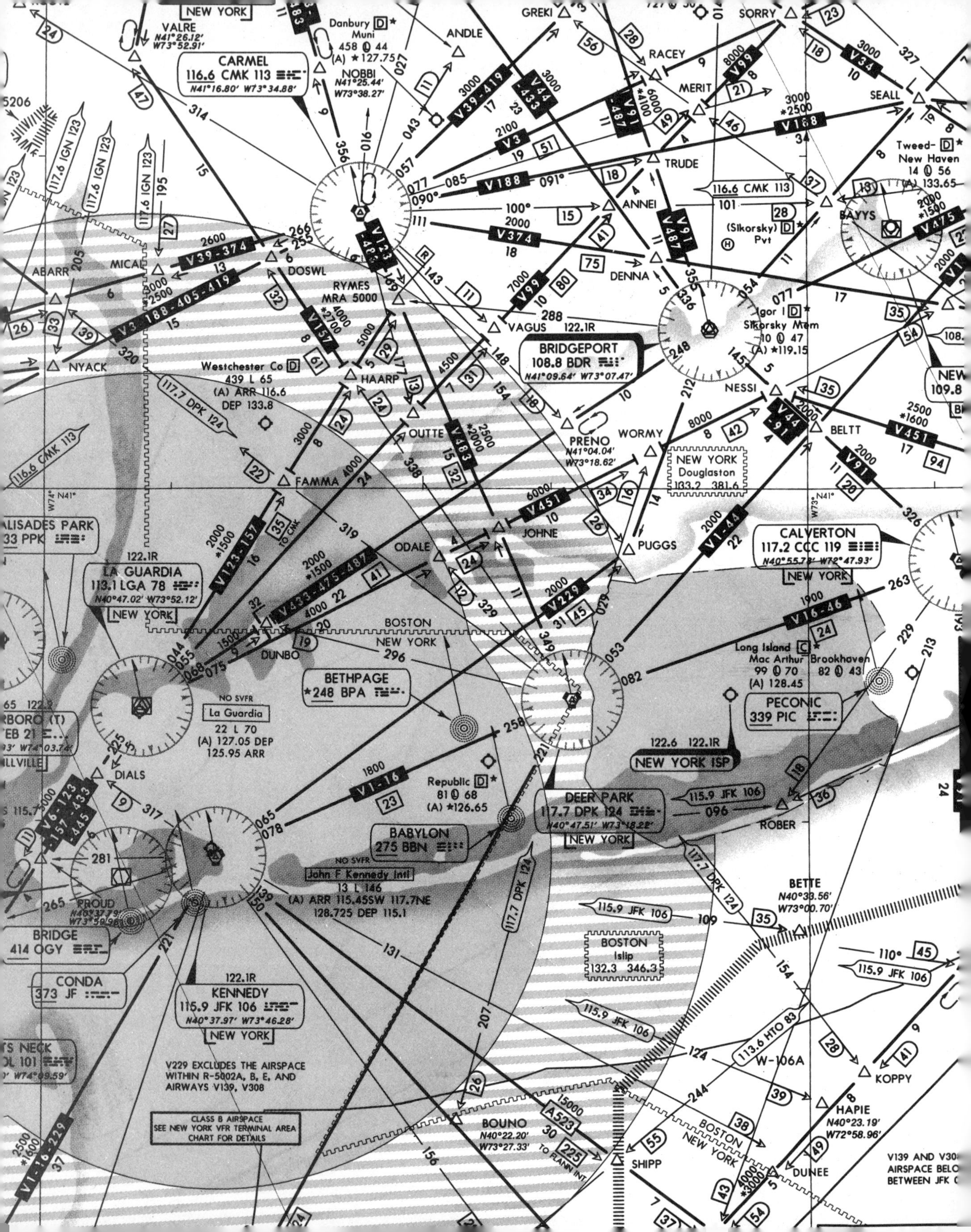

NEW YORK
VALRE
N41°26.12'
W73°52.91'
CARMEL
116.6 CMK 113
N41°16.80' W73°34.88'
Danbury
Muni
458 44
(A) ★127.75
NOBBI
N41°25.44'
W73°38.27'
ANDLE
GREKI
SORRY
RACEY
MERIT
SEALL
Tweed-New Haven
14 56
(A) 133.65
TRUDE
116.6 CMK 113
ANNEI
BAYYS
(Sikorsky)
Pvt
DENNA
V39-419
V44
V3
V188
V374
V99
V91
V34
V475
V451
V483
V157
V123
V39-374
V3-188-405-419
ABARR
MICAL
DOSWL
RYMES
MRA 5000
NYACK
Westchester Co
439 L 65
(A) ARR 116.6
DEP 133.8
VAGUS
122.1R
BRIDGEPORT
108.8 BDR
N41°09.64' W73°07.47'
Igor I
Sikorsky Mem
10 47
(A) ★119.15
NESSI
BELTT
HAARP
OUTTE
PRENO
N41°04.04'
W73°18.62'
WORMY
NEW YORK
Douglaston
133.2 381.6
117.7 DPK 124
116.6 CMK 113
FAMMA
JOHNE
PUGGS
ODALE
CALVERTON
117.2 CCC 119
N40°55.73' W72°47.93'
NEW YORK
PALISADES PARK
LA GUARDIA
113.1 LGA 78
N40°47.02' W73°52.12'
NEW YORK
V123-157
V433-475-487
V229
V1-44
V16-46
V1-16
V6-123-157-433-445
V1-16-229
A523
BOSTON
NEW YORK
DUNBO
BETHPAGE
★248 BPA
NO SVFR
La Guardia
22 L 70
(A) 127.05 DEP
125.95 ARR
Long Island
Mac Arthur
99 70
(A) 128.45
Brookhaven
82 43
PECONIC
339 PIC
122.6 122.1R
NEW YORK ISP
DIALS
Republic
81 68
(A) ★126.65
DEER PARK
117.7 DPK 124
N40°47.51' W73°18.22'
NEW YORK
115.9 JFK 106
ROBER
BABYLON
275 BBN
NO SVFR
John F Kennedy Intl
13 L 146
(A) ARR 115.45SW 117.7NE
128.725 DEP 115.1
PROUD
BRIDGE
414 OGY
CONDA
373 JF
BETTE
N40°38.56'
W73°00.70'
BOSTON
Islip
132.3 346.3
115.9 JFK 106
113.6 HTO 83
W-106A
KOPPY
HAPIE
N40°23.19'
W72°58.96'
122.1R
KENNEDY
115.9 JFK 106
N40°37.97' W73°46.28'
NEW YORK
V229 EXCLUDES THE AIRSPACE
WITHIN R-5002A, B, E, AND
AIRWAYS V139, V308
CLASS B AIRSPACE
SEE NEW YORK VFR TERMINAL AREA
CHART FOR DETAILS
BOUNO
N40°22.20'
W73°27.33'
TO FLANN INT
SHIPP
BOSTON
NEW YORK
DUNEE

APPENDIX B

San Diego/Los Angeles Low Altitude Enroute Chart L-3

The Low Altitude Enroute Chart, for the San Diego/Los Angeles and Oceanside/Van Nuys flight scenarios, is on the following page. The map scale is 1" = 10 NM. Study the chart, there is a wealth of information on it. The area that this section of the chart covers is illustrated in Figure B.2.

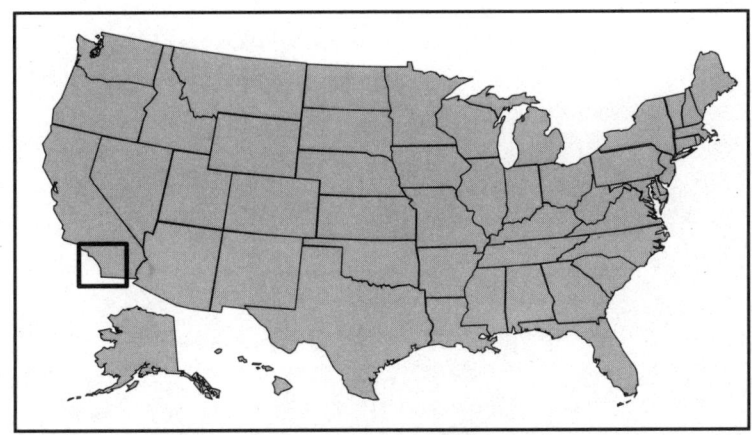

Figure B.2

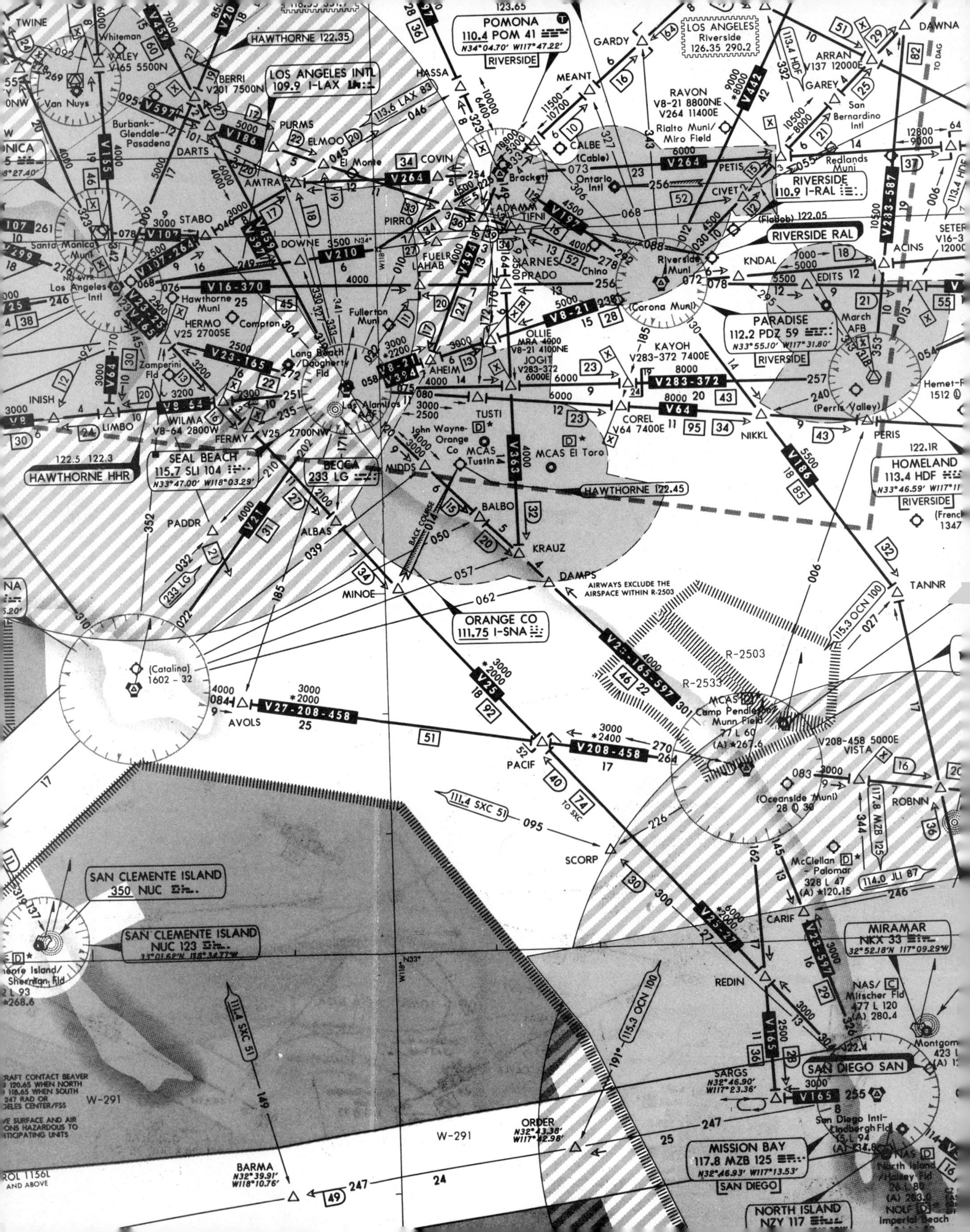

TWINE
Whiteman
VALEY
V165 5500N
Van Nuys
HAWTHORNE 122.35
BERRI
V201 7500N
LOS ANGELES INTL
109.9 I-LAX
POMONA
110.4 POM 41
N34°04.70' W117°47.22'
RIVERSIDE
123.65
LOS ANGELES
Riverside
126.35 290.2
GARDY
MEANT
HASSA
DAWNA
ARRAN
V137 12000E
GAREY
San Bernardino Intl
RAVON
V8-21 8800NE
V264 11400E
Rialto Muni/
Miro Field
Burbank-Glendale-Pasadena
PURMS
ELMOO
El Monte
COVIN
DARTS
AMTRA
CALBE
(Cable)
Brackett
Ontario Intl
PETIS
Redlands Muni
RIVERSIDE
110.9 I-RAL
CIVET
STABO
Santa Monica Muni
Los Angeles Intl
DOWNE
PIRRO
ADAMM
TIFNI
(Flabob) 122.05
RIVERSIDE RAL
ACINS
SETER
V16-3
FUELR
LAHAB
HARNES
PRADO
Chino
Riverside Muni
KNDAL
EDITS
Hawthorne Muni
Compton
HERMO
V25 2700SE
Fullerton Muni
(Corona Muni)
PARADISE
112.2 PDZ 59
N33°55.10' W117°31.80'
RIVERSIDE
March AFB
Zamperini Fld
Long Beach
/Daugherty Fld
AHEIM
OLLIE
MRA 4000
V8-21 4100NE
JOGIT
V283-372
6000E
KAYOH
V283-372 7400E
Hemet-R
1512
INISH
LIMBO
WILMA
V8-64 2800W
FERMY
V25 2700NW
Los Alamitos AAF
TUSTI
John Wayne-Orange Co
MCAS Tustin
MCAS El Toro
COREL
V64 7400E
NIKKL
(Perris Valley)
PERIS
122.1R
HOMELAND
113.4 HDF
N33°46.59' W117°1
RIVERSIDE
SEAL BEACH
115.7 SLI 104
N33°47.00' W118°03.29'
HAWTHORNE HHR
122.5 122.3
BECCA
233 LG
MIDDS
HAWTHORNE 122.45
BALBO
KRAUZ
PADDR
ALBAS
BACK COURSE
DAMPS
AIRWAYS EXCLUDE THE AIRSPACE WITHIN R-2503
MINOE
TANNR
ORANGE CO
111.75 I-SNA
(Catalina)
1602 – 32
AVOLS
V27-208-458
PACIF
V208-458
TO SXC
R-2503
R-2533
MCAS
Camp Pendleton
Munn Field
77 L 60
(A) *267.6
V208-458 5000E
VISTA
(Oceanside Muni)
28 30
ROBNN
111.4 SXC 51
SCORP
McClellan
- Palomar
328 L 47
(A) *120.15
114.0 JLI 87
117.8 MZB 125
115.3 OCN 100
SAN CLEMENTE ISLAND
350 NUC
SAN CLEMENTE ISLAND
NUC 123
33°01.62'N 118°34.77'W
San Clemente Island/
Sherman Fld
CARIF
MIRAMAR
NKX 33
32°52.18'N 117°09.29'W
REDIN
NAS/
Mitscher Fld
477 L 120
(A) 280.4
Montgom
SAN DIEGO SAN
SARGS
N32°46.90'
W117°23.36'
V165
San Diego Intl-Lindbergh Fld
W-291
ORDER
N32°43.38'
W117°42.98'
BARMA
N32°39.91'
W118°10.76'
MISSION BAY
117.8 MZB 125
N32°46.93' W117°13.53'
SAN DIEGO
NAS
North Island
/Halsey Fld
NOLF
Imperial Beach
NORTH ISLAND
NZY 117
AND ABOVE

APPENDIX B

Chicago Low Altitude Enroute Chart L-23

The Low Altitude Enroute Chart, for the Chicago flight scenario, is on the following page. The map scale is 1" = 12 NM. Study the chart, there is a wealth of information on it. The area that this section of the chart covers is illustrated in Figure B.3.

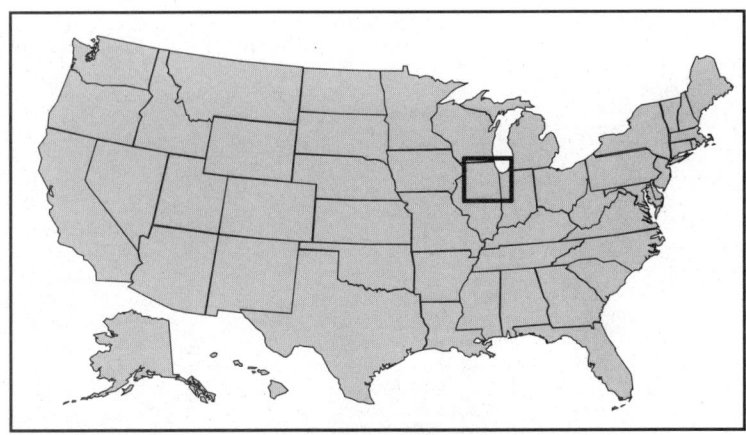

Figure B.3

B3

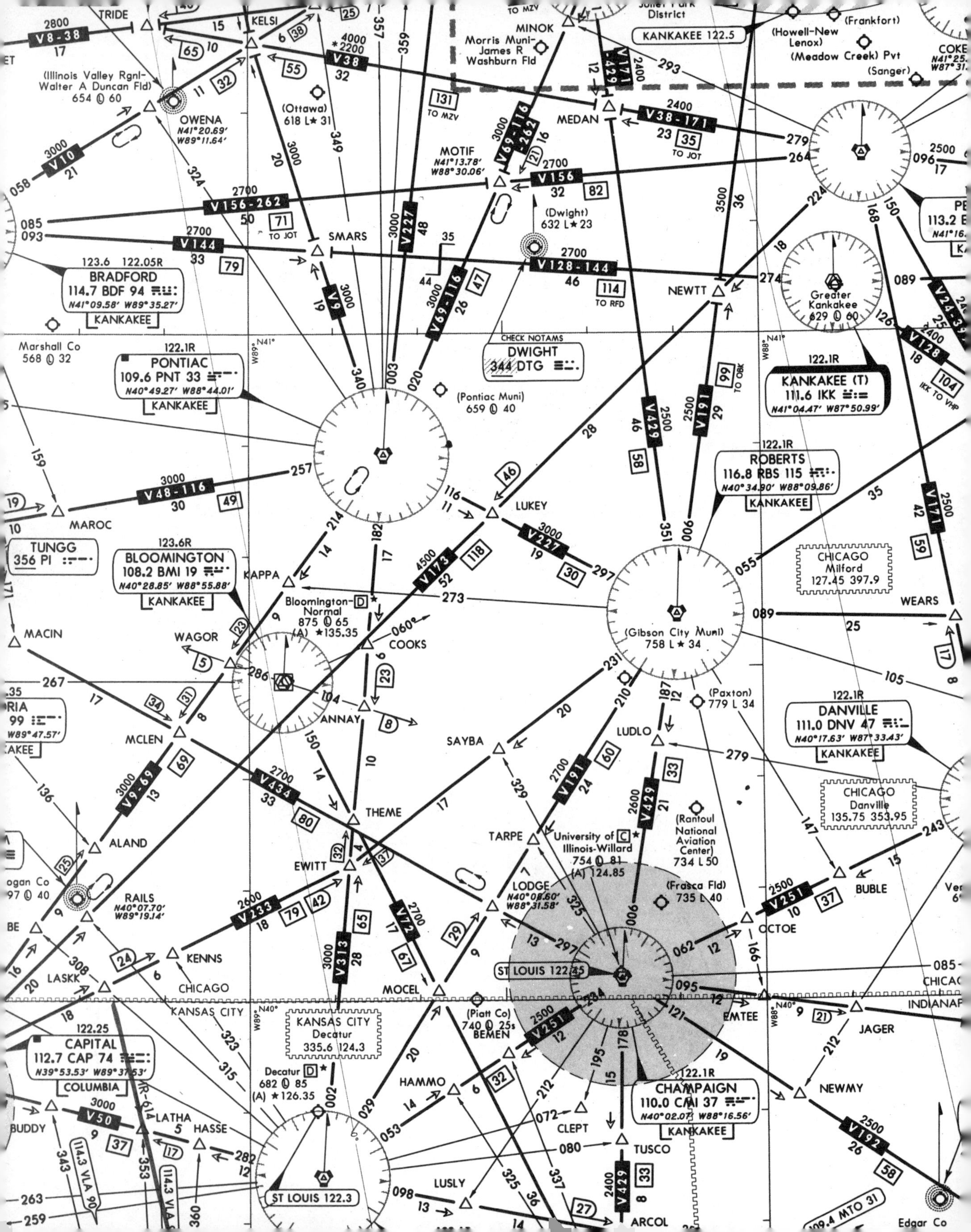

TRIDE
KELSI
V8-38
2800
MINOK
Morris Muni-James R Washburn Fld
Joliet Park District
KANKAKEE 122.5
(Howell-New Lenox)
(Frankfort)
(Meadow Creek) Pvt
(Sanger)
COKE
(Illinois Valley Rgnl-Walter A Duncan Fld)
654 L 60
OWENA
N41°20.69′
W89°11.64′
V38
4000
*2200
(Ottawa)
618 L★ 31
TO MZV
MEDAN
V38-171
2400
TO JOT
V10
3000
MOTIF
N41°13.78′
W88°30.06′
V69-116-262
V156
2700
V156-262
TO JOT
SMARS
V144
(Dwight)
632 L★ 23
V128-144
TO RFD
NEWTT
123.6 122.05R
BRADFORD
114.7 BDF 94
N41°09.58′ W89°35.27′
KANKAKEE
V9
V227
V69-116
Greater Kankakee
629 L 60
V128
V24-39
Marshall Co
568 L 32
122.1R
PONTIAC
109.6 PNT 33
N40°49.27′ W88°44.01′
KANKAKEE
CHECK NOTAMS
DWIGHT
344 DTG
(Pontiac Muni)
659 L 40
V429
V191
TO OBK
122.1R
KANKAKEE (T)
111.6 IKK
N41°04.47′ W87°50.99′
IKK TO VHP
122.1R
ROBERTS
116.8 RBS 115
N40°34.90′ W88°09.86′
KANKAKEE
V48-116
3000
MAROC
TUNGG
356 PI
LUKEY
V227
123.6R
BLOOMINGTON
108.2 BMI 19
N40°28.85′ W88°55.88′
KANKAKEE
KAPPA
V173
4500
Bloomington-Normal
875 L 65
(A) ★135.35
CHICAGO
Milford
127.45 397.9
V171
2500
MACIN
WAGOR
COOKS
(Gibson City Muni)
758 L ★ 34
WEARS
ANNAY
(Paxton)
779 L 34
122.1R
DANVILLE
111.0 DNV 47
N40°17.63′ W87°33.43′
KANKAKEE
MCLEN
SAYBA
LUDLO
V9-69
V434
2700
V191
V429
2600
CHICAGO
Danville
135.75 353.95
ALAND
THEME
TARPE
University of Illinois-Willard
754 L 81
(A) 124.85
(Rantoul National Aviation Center)
734 L 50
EWITT
LODGE
N40°08.60′
W88°31.58′
(Frasca Fld)
735 L 40
BUBLE
V251
Logan Co
RAILS
N40°07.70′
W89°19.14′
V233
V72
V313
OCTOE
KENNS
CHICAGO
LASKK
ST LOUIS 122.45
MOCEL
EMTEE
JAGER
INDIANAPOLIS
KANSAS CITY
KANSAS CITY
Decatur
335.6 124.3
(Piatt Co)
740 L 25s
BEMEN
122.25
CAPITAL
112.7 CAP 74
N39°53.53′ W89°37.53′
COLUMBIA
Decatur
682 L 85
(A) ★126.35
HAMMO
V251
122.1R
CHAMPAIGN
110.0 CMI 37
N40°02.07′ W88°16.56′
KANKAKEE
NEWMY
V50
3000
BUDDY
LATHA
HASSE
114.3 VLA 90
CLEPT
TUSCO
V192
2500
ST LOUIS 122.3
LUSLY
V429
2400
ARCOL
109.4 MTO 31
Edgar Co

APPENDIX B

San Francisco
Low Altitude Enroute Chart
L-2

The Low Altitude Enroute Chart, for the San Francisco and Watsonville flight scenarios, is on the following two pages. The map scale is 1" = 10 NM. Study the chart, there is a wealth of information on it. The area that this section of the chart covers is illustrated in Figure B.4.

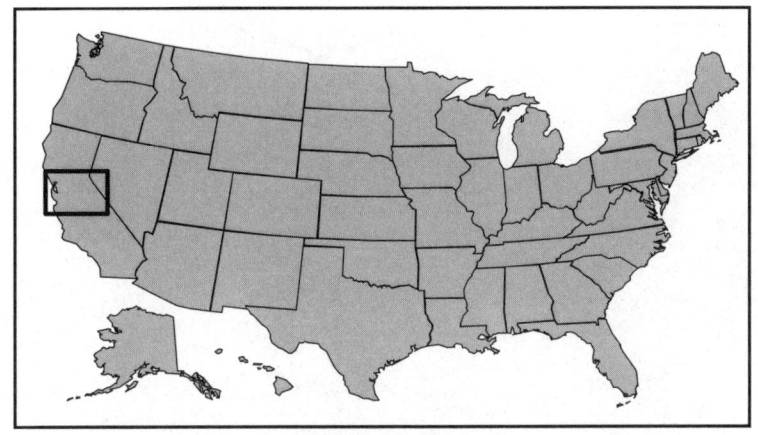

Figure B.4

LAMPSON
217 LOP
Cloverdale Muni
272 L 31
GETER
V25 12000 N
MRA 10000
114.4 ILA 91
SANTA ROSA
113.0 STS 77
N38°30.49' W122°48.64'
Sonoma Co
125 L 51
(A) ★120.55
FREES
KLOGE
V301 6000 NE
RUMSY
WILLIAMS
114.4 ILA 91
N39°04.27' W122°01.64'
(Pope Valley) Pvt
618 L 37
MAUCH
(Virgil O Parrett Field)
1848 L 32
POPES
BESSA
V195 7500 S
RAGGS
MRA 7500
TRAVIS
116.4 TZZ
115.2 SAC 99
SACRAMENTO
115.2 SAC 99
N38°26.82' W121°33.10'
RANCHO
OAKLAND
Sacramento
127.95 316.1
(Watts-Woodland)
125 L 38
Yolo County
98 L 60
(University)
68 L 32
CAPTO
Sacramento Metropolitan
24 L 86
(A) 126.75
Mc Clellan
MC CL
109.2 MCC
GRIME
(Vanderford Company)
TRAVIS
SUU 113
N38°14.73' W121°56.70'
Nut Tree
114 L 38
Sacramento Executive
21 L★ 55
(A) ★125.5
A-682
(Petaluma Muni)
SEE SAN FRANCISCO AREA CHART A-2
SCAGGS ISLAND
112.1 SGD 58
N38°10.76' W122°22.39'
Gnoss Field
Napa Co
CORDD
V195 6200 N
A-682
Travis AFB
EMBER
COUPS
POINT REYES
113.7 PYE 84
N38°04.79' W122°52.07'
Hamilton AAF
FLEAM
REJOY
2800 S
RYMAR
N38°06.60' W121°49.75'
VISTO
(Rio Vista Muni)
45 L 30
WAGER
N38°13.85' W121°25.09'
116.4 TZZ
MICRA
SAUSALITO
116.2 SAU 109
N37°51.32' W122°31.37'
GROIT
SABLO
Buchanan Field
PITTS
V6 3800 S
OAKEY
V334-392
3000 S
(Kingdon Airpark)
15 L 40
116.0 ECA 107
REBAS
OAKLAND
Mt Tamalpais
127.8 353.5
121.SGD 58
STINS
OAKLAND 122.5
COMMO
CONCORD (T)
117.0 CCR 117
N38°02.70' W122°02.71'
BERKS
COLLI
OAKLAND
116.8 OAK 115
N37°43.56' W122°13.42'
NAS Alameda Nimitz Field
Crissy AHP
GOBBS
SUTRO
SALAD
V28-109-244-392
4700 NE
ALTAM
N37°48.73' W121°44.83'
HAIRE
JANEY
BYRON
Metropolitan Oakland Intl
SAN FRANCISCO INTL
108.9 I-SIA
Livermore Muni
115.2 SAC 99
112.1 SGD 58
TRACY
Tracy Muni
190 L 37
BANTA
SEEMS
116.8 OAK 115
NO SVFR
San Francisco Intl
Hayward Air Terminal
116.2 SAU 109
Half Moon Bay
SAN FRANCISCO
115.8 SFO
DECOT
SUNOL
V301 6500 SE
AIRWAY EXCLUDES AIRSPACE WITHIN R-2531A AND
REIGA
New Jerusalem

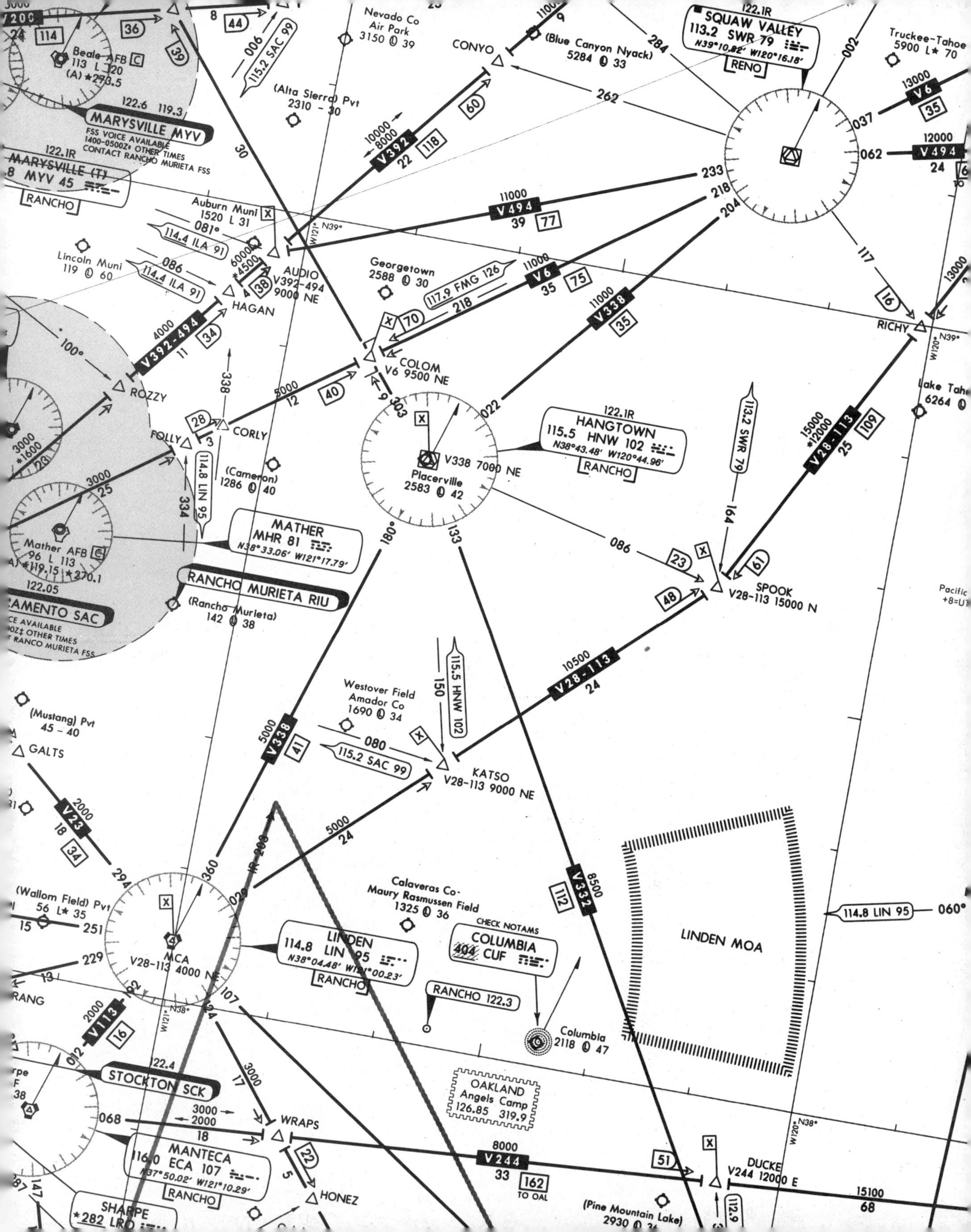

SQUAW VALLEY
122.1R
113.2 SWR 79
N39°10.82' W120°16.18'
RENO
Truckee-Tahoe
5900 L★ 70
Nevado Co
Air Park
3150 Ⓛ 39
CONYO
(Blue Canyon Nyack)
5284 Ⓛ 33
(Alta Sierra) Pvt
2310 - 30
115.2 SAC 99
Beale AFB
113 L 120
(A) ★273.5
122.6 119.3
MARYSVILLE MYV
FSS VOICE AVAILABLE
1400-0500Z‡ OTHER TIMES
CONTACT RANCHO MURIETA FSS
122.1R
MARYSVILLE (T)
MYV 45
RANCHO
Auburn Muni
1520 L 31
081°
114.4 ILA 91
Lincoln Muni
119 Ⓛ 60
086
AUDIO
V392-494
9000 NE
HAGAN
Georgetown
2588 Ⓛ 30
117.9 FMG 126
218
V392
V494
V338
V6
V392-494
ROZZY
COLOM
V6 9500 NE
CORLY
FOLLY
RICHY
Lake Tahoe
6264 Ⓛ
122.1R
HANGTOWN
115.5 HNW 102
N38°43.48' W120°44.96'
RANCHO
V338 7000 NE
Placerville
2583 Ⓛ 42
113.2 SWR 79
114.8 LIN 95
(Cameron)
1286 Ⓛ 40
MATHER
MHR 81
N38° 33.06' W121°17.79'
Mather AFB
96 L 113
★119.15 ★270.1
122.05
RANCHO MURIETA RIU
(Rancho Murieta)
142 Ⓛ 38
SACRAMENTO SAC
SPOOK
V28-113 15000 N
V28-113
Pacific
+8=UT
115.5 HNW 102
Westover Field
Amador Co
1690 Ⓛ 34
080
115.2 SAC 99
KATSO
V28-113 9000 NE
(Mustang) Pvt
45 - 40
GALTS
V23
V332
LINDEN MOA
114.8 LIN 95
060°
(Wallom Field) Pvt
56 L★ 35
LINDEN
114.8 LIN 95
N38°04.48' W121°00.23'
RANCHO
V28-113 4000 N
Calaveras Co-
Maury Rasmussen Field
1325 Ⓛ 36
CHECK NOTAMS
COLUMBIA
404 CUF
RANCHO 122.3
Columbia
2118 Ⓛ 47
RANG
V113
122.4
STOCKTON SCK
OAKLAND
Angels Camp
126.85 319.9
WRAPS
MANTECA
116.0 ECA 107
N37°50.02' W121°10.29'
RANCHO
HONEZ
V244
TO OAL
DUCKE
V244 12000 E
(Pine Mountain Lake)
2930
SHARPE
★282 LRO

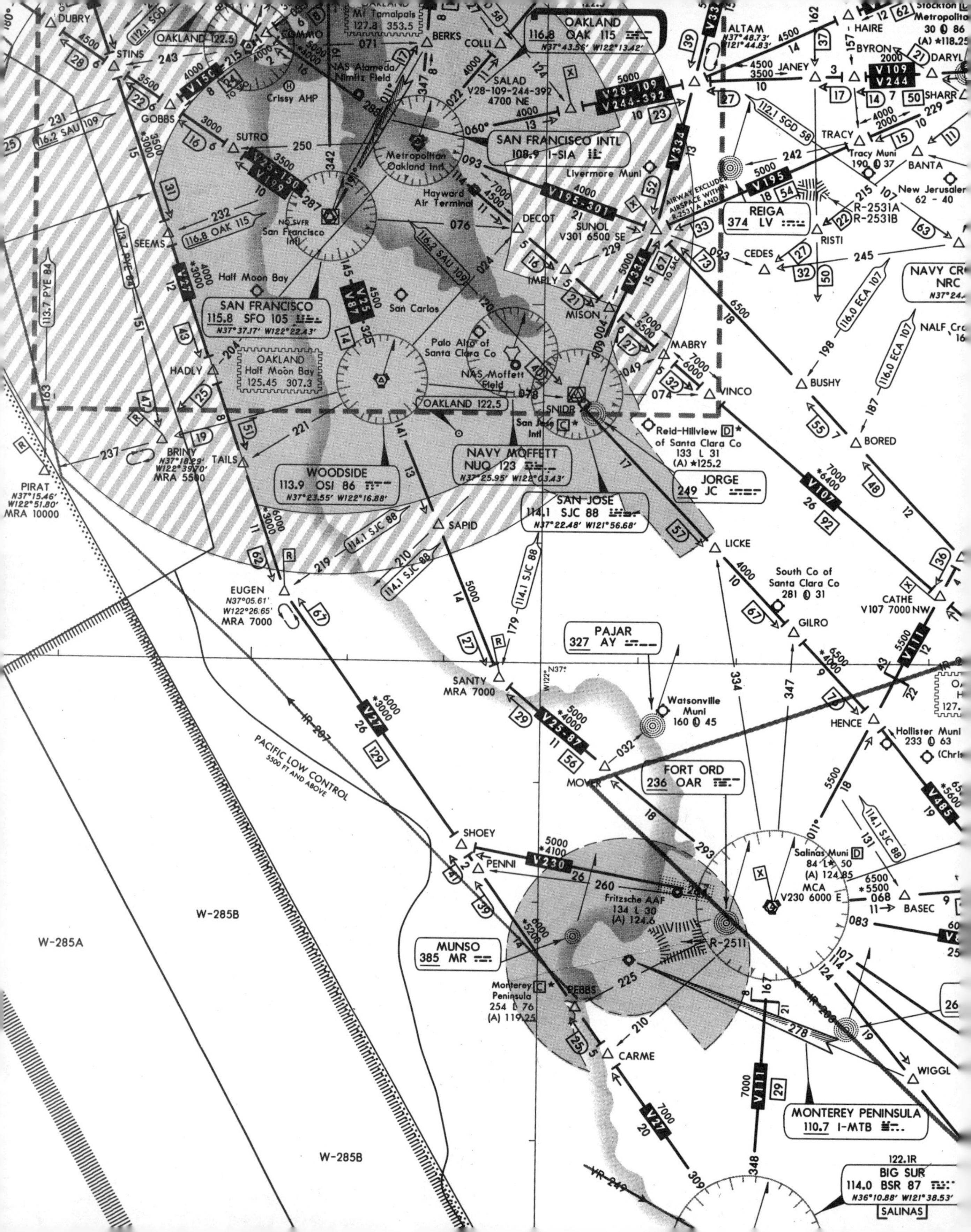
OAKLAND 122.5
Mt Tamalpais 127.8 353.5
OAKLAND 116.8 OAK 115 N37°43.56' W122°13.42'
DUBRY
STINS
COMMO
BERKS
COLLI
SALAD V28-109-244-392 4700 NE
GOBBS
SUTRO
Crissy AHP
NAS Alameda Nimitz Field
Metropolitan Oakland Intl
SAN FRANCISCO INTL 108.9 I-SIA
Livermore Muni
Hayward Air Terminal
DECOT
SUNOL V301 6500 SE
NO SVFR San Francisco Intl
SEEMS
116.8 OAK 115
116.2 SAU 109
113.7 PYE 84
Half Moon Bay
SAN FRANCISCO 115.8 SFO 105 N37°37.17' W122°22.43'
San Carlos
IMPLY
MISON
MABRY
Palo Alto of Santa Clara Co
NAS Moffett Field
HADLY
OAKLAND Half Moon Bay 125.45 307.3
OAKLAND 122.5
SNIDR
San Jose Intl
VINCO
BUSHY
Reid-Hillview of Santa Clara Co 133 L 31 (A) *125.2
JORGE 249 JC
BORED
BRINY N37°18.29' W122°39.70' MRA 5500
TAILS
PIRAT N37°15.46' W122°51.80' MRA 10000
WOODSIDE 113.9 OSI 86 N37°23.55' W122°16.88'
NAVY MOFFETT NUQ 123 N37°25.95' W122°03.43'
SAN JOSE 114.1 SJC 88 N37°22.48' W121°56.68'
SAPID
114.1 SJC 88
LICKE
South Co of Santa Clara Co 281 L 31
GILRO
CATHE V107 7000 NW
EUGEN N37°05.61' W122°26.65' MRA 7000
SANTY MRA 7000
PAJAR 327 AY
Watsonville Muni 160 L 45
HENCE
Hollister Muni 233 L 63
MOVER
FORT ORD 236 OAR
IR-207
PACIFIC LOW CONTROL 5500 FT AND ABOVE
SHOEY
PENNI
Salinas Muni 84 L* 50 (A) 124.85
MCA V230 6000 E
BASEC
Fritzsche AAF 134 L 30 (A) 124.6
R-2511
W-285A
W-285B
MUNSO 385 MR
Monterey Peninsula 254 L 76 (A) 119.25
PEBBS
CARME
WIGGL
MONTEREY PENINSULA 110.7 I-MTB
122.1R BIG SUR 114.0 BSR 87 N36°10.88' W121°38.53'
SALINAS
VR-249
ALTAM N37°48.73' W121°44.83'
HAIRE
BYRON
JANEY
DARYL
SHARR
TRACY
Tracy Muni 190 L 37
BANTA
112.1 SGD 58
New Jerusalem 62 - 40
REIGA 374 LV
R-2531A
R-2531B
RISTI
CEDES
NAVY CROWS NRC
116.0 ECA 107
Stockton Metropolitan

APPENDIX B

Seattle
Low Altitude Enroute Chart
L-1

The Low Altitude Enroute Chart, for the Seattle flight scenario, is on the following page. The map scale is 1" = 12 NM. Study the chart, there is a wealth of information on it. The area that this section of the chart covers is illustrated in Figure B.5.

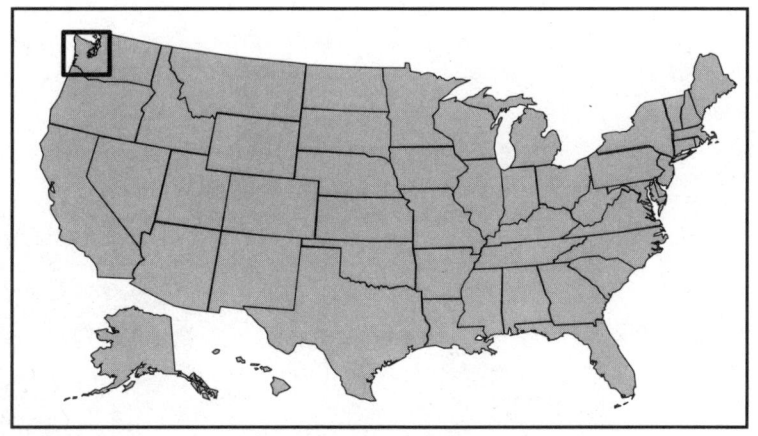

Figure B.5

B5

VANCOUVER
Victoria
133.85 308.4
MILL BAY
293 MB
VICTORIA
200 YJ
N48°38.64' W123°23.97'
Victoria
63 L 70
(A) ★118.8
IDNEY
CONDI
EVEN
4000
24
126.7
VICTORIA HARBOUR
FSS OPERATES
1345-0530Z‡
CYR 104
IMPOR
(Roche Harbor) Pvt
100 L★ 43
VICTORIA
108.7 I-YJ
CHATM
N48°27.31'
W123°13.87'
113.7 YYJ 84
N48°43.62' W123°29.06'
100°
DISCO
N48°23.56'
W123°10.32'
MRA 3000
CYR 109
058
062
CYR 156
CYR 139
CYR 108
CYR 103
CYA 102
V495
5400
*4300
17
67
Friday Harbor
109 L 3d
(A) ★134.15 ★280.3
ISLND
Whidbey Island
NAS/Ault Fld
47 L 80
(A) ★134.15 ★280.3
NAVY W
NUW
N48°21.30'
Anacortes
241 L 30
Skagit Regio
Bay View
140 L 55
(A) ★134.15
V287
5000
18
V23
4500
*3400
49
63
(Oak Harbor
Airpark)
189 L 32
(A) ★134.15 ★280.3
OLF Coupeville
199 L★ 54
A-680
5400
V4
73
115
TO SEA
(Port Angeles CGAS)
13 L★ 45
249
CHINOOK B
WATTR
William R
Fairchild Intl
288 L 63
(A) ★134.15 ★280.3
ELWHA
515 CL
(Sequim Valley)
144 L 35
SEATTLE 122.6
JAWBN
N49°01.91'
W122°50.50'
Jefferson
County Intl
110 L 30
R-6701
Arling
137
EDIZ HOOK
317
TRANSMITS CHARACTERISTIC
IDENTIFIER FOR 50 SECONDS
FOLLOWED BY A 10 SECOND DASH
V4-495
5400
*4300
42
13
CHINOOK A
B MOA
SEATTLE
Neah Bay
125.1 319.2
RX
4000
*1700
V287
236
17
LOFAL
MRA 6000
V287 7000E
Snohomish Co/
Paine Fld
606 L 90
(A) 128.65
SEATTLE
Ft Lawton
128.5 306.9
7000
V287
34
54
OLM TO PAE
V4-495
4000
29
3000
V23
29
163
KITSAP
206 PWT
Boeing Field/
King Co Intl
18 L 100
(A) 127.75
R-6707
CARNEY
274 CAN
Bremerton
National
439 L 62
DONDO
224 SE
NO SVFR
Seattle-
Tacoma Intl
429 L 119
(A) 118.0
OLYMPIC A MOA
MASON CO
348 MNC
CARRO
N47°18.24'
W122°49.15'
MRA 4000
V287 5400N
RX
3000
V27-165
227
22
42
TO OLM
Tacoma Narrows
292 L 50
(A) ★124.05
Auburn
57 L 34
GRAYE
216 GR
Sanderson Fld
269 L 50
24
SANDR
N47°09.79'
W123°21.19'
283MCA
V204 3200W
V165-287
4000
20
PUGET
260
Mc Chord AFB
328 L 101
(A) ★109.6 ★270.1
3000
175
165
5000
36
26
141
20
253
11
(Hogans Corner) Pvt
50 - 37
ULESS
181
3200
V27
18
81
35
TO SEA
CHECK NOTAMS
ABERN
414 HQ
OLYMPIA
113.4 OLM 81
N46°58.30' W122°54.11'
351
353
6000
V187
13
24
Gray AAF
302 L 61
(A) ★124.65 ★248.2
074
6000
13
134
Pier
Thun
534
049
17
Olympia
206 L 54
Bowerman
14 L 50
069
15
SOUPY
4500
V204
36
51
31
20
250
314
A
B
C
1
2
3
CHUCK
R-6703
A,B,C,D
RAINER 1,2,3
MOA
4000
095
15
9000
5000
37
LA
328
5800
MCKEN
SEATTLE
Larch Mountain
128.3 269.0
122.2
201
012
W124°
N48°
W123°
N47°

APPENDIX B

New York Low Altitude Enroute Chart L-25

The Low Altitude Enroute Chart, for the Block Island scenario, is on the following page. The map scale is 1" = 8 NM. Study the chart, there is a wealth of information on it. The area that this section of the chart covers is illustrated in Figure B.6.

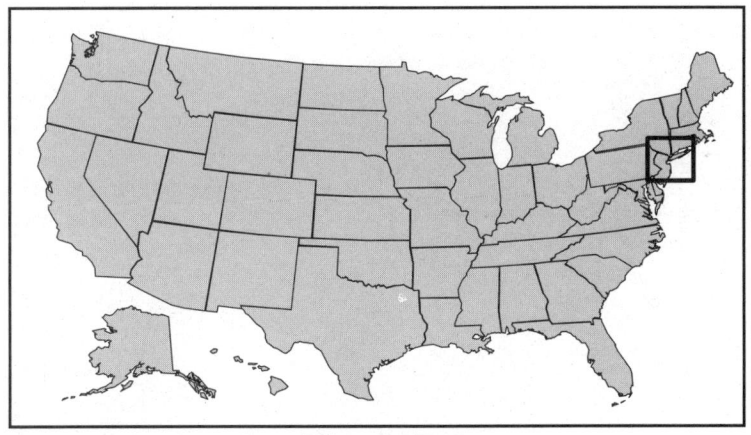

Figure B.6

B6

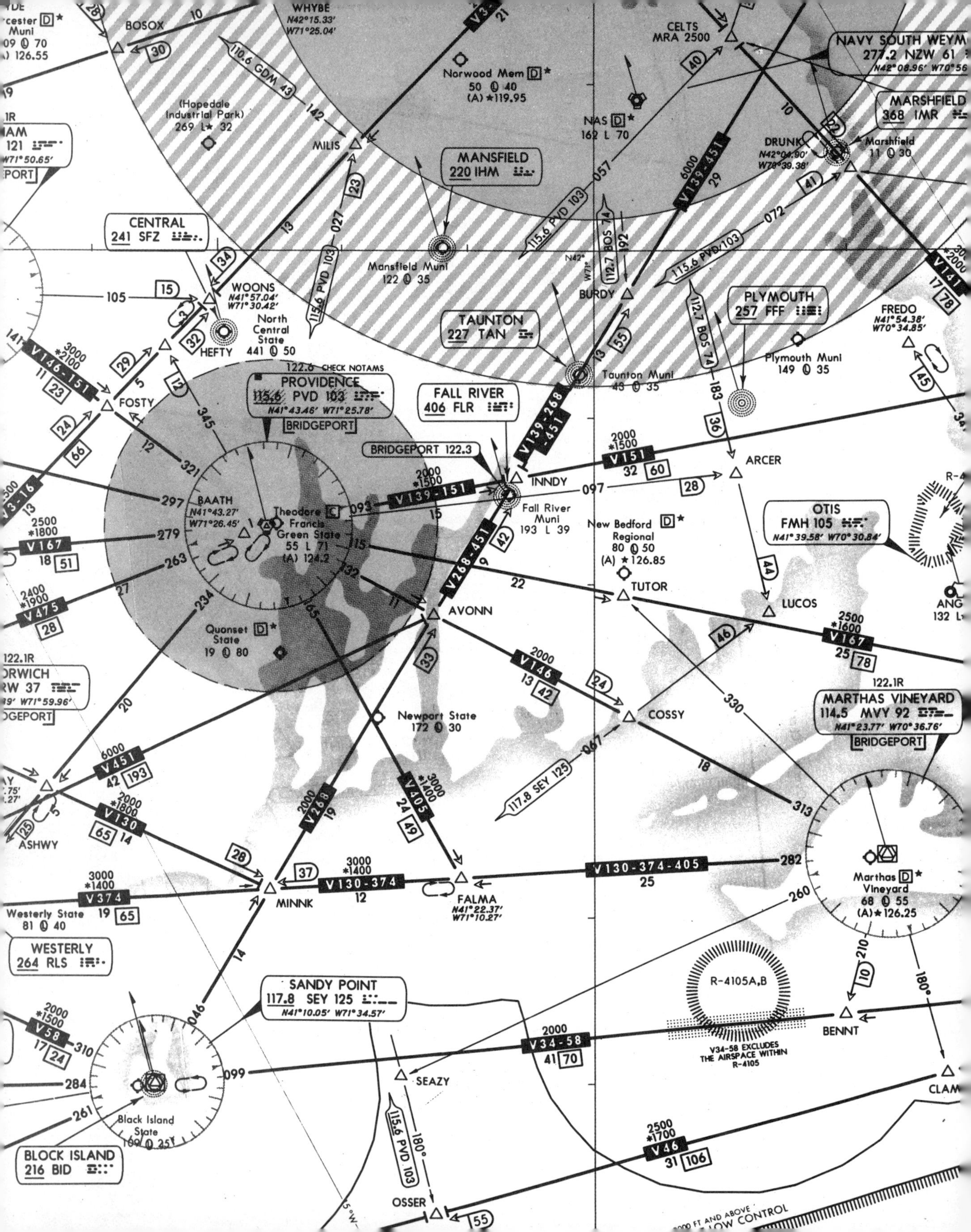
WHYBE
N42°15.33'
W71°25.04'
BOSOX
Worcester Muni
(Hopedale Industrial Park)
269 L★ 32
110.6 GDM 43
Norwood Mem
50 40
(A) ★119.95
CELTS
MRA 2500
NAVY SOUTH WEYM
277.2 NZW 61
N42°08.96' W70°56
MARSHFIELD
368 IMR
NAS
162 L 70
DRUNK
N42°04.90'
W70°39.38'
Marshfield
11 30
MILIS
MANSFIELD
220 IHM
CENTRAL
241 SFZ
Mansfield Muni
122 35
115.6 PVD 103
112.7 BOS 74
115.6 PVD/103
V139-451
WOONS
N41°57.04'
W71°30.42'
North Central State
441 50
HEFTY
BURDY
TAUNTON
227 TAN
Taunton Muni
45 35
PLYMOUTH
257 FFF
Plymouth Muni
149 35
FREDO
N41°54.38'
W70°34.85'
V141
FOSTY
V146-151
122.6 CHECK NOTAMS
PROVIDENCE
115.6 PVD 103
N41°43.46' W71°25.78'
BRIDGEPORT
FALL RIVER
406 FLR
BRIDGEPORT 122.3
V139-268-451
INNDY
V151
ARCER
BAATH
N41°43.27'
W71°26.45'
Theodore Francis Green State
55 L 71
(A) 124.2
V139-151
Fall River Muni
193 L 39
New Bedford Regional
80 50
(A) ★126.85
OTIS
FMH 105
N41°39.58' W70°30.84'
V167
V475
V268-451
TUTOR
LUCOS
AVONN
Quonset State
19 80
V146
122.1R
NORWICH
ORW 37
W71°59.96'
BRIDGEPORT
Newport State
172 30
COSSY
MARTHAS VINEYARD
114.5 MVY 92
N41°23.77' W70°36.76'
BRIDGEPORT
V451
117.8 SEY 125
V130
V268
V405
ASHWY
V130-374
V130-374-405
V374
MINNK
FALMA
N41°22.37'
W71°10.27'
Westerly State
81 40
WESTERLY
264 RLS
Marthas Vineyard
68 55
(A) ★ 126.25
SANDY POINT
117.8 SEY 125
N41°10.05' W71°34.57'
R-4105A,B
V58
V34-58
V34-58 EXCLUDES THE AIRSPACE WITHIN R-4105
BENNT
SEAZY
CLAM
Black Island State
109 35
BLOCK ISLAND
216 BID
115.6 PVD 103
V46
OSSER
LOW CONTROL

APPENDIX C

Scenario One Approach Plates

Islip to Westchester County

1. **TAKE-OFF MINS**

2. **ISLIP/LONG ISLAND MACARTHUR (ISP) AIRPORT DIAGRAM**

3. **BOUNO TWO ARRIVAL (BOUNO.BOUNO2) WESTCHESTER COUNTY**

4. **WHITE PLAINS/WESTCHESTER COUNTY (HPN) AIRPORT DIAGRAM**

▼ **TAKE-OFF MINS**

94006

HAZLETON, PA
HAZLETON MUNI
TAKE-OFF MINIMUMS: **Rwys 10,28**, 300-1.
DEPARTURE PROCEDURE: **Rwys 10, 28** climb runway heading 2200 before turning on course.

HONESDALE, PA
CHERRY RIDGE
TAKE-OFF MINIMUMS: **Rwy 17**, 300-1. **Rwy 35**, 400-1.

HORNELL, NY
HORNELL MUNI
TAKE-OFF MINIMUMS: **Rwy 35**, 900-1. **Rwy 17**, 1200-1.
DEPARTURE PROCEDURE: **Rwys 35, 17** climb runway heading to 2500 before proceeding on course.

INDIANA, PA
INDIANA COUNTY-JIMMY STEWART FIELD
TAKE-OFF MINIMUMS: **Rwy 10**, 600-1. **Rwy 28**, 300-1.
DEPARTURE PROCEDURE: **Rwy 10**, climb runway heading to 2300 before proceeding on course.

ISLIP, NY
LONG ISLAND MACARTHUR
TAKE-OFF MINIMUMS: **Rwy 33R**, 300-1.
DEPARTURE PROCEDURE: **Rwy 33L**, climb runway heading to 500 feet before turning.

ITHACA, NY
TOMPKINS COUNTY
TAKE-OFF MINIMUMS: **Rwy 14**, 1100-1 or std. with min. climb of 370' per NM to 2200.
DEPARTURE PROCEDURE: **Rwy 14**, climbing right turn to 2500' via ITH VOR/DME R-200 before proceeding on course.

JAMESTOWN, NY
CHAUTAUQUA COUNTY/JAMESTOWN
TAKE-OFF MINIMUMS: **Rwys 13,31,25**, 300-1.

JOHNSTOWN, NY
FULTON COUNTY
TAKE-OFF MINIMUMS: **Rwy 10**, 300-1 or std. with min. climb of 410' per NM to 1000. **Rwy 28**, 300-1 or std. with min. climb of 270' per NM to 1200.

JOHNSTOWN, PA
JOHNSTOWN-CAMBRIA COUNTY
TAKE-OFF MINIMUMS: **Rwy 10**, 300-1.

LANGHORN, PA
BUEHL FIELD
TAKE-OFF MINIMUMS: **Rwys 6,24**, 300-1.
NOTE: **Rwy 6**, 250' power line 500' from departure end of runway. **Rwy 24**, 286' trees 1000' from departure end of runway.

LATROBE, PA
WESTMORELAND COUNTY
TAKE-OFF MINIMUMS: **Rwys 21,23**, 300-1.
DEPARTURE PROCEDURE: **Rwys 3,5**, climb runway heading to 2000, then climbing left turn to 4000 via heading 360° to intercept IHD VORTAC R-002. **Rwys 21,23**, climb to 4000 via BHU NDB 233° bearing.

LEHIGHTON, PA
JAKE ARNER MEMORIAL
DEPARTURE PROCEDURE: **Rwy 8**, climb to 2500 via LQX NDB bearing 070° before departing on course. **Rwy 26**, climb to 2500 via LQX NDB bearing 248° before departing on course.

MALONE, NY
MALONE-DUFORT
TAKE-OFF MINIMUMS: **Rwy 23**, 400-1 or std. with min. climb of 240' per NM to 1300.
DEPARTURE PROCEDURE: **Rwy 23**, climb on runway heading to 1500 before proceeding southbound.

MASSENA, NY
MASSENA INTL-RICHARDS FIELD
TAKE-OFF MINIMUMS: **Rwys 5, 27**, 300-1. **Rwy 9**, 300-1 or std. with min. climb of 260' per NM to 500. **Rwy 23**, 300-1 or std. with min. climb of 230' per NM to 800.

MEADVILLE, PA
PORT MEADVILLE
DEPARTURE PROCEDURE: **Rwy 7**, climb runway heading to 2000 before proceeding on course.

MIDDLETOWN, NY
RANDALL
TAKE-OFF MINIMUMS: **Rwys 8,22,26**, 300-1.

MILLBROOK, NY
SKY ACRES
TAKE-OFF MINIMUMS: **Rwy 17**, 600-1. **Rwy 35**, 300-1.
DEPARTURE PROCEDURE: **Rwy 17**, climb runway heading to 1300, then climbing right turn to cross IGN VORTAC at or above 2000. **Rwy 35**, climb runway heading to 1300, then climbing left turn to cross IGN VORTAC at or above 2000.

MONTAUK, NY
MONTAUK
TAKE-OFF MINIMUMS: **Rwy 24**, 300-1.

MONTGOMERY, NY
ORANGE COUNTY
TAKE-OFF MINIMUMS: **Rwys 3,26,29**, 500-1. **Rwys 8, 21**, 300-1. **Rwy 11**, take-off minimums not authorized.
DEPARTURE PROCEDURE: **Rwys 3,8,21,26,29**, climb to 900 on runway heading before proceeding on course.

NE-2

▼ **TAKE-OFF MINS**

C4

AIRPORT DIAGRAM

AL-948 (FAA)

ISLIP/LONG ISLAND MACARTHUR (ISP)
ISLIP, NEW YORK

ATIS 128.45
LONG ISLAND TOWER*
119.3 335.5
GND CON
135.3
CLNC DEL
121.85

VAR 13.7°W
JANUARY 1990
ANNUAL RATE OF CHANGE
0.0°W

FIELD ELEV 99

ELEV 99
ELEV 92
ELEV 82
ELEV 90
ELEV 83
ELEV 79
ELEV 93

148.7°
238.7°
148.7°
328.7°
283.7°
058.7°
103.7°

5186
3212
7002 X 150
5036
X 150
X 75

HANGARS
T HANGARS
WEST TAXIWAY
CHARLIE TAXIWAY
EAST TAXIWAY
SOUTH TAXIWAY EAST
CONTROL TOWER
TERMINAL
HANGARS

UP ←0.4%

40°48'N
40°47'N
73°07'W
73°06'W

Rwy 6 ldg 6000'

RWY 6-24
  S100, T170, TT300, ST175
RWY 10-28
  S32, T56, TT92
RWY 15R-33L
  S100, T170, TT300, ST175
RWY 15L-33R
  S25

△226

CAUTION: BE ALERT TO RUNWAY CROSSING CLEARANCES.
READBACK OF ALL RUNWAY HOLDING INSTRUCTIONS IS REQUIRED.

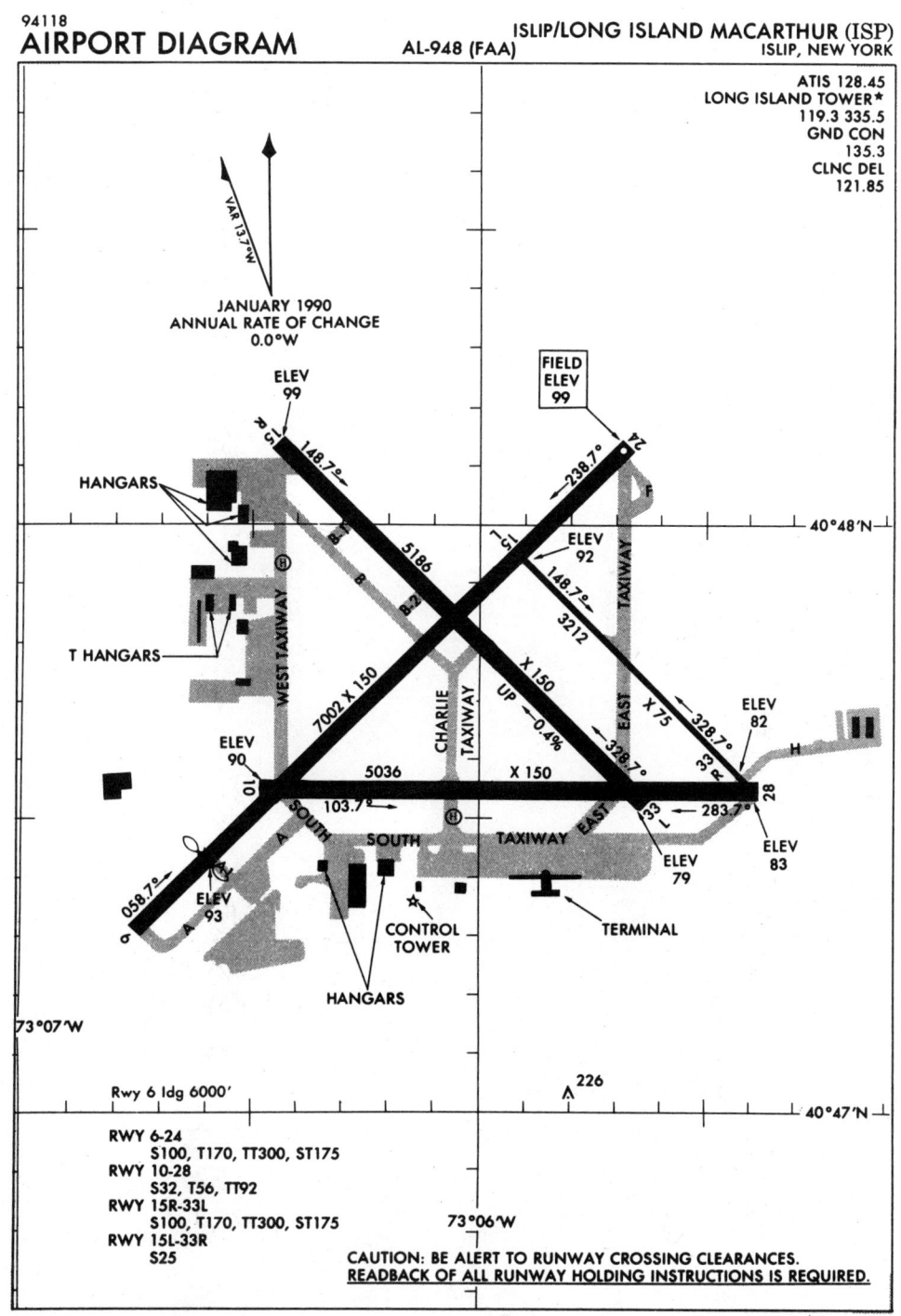

AIRPORT DIAGRAM

ISLIP, NEW YORK
ISLIP/LONG ISLAND MACARTHUR (ISP)

93091
ST-651 (FAA)

BOUNO TWO ARRIVAL (BOUNO.BOUNO2)

WESTCHESTER COUNTY
WHITE PLAINS, NEW YORK

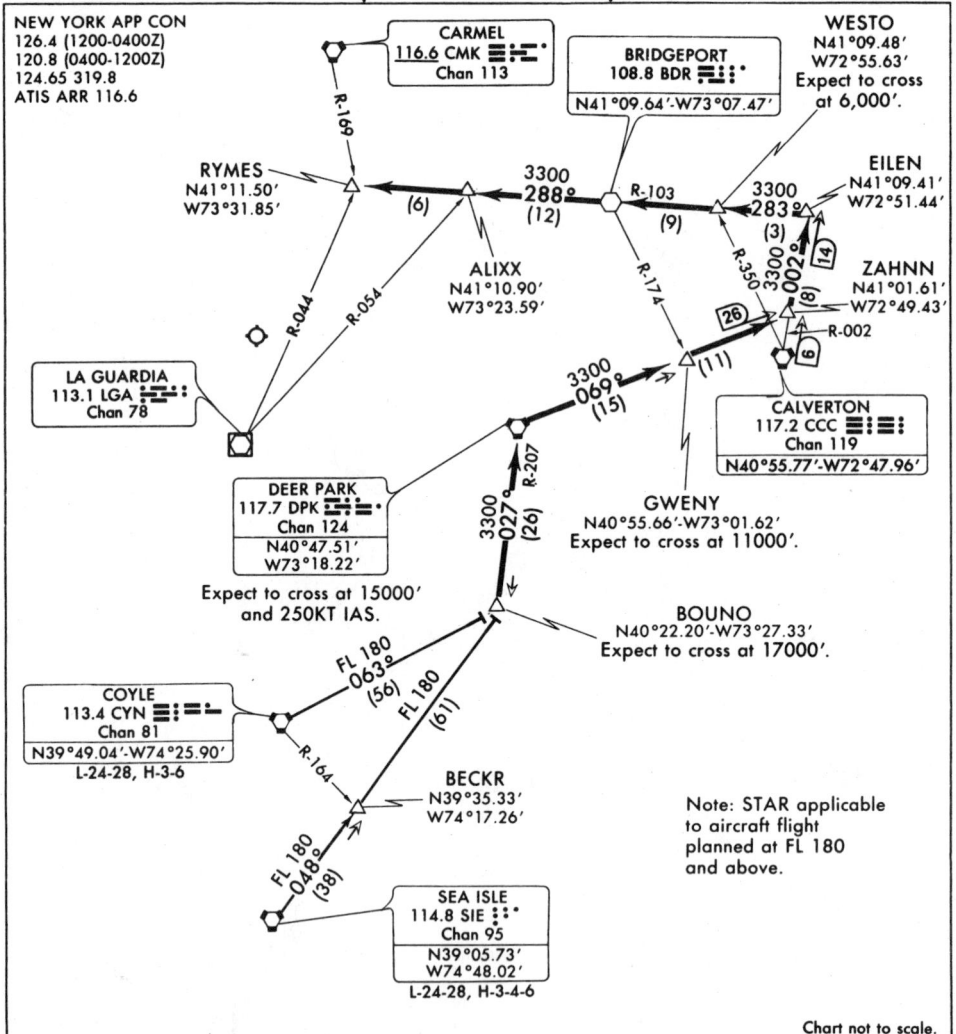

NEW YORK APP CON
126.4 (1200-0400Z)
120.8 (0400-1200Z)
124.65 319.8
ATIS ARR 116.6

CARMEL
116.6 CMK
Chan 113

BRIDGEPORT
108.8 BDR
N41°09.64'-W73°07.47'

WESTO
N41°09.48'
W72°55.63'
Expect to cross
at 6,000'.

RYMES
N41°11.50'
W73°31.85'

ALIXX
N41°10.90'
W73°23.59'

EILEN
N41°09.41'
W72°51.44'

ZAHNN
N41°01.61'
W72°49.43'

LA GUARDIA
113.1 LGA
Chan 78

CALVERTON
117.2 CCC
Chan 119
N40°55.77'-W72°47.96'

DEER PARK
117.7 DPK
Chan 124
N40°47.51'
W73°18.22'

GWENY
N40°55.66'-W73°01.62'
Expect to cross at 11000'.

Expect to cross at 15000'
and 250KT IAS.

BOUNO
N40°22.20'-W73°27.33'
Expect to cross at 17000'.

COYLE
113.4 CYN
Chan 81
N39°49.04'-W74°25.90'
L-24-28, H-3-6

BECKR
N39°35.33'
W74°17.26'

Note: STAR applicable
to aircraft flight
planned at FL 180
and above.

SEA ISLE
114.8 SIE
Chan 95
N39°05.73'
W74°48.02'
L-24-28, H-3-4-6

Chart not to scale.

COYLE TRANSITION (CYN.BOUNO2): From over CYN VORTAC via CYN R-063 to BOUNO FIX. Thence . . . .
SEA ISLE TRANSITION (SIE.BOUNO2): From over SIE VORTAC via SIE R-048 to BOUNO FIX. Thence . . . .
. . . . From over BOUNO FIX via DPK R-207 to DPK VORTAC, then via DPK R-069 to ZAHNN INT, then via CCC R-002 to EILEN INT, then via BDR R-103 to BDR VOR, then via BDR R-288 to RYMES INT. Expect radar vectors to final approach fix in use.

BOUNO TWO ARRIVAL (BOUNO.BOUNO2)

WHITE PLAINS, NEW YORK
WESTCHESTER COUNTY

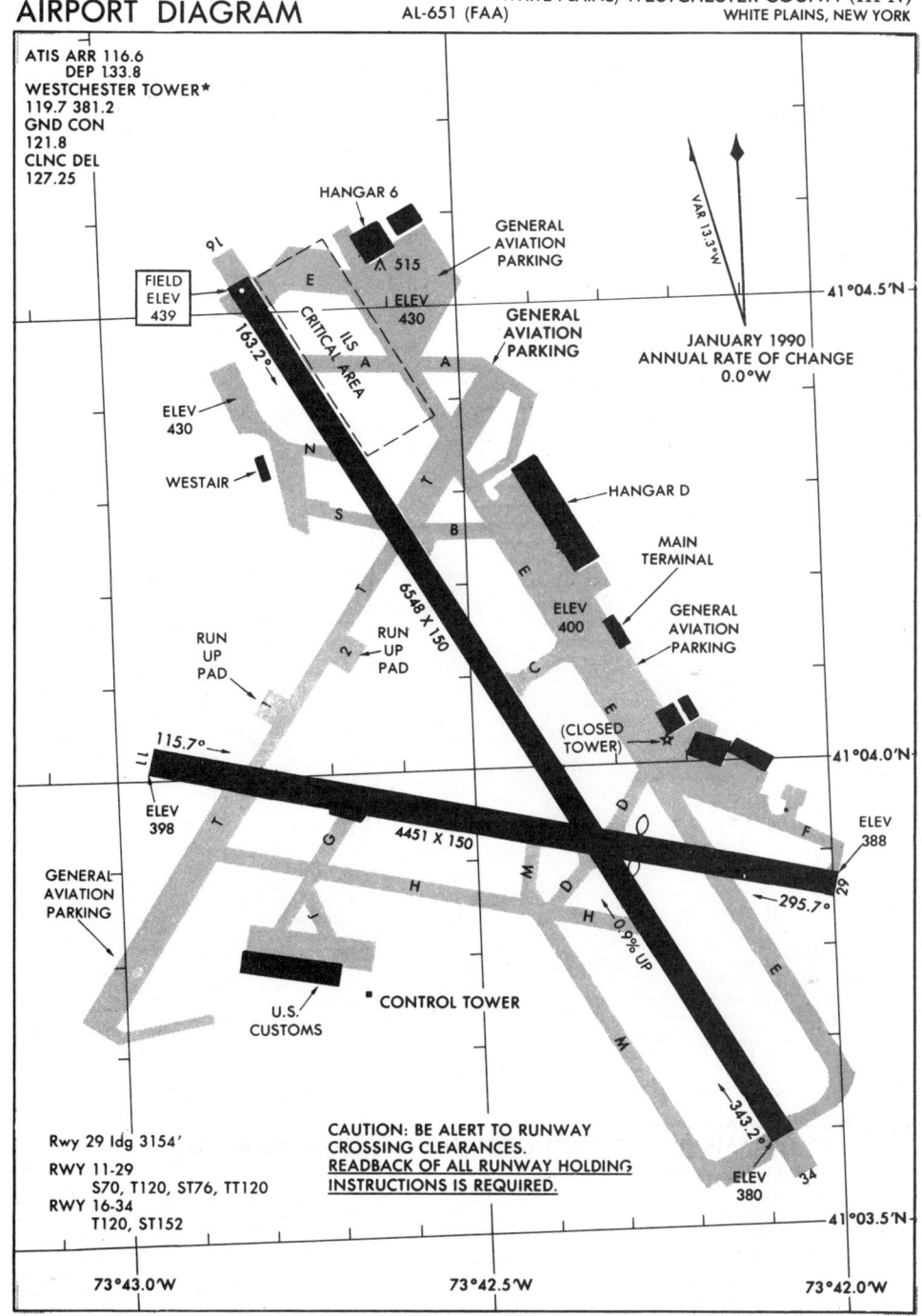

AIRPORT DIAGRAM

WHITE PLAINS/WESTCHESTER COUNTY (HPN)
WHITE PLAINS, NEW YORK
AL-651 (FAA)

ATIS ARR 116.6
DEP 133.8
WESTCHESTER TOWER*
119.7 381.2
GND CON
121.8
CLNC DEL
127.25

FIELD ELEV 439

JANUARY 1990
ANNUAL RATE OF CHANGE
0.0°W
VAR 13.3°W

HANGAR 6
GENERAL AVIATION PARKING
ELEV 430
GENERAL AVIATION PARKING
ELEV 430
WESTAIR
HANGAR D
MAIN TERMINAL
ELEV 400
GENERAL AVIATION PARKING
(CLOSED TOWER)
RUN UP PAD
RUN UP PAD
ELEV 398
ELEV 388
GENERAL AVIATION PARKING
U.S. CUSTOMS
CONTROL TOWER
ELEV 380

163.2°
6548 X 150
115.7°
4451 X 150
295.7°
343.2°
0.9% UP

ILS CRITICAL AREA

Rwy 29 ldg 3154'
RWY 11-29
 S70, T120, ST76, TT120
RWY 16-34
 T120, ST152

CAUTION: BE ALERT TO RUNWAY CROSSING CLEARANCES.
READBACK OF ALL RUNWAY HOLDING INSTRUCTIONS IS REQUIRED.

AIRPORT DIAGRAM
WHITE PLAINS, NEW YORK
WHITE PLAINS/WESTCHESTER COUNTY (HPN)

276 IFR Flights of "13MIKE"

APPENDIX C

Scenario Two
Approach Plates

San Diego to Los Angeles

1. **SAN DIEGO INTL-LINDBERGH FIELD (SAN)**
   AIRPORT DIAGRAM

2. **HARBR TWO DEPARTURE (HARBR2.HARBR)**
   SAN DIEGO INTL-LINDBERGH FIELD

3. **VOR or TACAN or GPS RWY 25L/R**
   LOS ANGELES INTL (LAX)

4. **LOS ANGELES INTL (LAX)**
   AIRPORT DIAGRAM

C2

AIRPORT DIAGRAM

SAN DIEGO INTL-LINDBERGH FIELD (SAN)
SAN DIEGO, CALIFORNIA
AL-373 (FAA)

ATIS 134.8
LINDBERGH TOWER
118.3 270.9
GND CON
123.9
CLNC DEL
125.9

FIELD ELEV 14

ELEV 14 (Rwy 13)
ELEV 10 (Rwy 31)
ELEV 14 (Rwy 27)
ELEV 10 (Rwy 9 east)
ELEV 12 (Rwy 9 west)

Runway 9-27: 9400 X 200
Runway 13-31: 4439 X 75

272.6°
131.5°
311.5°
092.6°

VAR 13.4°E
JANUARY 1990
ANNUAL RATE OF CHANGE 0.0°W

Rwy 9 ldg 8700'
Rwy 13 ldg 3890'
Rwy 27 ldg 7590'
Rwy 31 ldg 4039'

RWY 9-27
S100, T150, ST175, TT250, DDT720
RWY 13-31
S30

CAUTION: BE ALERT TO RUNWAY CROSSING CLEARANCES. READBACK OF ALL RUNWAY HOLDING INSTRUCTIONS IS REQUIRED.

GENERAL AVIATION PARKING
NWS
U.S. CUSTOMS
U.S. COAST GUARD AIR STATION
TELEDYNE RYAN
CONTROL TOWER
FIRE STATION
EAST TERMINAL
WEST TERMINAL AND ADMINISTRATION BUILDING

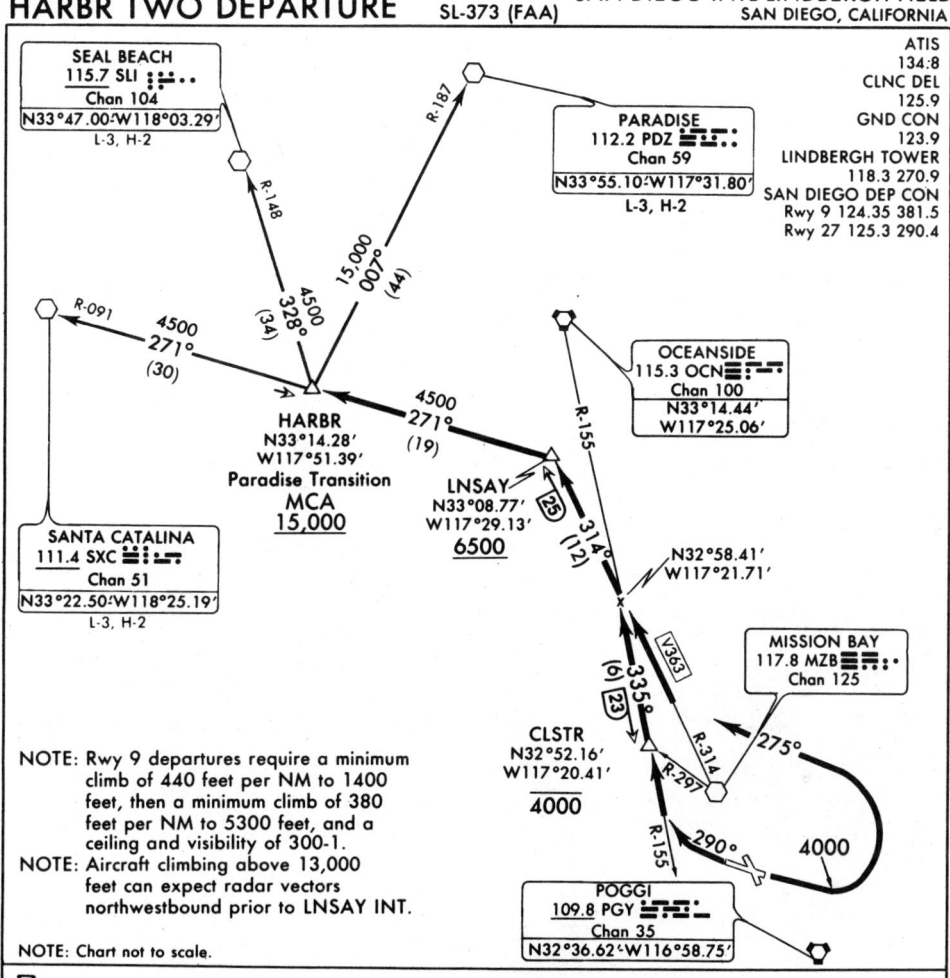

HARBR TWO DEPARTURE
(PILOT NAV)(HARBR2.HARBR) 93035

SL-373 (FAA)

SAN DIEGO INTL-LINDBERGH FIELD
SAN DIEGO, CALIFORNIA

ATIS 134.8
CLNC DEL 125.9
GND CON 123.9
LINDBERGH TOWER 118.3 270.9
SAN DIEGO DEP CON
Rwy 9 124.35 381.5
Rwy 27 125.3 290.4

SEAL BEACH 115.7 SLI Chan 104
N33°47.00' W118°03.29'
L-3, H-2

PARADISE 112.2 PDZ Chan 59
N33°55.10' W117°31.80'
L-3, H-2

OCEANSIDE 115.3 OCN Chan 100
N33°14.44' W117°25.06'

HARBR N33°14.28' W117°51.39'
Paradise Transition
MCA **15,000**

LNSAY N33°08.77' W117°29.13'
6500

N32°58.41' W117°21.71'

SANTA CATALINA 111.4 SXC Chan 51
N33°22.50' W118°25.19'
L-3, H-2

MISSION BAY 117.8 MZB Chan 125

CLSTR N32°52.16' W117°20.41'
4000

NOTE: Rwy 9 departures require a minimum climb of 440 feet per NM to 1400 feet, then a minimum climb of 380 feet per NM to 5300 feet, and a ceiling and visibility of 300-1.
NOTE: Aircraft climbing above 13,000 feet can expect radar vectors northwestbound prior to LNSAY INT.
NOTE: Chart not to scale.

POGGI 109.8 PGY Chan 35
N32°36.62' W116°58.75'

DEPARTURE ROUTE DESCRIPTION

<u>TAKE-OFF RUNWAY 9:</u> Climb via runway heading until leaving 4,000, then turn left heading 275° to intercept and proceed via the MZB R-314 to LNSAY INT at or above 6500, then via SXC R-091 to HARBR INT. Then via (transition) or (assigned route).
<u>TAKE-OFF RUNWAY 27:</u> As soon as practical after takeoff, make climbing right turn heading 290° to intercept and proceed via OCN VORTAC R-155 to CLSTR INT at or below 4,000', then via the OCN VORTAC R-155 to intercept and proceed via MZB VORTAC R-314 to LNSAY INT at or above 6500', then via SXC VORTAC R-091 to HARBR INT. Then via (transition) or (assigned route).
<u>PARADISE TRANSITION (HARBR2.PDZ)</u>
<u>SANTA CATALINA TRANSITION (HARBR2.SXC)</u>
<u>SEAL BEACH TRANSITION (HARBR2.SLI)</u>

HARBR TWO DEPARTURE
(PILOT NAV)(HARBR2.HARBR)

SAN DIEGO, CALIFORNIA
SAN DIEGO INTL-LINDBERGH FIELD

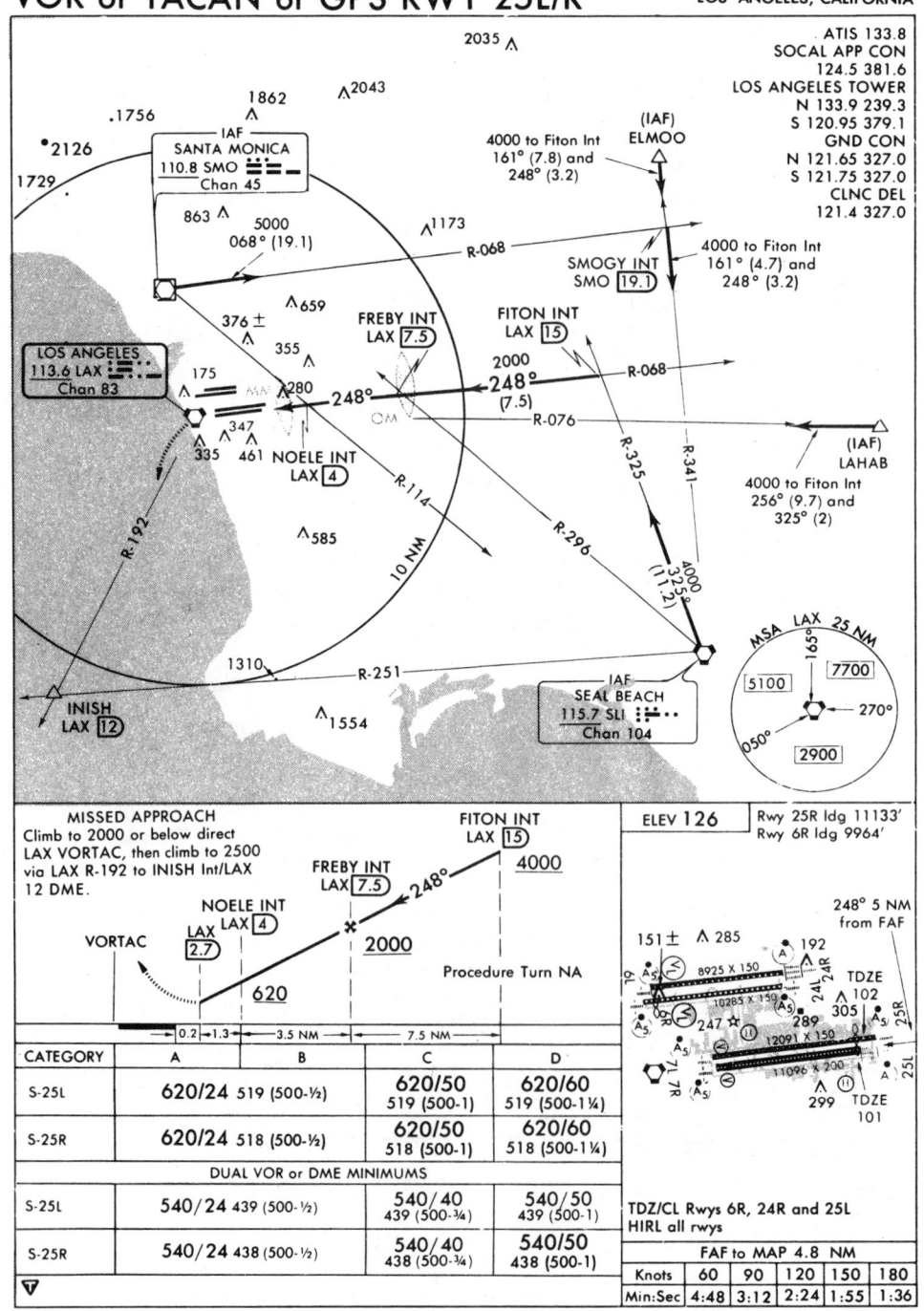

Amdt 15 94118 AL-237 (FAA) LOS ANGELES INTL (LAX)
LOS ANGELES, CALIFORNIA

VOR or TACAN or GPS RWY 25L/R

ATIS 133.8
SOCAL APP CON 124.5 381.6
LOS ANGELES TOWER
 N 133.9 239.3
 S 120.95 379.1
GND CON
 N 121.65 327.0
 S 121.75 327.0
CLNC DEL 121.4 327.0

MISSED APPROACH
Climb to 2000 or below direct LAX VORTAC, then climb to 2500 via LAX R-192 to INISH Int/LAX 12 DME.

ELEV 126   Rwy 25R ldg 11133'
            Rwy 6R ldg 9964'

CATEGORY	A	B	C	D
S-25L	620/24 519 (500-½)		620/50 519 (500-1)	620/60 519 (500-1¼)
S-25R	620/24 518 (500-½)		620/50 518 (500-1)	620/60 518 (500-1¼)
DUAL VOR or DME MINIMUMS				
S-25L	540/24 439 (500-½)		540/40 439 (500-¾)	540/50 439 (500-1)
S-25R	540/24 438 (500-½)		540/40 438 (500-¾)	540/50 438 (500-1)

TDZ/CL Rwys 6R, 24R and 25L
HIRL all rwys

FAF to MAP 4.8 NM

Knots	60	90	120	150	180
Min:Sec	4:48	3:12	2:24	1:55	1:36

VOR or TACAN or GPS RWY 25L/R
33°57'N–118°24'W

LOS ANGELES, CALIFORNIA
LOS ANGELES INTL (LAX)

125

AIRPORT DIAGRAM

AL-237 (FAA)

LOS ANGELES INTL (LAX)
LOS ANGELES, CALIFORNIA

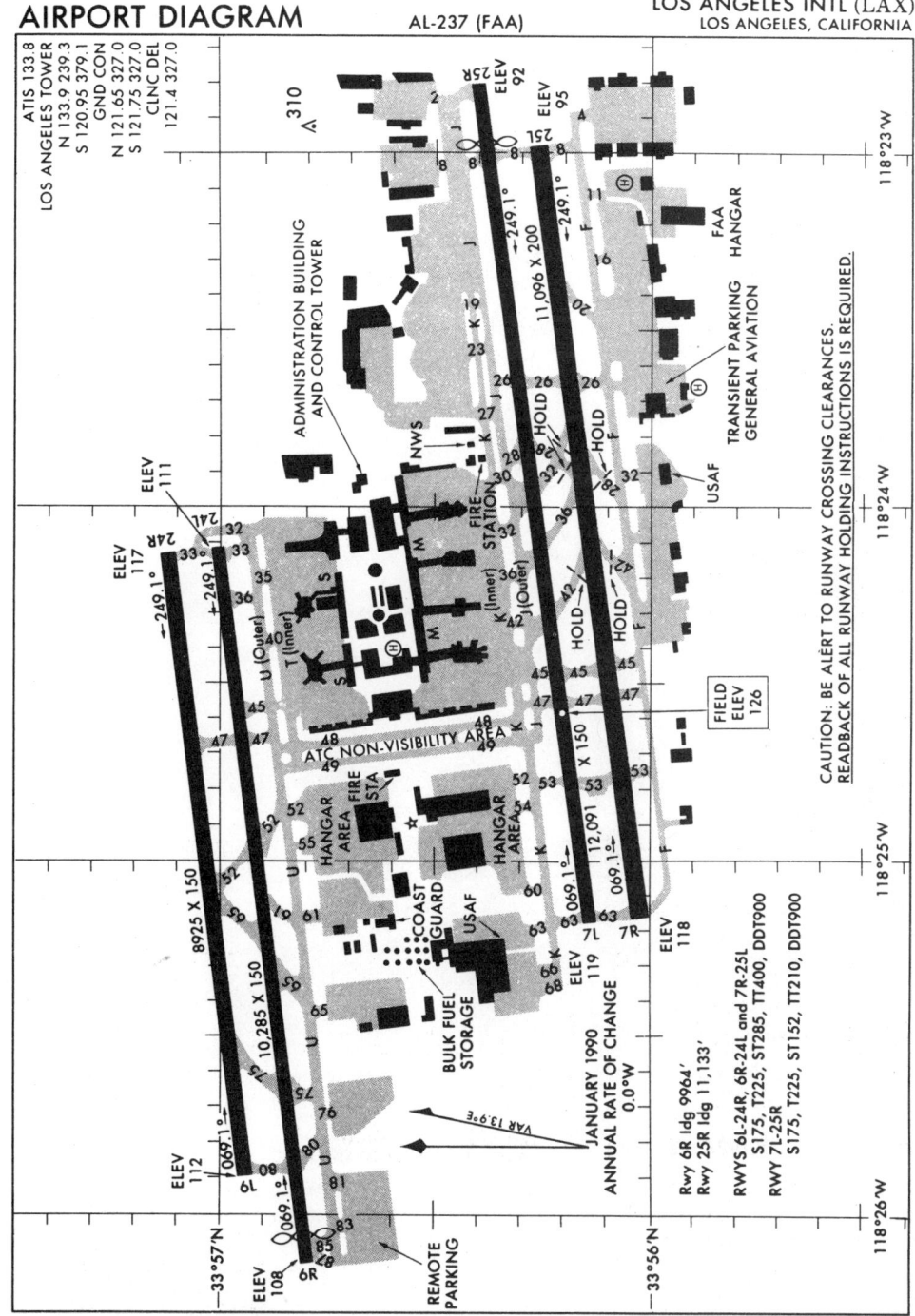

282 IFR Flights of "13MIKE"

APPENDIX C

Scenario Three Approach Plates

Kankakee to Champaign

1. KANKAKEE/**GREATER KANKAKEE (IKK)**
   AIRPORT DIAGRAM (On VOR RWY 4 plate)

2. **VOR/DME RWY 22R**
   CHAMPAIGN - URBANA/**UNIVERSITY OF ILLINOIS -WILLARD (CMI)**

3. CHAMPAIGN - URBANA/**UNIVERSITY OF ILLINOIS -WILLARD (CMI) AIRPORT DIAGRAM**

C3

Amdt 5 93147

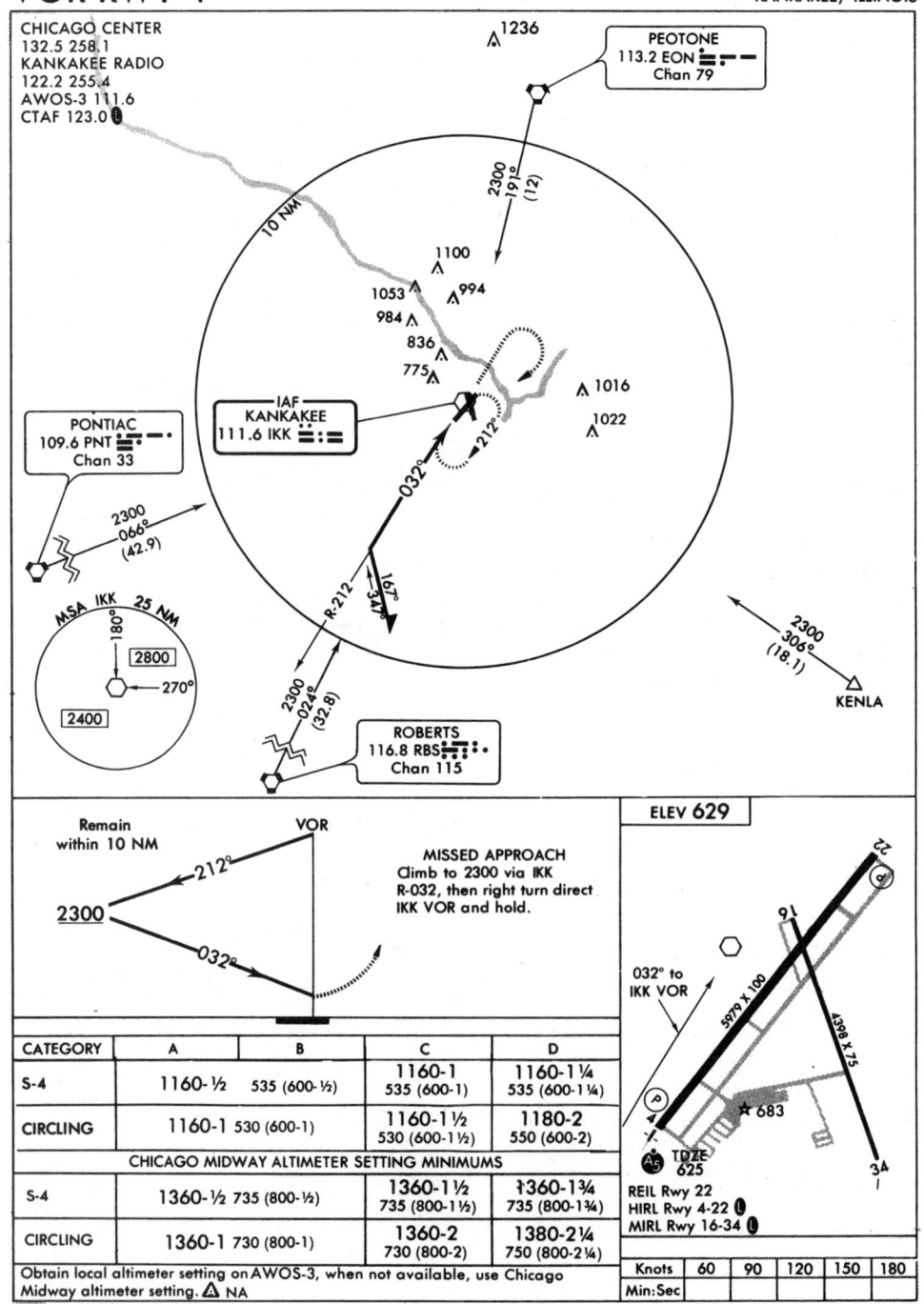

VOR RWY 4

AL-5278 (FAA)

KANKAKEE/GREATER KANKAKEE (IKK)
KANKAKEE, ILLINOIS

CHICAGO CENTER
132.5 258.1
KANKAKEE RADIO
122.2 255.4
AWOS-3 111.6
CTAF 123.0

PEOTONE
113.2 EON
Chan 79

PONTIAC
109.6 PNT
Chan 33

IAF
KANKAKEE
111.6 IKK

ROBERTS
116.8 RBS
Chan 115

MSA IKK 25 NM
180°: 2800
270°: 2400

ELEV 629

Remain within 10 NM

MISSED APPROACH
Climb to 2300 via IKK R-032, then right turn direct IKK VOR and hold.

032° to IKK VOR

TDZE 625

REIL Rwy 22
HIRL Rwy 4-22
MIRL Rwy 16-34

CATEGORY	A	B	C	D
S-4	1160-½	535 (600-½)	1160-1 535 (600-1)	1160-1¼ 535 (600-1¼)
CIRCLING	1160-1	530 (600-1)	1160-1½ 530 (600-1½)	1180-2 550 (600-2)
CHICAGO MIDWAY ALTIMETER SETTING MINIMUMS				
S-4	1360-½	735 (800-½)	1360-1½ 735 (800-1½)	1360-1¾ 735 (800-1¾)
CIRCLING	1360-1	730 (800-1)	1360-2 730 (800-2)	1380-2¼ 750 (800-2¼)

Obtain local altimeter setting on AWOS-3, when not available, use Chicago Midway altimeter setting. △ NA

Knots	60	90	120	150	180
Min:Sec					

VOR RWY 4

41°04'N – 87°51'W

KANKAKEE, ILLINOIS
KANKAKEE/GREATER KANKAKEE (IKK)

195

Amdt 7 93259

VOR/DME RWY 22R

CHAMPAIGN-URBANA/UNIVERSITY OF ILLINOIS-WILLARD (CMI)
AL-709 (FAA)
CHAMPAIGN-URBANA, ILLINOIS

ATIS 124.85
CHAMPAIGN APP CON 121.35 291.0
CHAMPAIGN TOWER* 120.4 (CTAF) 229.4
GND CON 121.8
CLNC DEL 128.75
ASR
UNICOM 122.95

IAF ROBERTS 116.8 RBS Chan 115

IAF DANVILLE 111.0 DNV Chan 47

VINEY INT

LODGE CMI 13

STADI CMI 6

CHAMPAIGN 110.0 CMI Chan 37

MSA CMI 25 NM 3000

When control tower closed, except for operators with approved weather reporting service, use Decatur altimeter setting

MISSED APPROACH
Climb to 2700 then right turn via CMI R-297 to LODGE Int and hold.

Remain within 10 NM

*1540 when using Decatur altimeter setting.

ELEV 754

207° to CMI VORTAC
TDZE 749
TWR 825

MIRL Rwy 18-36
MIRL Rwys 4L-22R
HIRL Rwy 14R-32L

CATEGORY	A	B	C	D
S-22R	1100-1 351 (400-1)			1100-1¼ 351 (400-1¼)
CIRCLING	1160-1 406 (500-1)	1220-1 466 (500-1)	1220-1½ 466 (500-1½)	1320-2 566 (600-2)
DECATUR ALTIMETER SETTING MINIMUMS				
S-22R	1240-1 491 (500-1)		1240-1¼ 491 (500-1¼)	1240-1½ 491 (500-1½)
CIRCLING	1280-1 526 (600-1)		1280-1½ 526 (600-1½)	1320-2 566 (600-2)

Knots	60	90	120	150	180
Min:Sec					

VOR/DME RWY 22R

40°02'N-88°17'W
CHAMPAIGN-URBANA, ILLINOIS
CHAMPAIGN-URBANA/UNIVERSITY OF ILLINOIS-WILLARD (CMI)

69

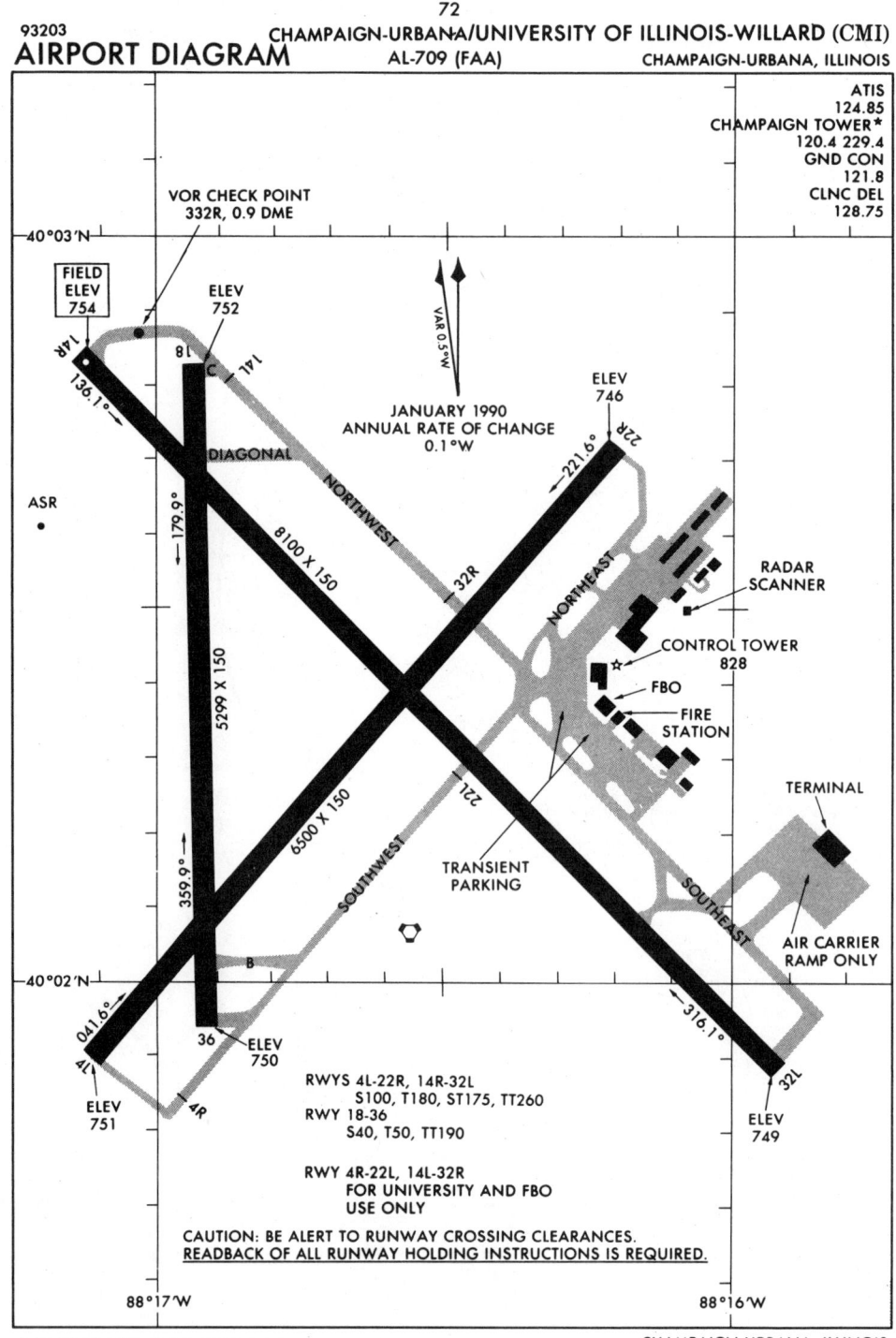

AIRPORT DIAGRAM

CHAMPAIGN-URBANA/UNIVERSITY OF ILLINOIS-WILLARD (CMI)
AL-709 (FAA)
CHAMPAIGN-URBANA, ILLINOIS

ATIS 124.85
CHAMPAIGN TOWER* 120.4 229.4
GND CON 121.8
CLNC DEL 128.75

FIELD ELEV 754
VOR CHECK POINT 332R, 0.9 DME
ELEV 752
ELEV 746
ELEV 750
ELEV 751
ELEV 749

JANUARY 1990 ANNUAL RATE OF CHANGE 0.1°W
VAR 0.5°W

DIAGONAL
NORTHWEST 8100 X 150
5299 X 150
6500 X 150
SOUTHWEST
NORTHEAST
SOUTHEAST

ASR
RADAR SCANNER
CONTROL TOWER 828
FBO
FIRE STATION
TRANSIENT PARKING
TERMINAL
AIR CARRIER RAMP ONLY

RWYS 4L-22R, 14R-32L
S100, T180, ST175, TT260
RWY 18-36
S40, T50, TT190

RWY 4R-22L, 14L-32R
FOR UNIVERSITY AND FBO USE ONLY

CAUTION: BE ALERT TO RUNWAY CROSSING CLEARANCES.
READBACK OF ALL RUNWAY HOLDING INSTRUCTIONS IS REQUIRED.

40°03'N 40°02'N
88°17'W 88°16'W

AIRPORT DIAGRAM
CHAMPAIGN-URBANA, ILLINOIS
CHAMPAIGN-URBANA/UNIVERSITY OF ILLINOIS-WILLARD (CMI)

APPENDIX C

Scenario Four
Approach Plates

San Francisco to South Lake Tahoe

1.   SAN FRANCISCO INTL (SFO)
   AIRPORT DIAGRAM

2.   SHORELINE NINE DEPARTURE
   (PILOT NAV) (SHOR9.OAK)
   SAN FRANCISCO INTL (SFO)

3.   VOR/DME-A
   SOUTH LAKE TAHOE/LAKE TAHOE (TVL)

C4

AIRPORT DIAGRAM

AL-375 (FAA)

SAN FRANCISCO INTL (SFO)
SAN FRANCISCO, CALIFORNIA

ATIS 108.9 113.7 118.85
SAN FRANCISCO TOWER
120.5 269.1
GND CON
124.25 (EAST)
121.8 (WEST)
CLNC DEL
118.2

VAR 15.7°E
JANUARY 1990
ANNUAL RATE OF CHANGE
0.0°W

NOTE: Several runway hold position signs are on the right rather than the left side of taxiways.

CAUTION: BE ALERT TO RUNWAY CROSSING CLEARANCES. READBACK OF ALL RUNWAY HOLDING INSTRUCTIONS IS REQUIRED.

FIELD ELEV 11

Rwy 1R ldg 8409'
RWY 1L-19R
 S60, T170, ST175, TT270, DDT710
RWY 1R-19L
 S60, T195, ST175, TT325, DDT710
RWYS 10L-28R and 10R-28L
 S60, T200, ST175, TT355, DDT710

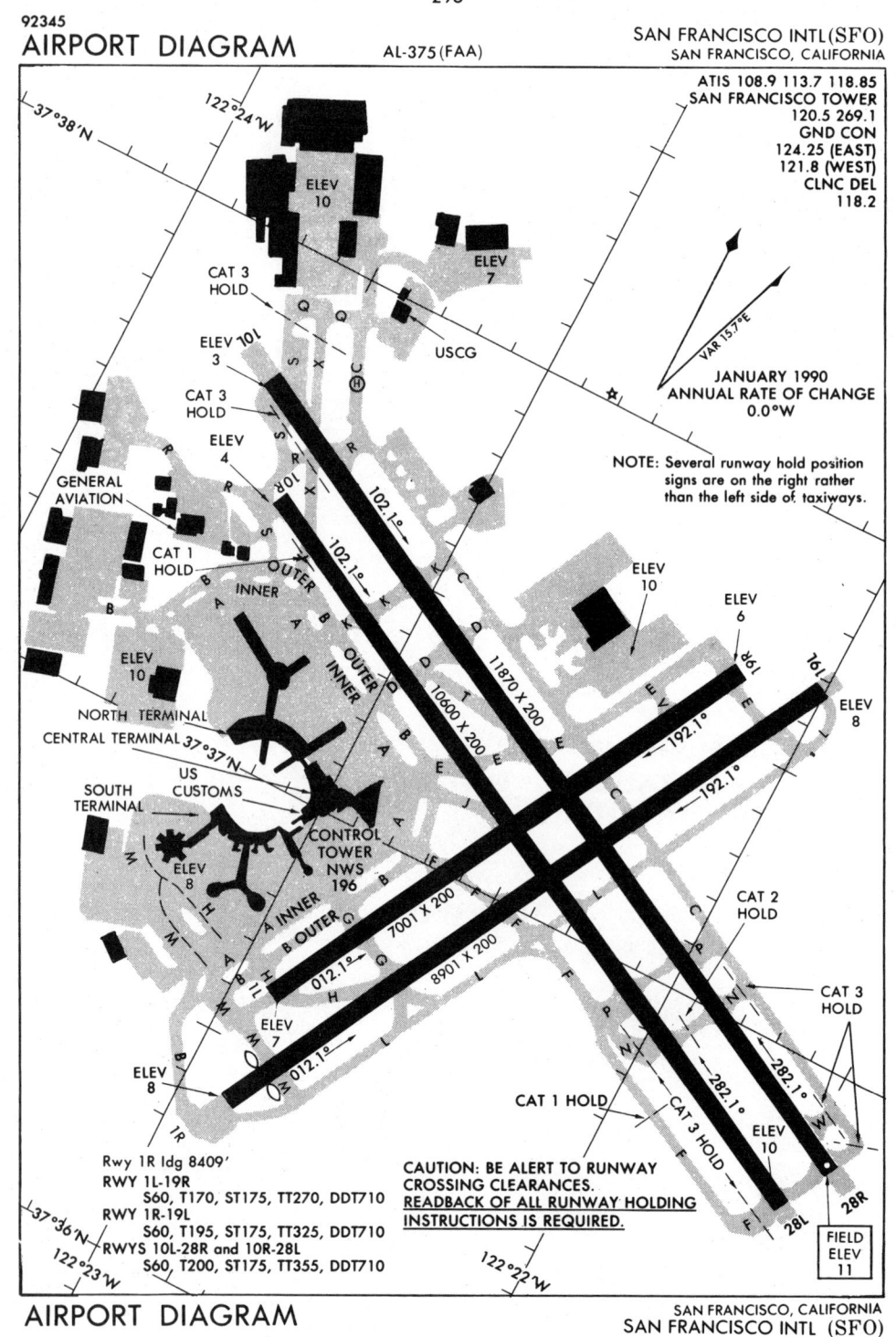

AIRPORT DIAGRAM

SAN FRANCISCO, CALIFORNIA
SAN FRANCISCO INTL (SFO)

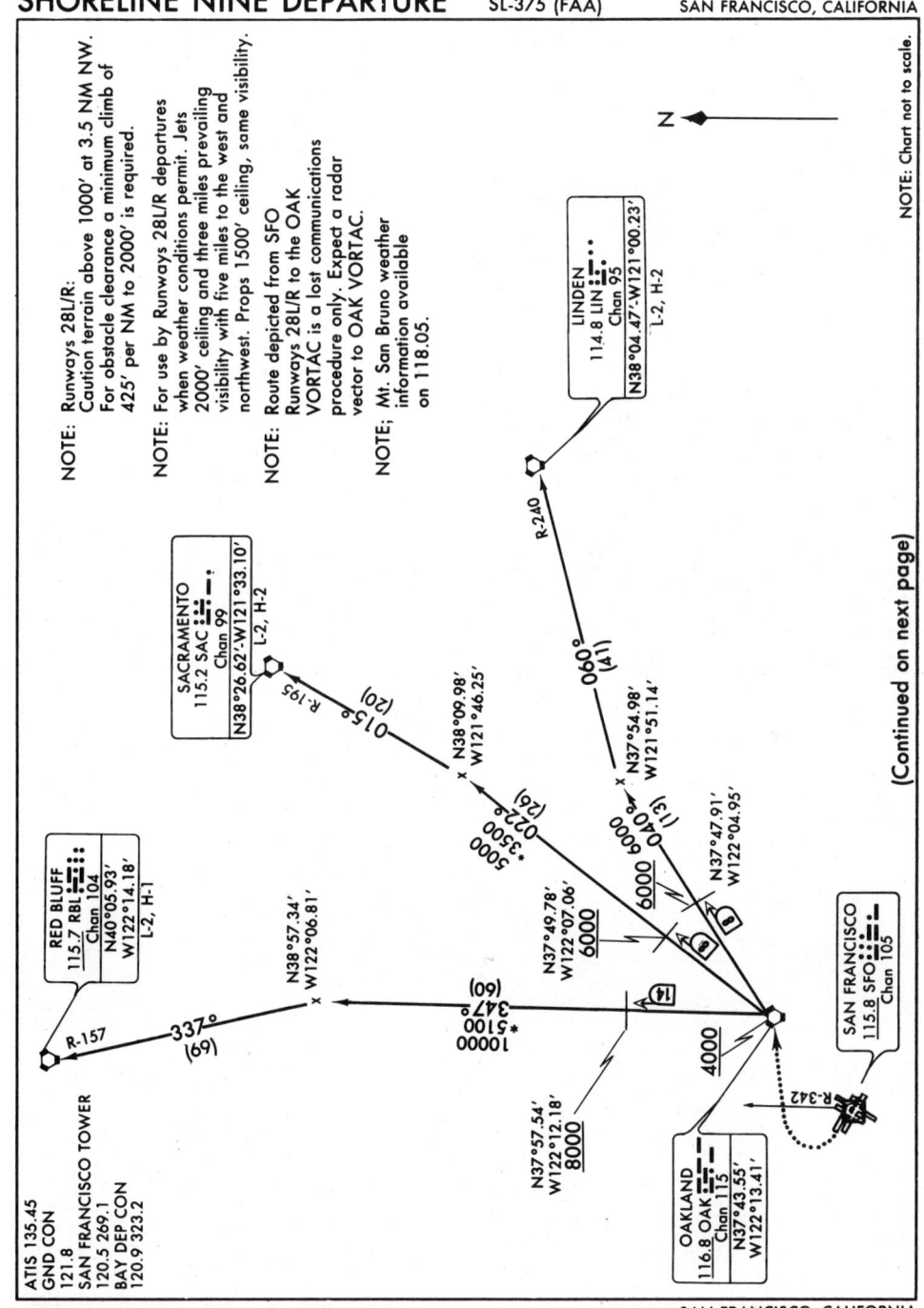

(PILOT NAV) (SHOR9.OAK)
SHORELINE NINE DEPARTURE

SL-375 (FAA)

SAN FRANCISCO INTL
SAN FRANCISCO, CALIFORNIA

NOTE: Chart not to scale.

NOTE: Runways 28L/R:
Caution terrain above 1000' at 3.5 NM NW. For obstacle clearance a minimum climb of 425' per NM to 2000' is required.

NOTE: For use by Runways 28L/R departures when weather conditions permit. Jets 2000' ceiling and three miles prevailing visibility with five miles to the west and northwest. Props 1500' ceiling, same visibility.

NOTE: Route depicted from SFO Runways 28L/R to the OAK VORTAC is a lost communications procedure only. Expect a radar vector to OAK VORTAC.

NOTE: Mt. San Bruno weather information available on 118.05.

LINDEN 114.8 LIN Chan 95
N38°04.47'-W121°00.23'
L-2, H-2

SACRAMENTO 115.2 SAC Chan 99
N38°26.62'-W121°33.10'
L-2, H-2

RED BLUFF 115.7 RBL Chan 104
N40°05.93'-W122°14.18'
L-2, H-1

SAN FRANCISCO 115.8 SFO Chan 105

OAKLAND 116.8 OAK Chan 115
N37°43.55'-W122°13.41'

ATIS 135.45
GND CON 121.8
SAN FRANCISCO TOWER 120.5 269.1
BAY DEP CON 120.9 323.2

(Continued on next page)

SHORELINE NINE DEPARTURE
(PILOT NAV) (SHOR9.OAK)

SAN FRANCISCO, CALIFORNIA
SAN FRANCISCO INTL

(PILOT NAV) (SHOR9.OAK) 91094
SHORELINE NINE DEPARTURE   SL-375 (FAA)   SAN FRANCISCO INTL
SAN FRANCISCO, CALIFORNIA

DEPARTURE ROUTE DESCRIPTION

<u>TAKE-OFF RUNWAYS 28L/R:</u> Turn right as soon as feasible heading 040° or as assigned, for vector to OAK VORTAC. Then via (transition) or (assigned route). Expect further clearance to filed altitude 10 minutes after departure.

<u>LINDEN TRANSITION (SHOR9.LIN):</u> Climb via OAK R-040 and LIN R-240 to LIN VORTAC. Cross the OAK R-040 8 DME fix at or above 6000'. Thence via (assigned route).

<u>RED BLUFF TRANSITION (SHOR9.RBL):</u> Climb via OAK R-347 and RBL R-157 to RBL VORTAC. Cross the OAK R-347 14 DME fix at or above 8000'. Maintain (assigned altitude) or (flight level). Thence via (assigned route).

<u>SACRAMENTO TRANSITION (SHOR9.SAC):</u> Climb via OAK R-022 and SAC R-195 to SAC VORTAC. Cross the OAK R-022 8 DME fix at or above 6000'. Maintain (assigned altitude) or (flight level). Thence via (assigned route).

<u>LOST COMMUNICATIONS:</u>
Take-off runways 28L/R: If not in contact with departure control one minute after crossing the SFO R-342, proceed direct to OAK VORTAC. Cross OAK VORTAC at or above 4000'.

SHORELINE NINE DEPARTURE
(PILOT NAV) (SHOR9.OAK)

SAN FRANCISCO, CALIFORNIA
SAN FRANCISCO INTL

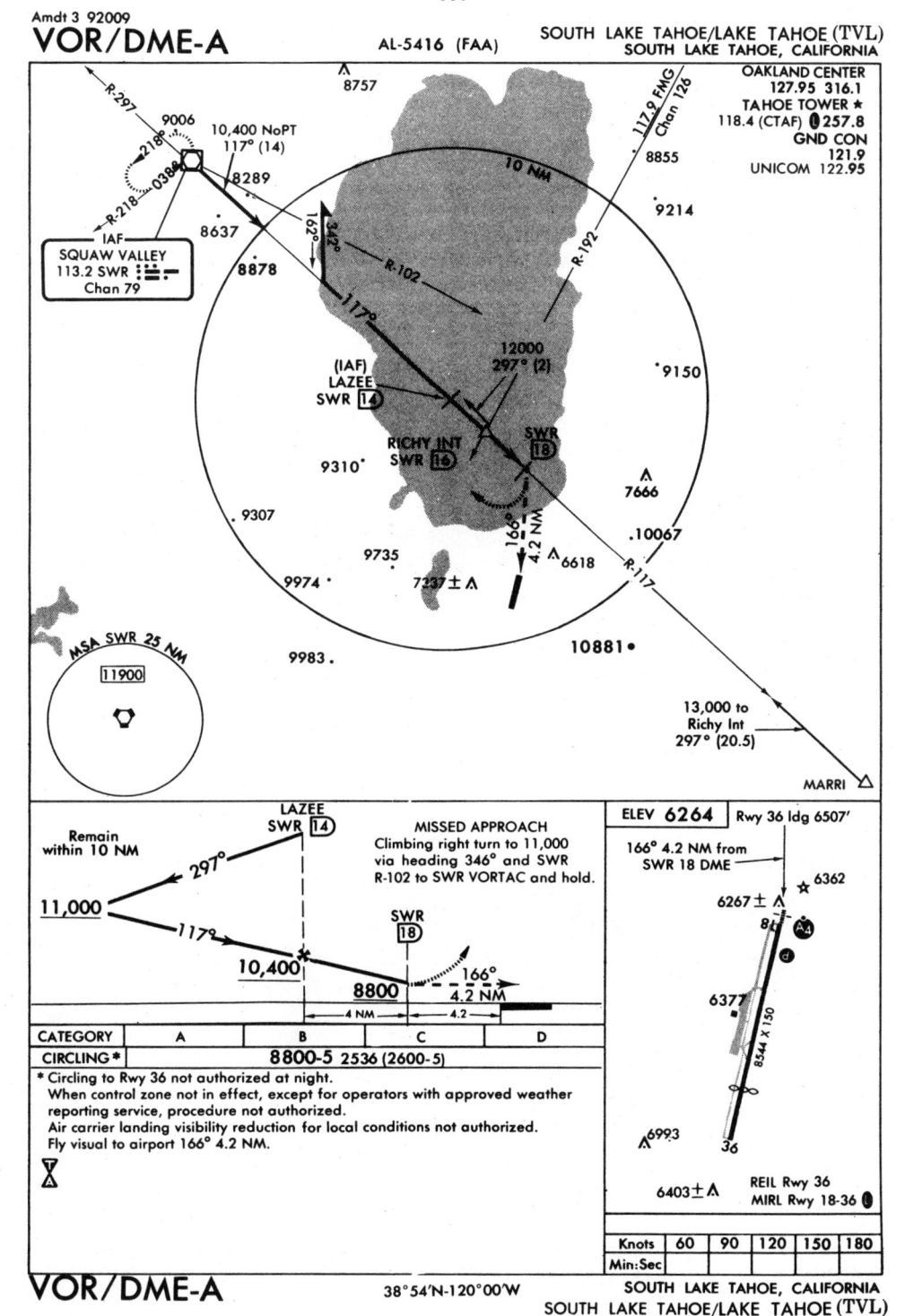

VOR/DME-A

Amdt 3 92009
AL-5416 (FAA)
SOUTH LAKE TAHOE/LAKE TAHOE (TVL)
SOUTH LAKE TAHOE, CALIFORNIA

OAKLAND CENTER 127.95 316.1
TAHOE TOWER ★ 118.4 (CTAF) 257.8
GND CON 121.9
UNICOM 122.95

IAF SQUAW VALLEY 113.2 SWR Chan 79

10,400 NoPT 117° (14)

(IAF) LAZEE SWR [14]

RICHY INT SWR [16]

SWR [18]

166° 4.2 NM

MSA SWR 25 NM — 11900

13,000 to Richy Int 297° (20.5)

MARRI

MISSED APPROACH
Climbing right turn to 11,000 via heading 346° and SWR R-102 to SWR VORTAC and hold.

Remain within 10 NM

LAZEE SWR [14]

11,000 — 297°
117°
10,400
SWR [18]
8800
166° 4.2 NM
4 NM — 4.2

ELEV 6264 Rwy 36 ldg 6507'
166° 4.2 NM from SWR 18 DME

REIL Rwy 36
MIRL Rwy 18-36

CATEGORY	A	B	C	D
CIRCLING*		8800-5 2536 (2600-5)		

* Circling to Rwy 36 not authorized at night.
When control zone not in effect, except for operators with approved weather reporting service, procedure not authorized.
Air carrier landing visibility reduction for local conditions not authorized.
Fly visual to airport 166° 4.2 NM.

Knots	60	90	120	150	180
Min:Sec					

VOR/DME-A
38°54'N-120°00'W
SOUTH LAKE TAHOE, CALIFORNIA
SOUTH LAKE TAHOE/LAKE TAHOE (TVL)

292 IFR Flights of "13MIKE"

APPENDIX C

Scenario Five Approach Plates

Port Angeles to Seattle-Tacoma

1. **PORT ANGELES/WILLIAM R. FAIRCHILD INTL (CLM) AIRPORT DIAGRAM** (On ILS-2 plate)

2. **PORT ANGELES ONE DEPARTURE (VECTOR)**
   PORT ANGELES/WILLIAM R. FAIRCHILD INTL (CLM)

3. **MALL VISUAL RWY 34R**
   SEATTLE-TACOMA INTL (SEA)

4. **SEATTLE-TACOMA INTL (SEA) AIRPORT DIAGRAM**

C5

Amdt 1A 93147
ILS-2 RWY 8
AL-886 (FAA)

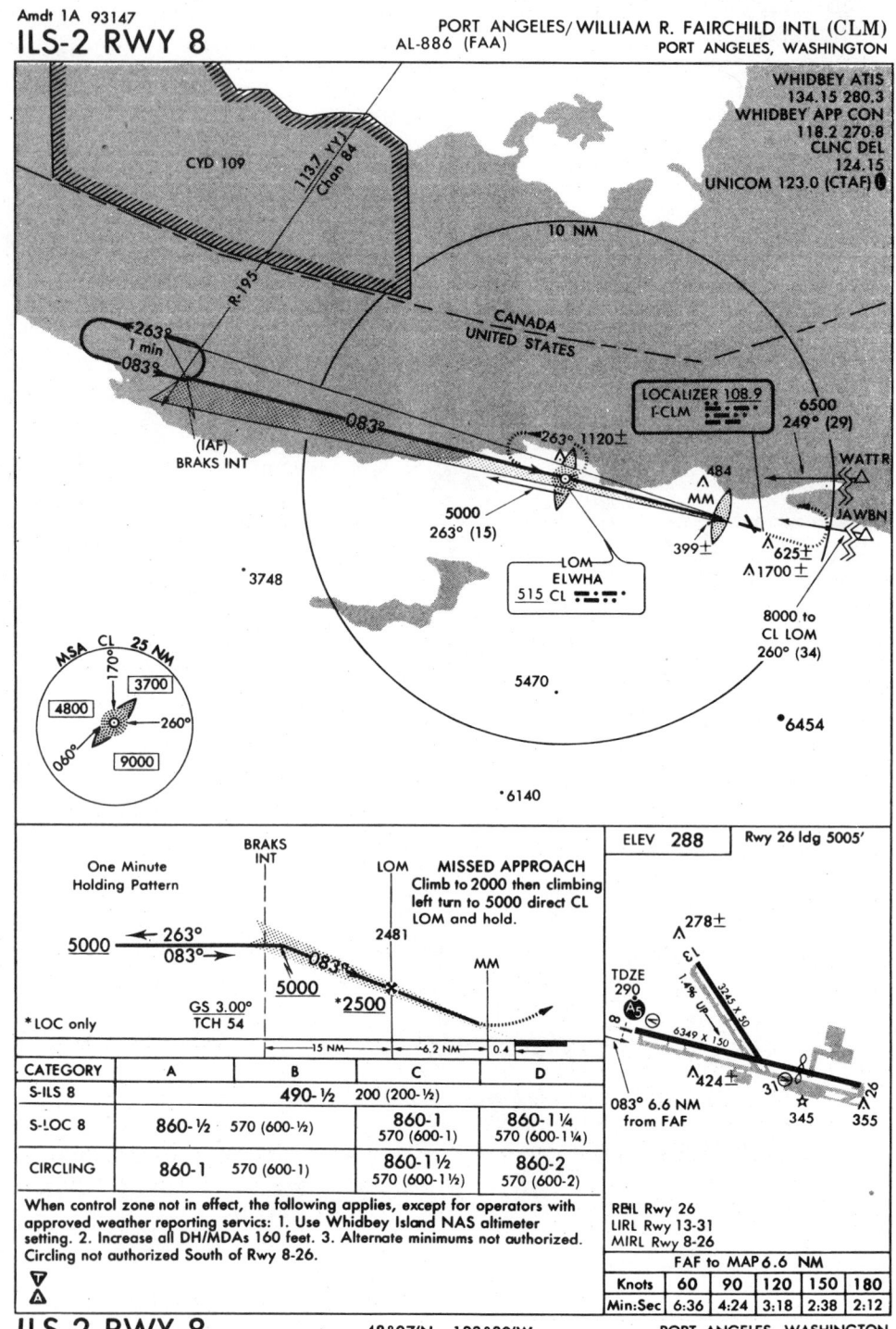

PORT ANGELES/WILLIAM R. FAIRCHILD INTL (CLM)
PORT ANGELES, WASHINGTON

WHIDBEY ATIS 134.15 280.3
WHIDBEY APP CON 118.2 270.8
CLNC DEL 124.15
UNICOM 123.0 (CTAF)

CYD 109
113.7 YYJ Chan 84
R-195
10 NM
CANADA / UNITED STATES
*2638 1 min 083°
083°
(IAF) BRAKS INT
263° 1120±
LOCALIZER 108.9 I-CLM
6500 249° (29)
WATTR
MM 484
399±
JAWBN
5000 263° (15)
625±
1700±
LOM ELWHA 515 CL
8000 to CL LOM 260° (34)
*3748
5470
*6454
*6140

MSA CL 25 NM
170° 3700
060° 260°
9000 4800

One Minute Holding Pattern
5000 ← 263° / 083°
BRAKS INT
083°
5000
*2500
GS 3.00° TCH 54
*LOC only

LOM 2481
MM

MISSED APPROACH
Climb to 2000 then climbing left turn to 5000 direct CL LOM and hold.

|←— 15 NM —→|←— 6.2 NM —→|←0.4→|

CATEGORY	A	B	C	D
S-ILS 8		490-½ 200 (200-½)		
S-LOC 8	860-½	570 (600-½)	860-1 570 (600-1)	860-1¼ 570 (600-1¼)
CIRCLING	860-1	570 (600-1)	860-1½ 570 (600-1½)	860-2 570 (600-2)

When control zone not in effect, the following applies, except for operators with approved weather reporting services: 1. Use Whidbey Island NAS altimeter setting. 2. Increase all DH/MDAs 160 feet. 3. Alternate minimums not authorized. Circling not authorized South of Rwy 8-26.

ELEV 288 | Rwy 26 ldg 5005'
278±
TDZE 290
A5
424±
083° 6.6 NM from FAF
345 355
31
26

REIL Rwy 26
LIRL Rwy 13-31
MIRL Rwy 8-26

FAF to MAP 6.6 NM					
Knots	60	90	120	150	180
Min:Sec	6:36	4:24	3:18	2:38	2:12

ILS-2 RWY 8
48°07'N – 123°30'W

PORT ANGELES, WASHINGTON
PORT ANGELES/WILLIAM R. FAIRCHILD INTL (CLM)

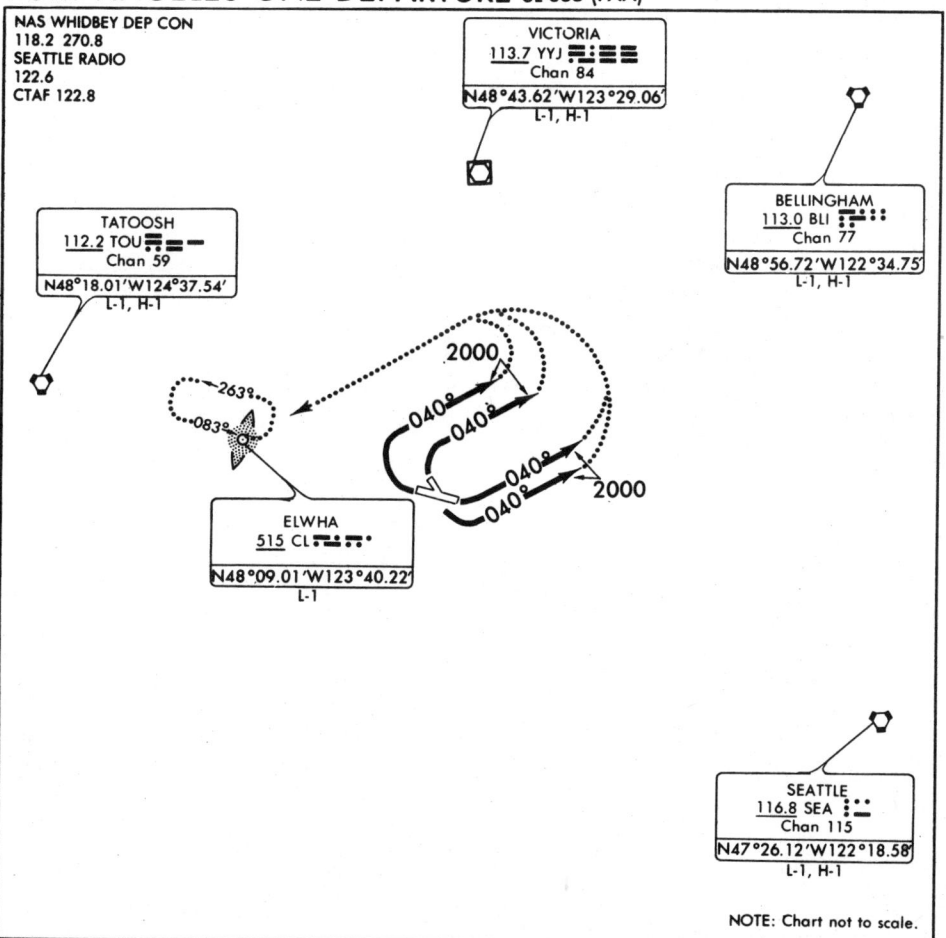

(VECTOR) 92289
PORT ANGELES ONE DEPARTURE SL-886 (FAA)

PORT ANGELES/WILLIAM R. FAIRCHILD INTL
PORT ANGELES, WASHINGTON

NAS WHIDBEY DEP CON
118.2 270.8
SEATTLE RADIO
122.6
CTAF 122.8

VICTORIA
113.7 YYJ
Chan 84
N48°43.62'W123°29.06'
L-1, H-1

TATOOSH
112.2 TOU
Chan 59
N48°18.01'W124°37.54'
L-1, H-1

BELLINGHAM
113.0 BLI
Chan 77
N48°56.72'W122°34.75'
L-1, H-1

ELWHA
515 CL
N48°09.01'W123°40.22'
L-1

SEATTLE
116.8 SEA
Chan 115
N47°26.12'W122°18.58'
L-1, H-1

NOTE: Chart not to scale.

DEPARTURE ROUTE DESCRIPTION

RUNWAYS 8 and 13: Turn left heading 040° as soon as practicable after take off for vector to assigned route/fix.

RUNWAYS 26 and 31: Turn right heading 040° as soon as practicable after takeoff for vector to assigned route/fix.

LOST COMMUNICATIONS: If no contact with ATC upon leaving 2000 feet, turn left, proceed direct to CL NDB. Continue climb in holding pattern (west, left turns, 083° inbound) to MEA for direction of flight.

PORT ANGELES ONE DEPARTURE
(VECTOR)

PORT ANGELES, WASHINGTON
PORT ANGELES/WILLIAM R. FAIRCHILD INTL

Amdt 2 93259

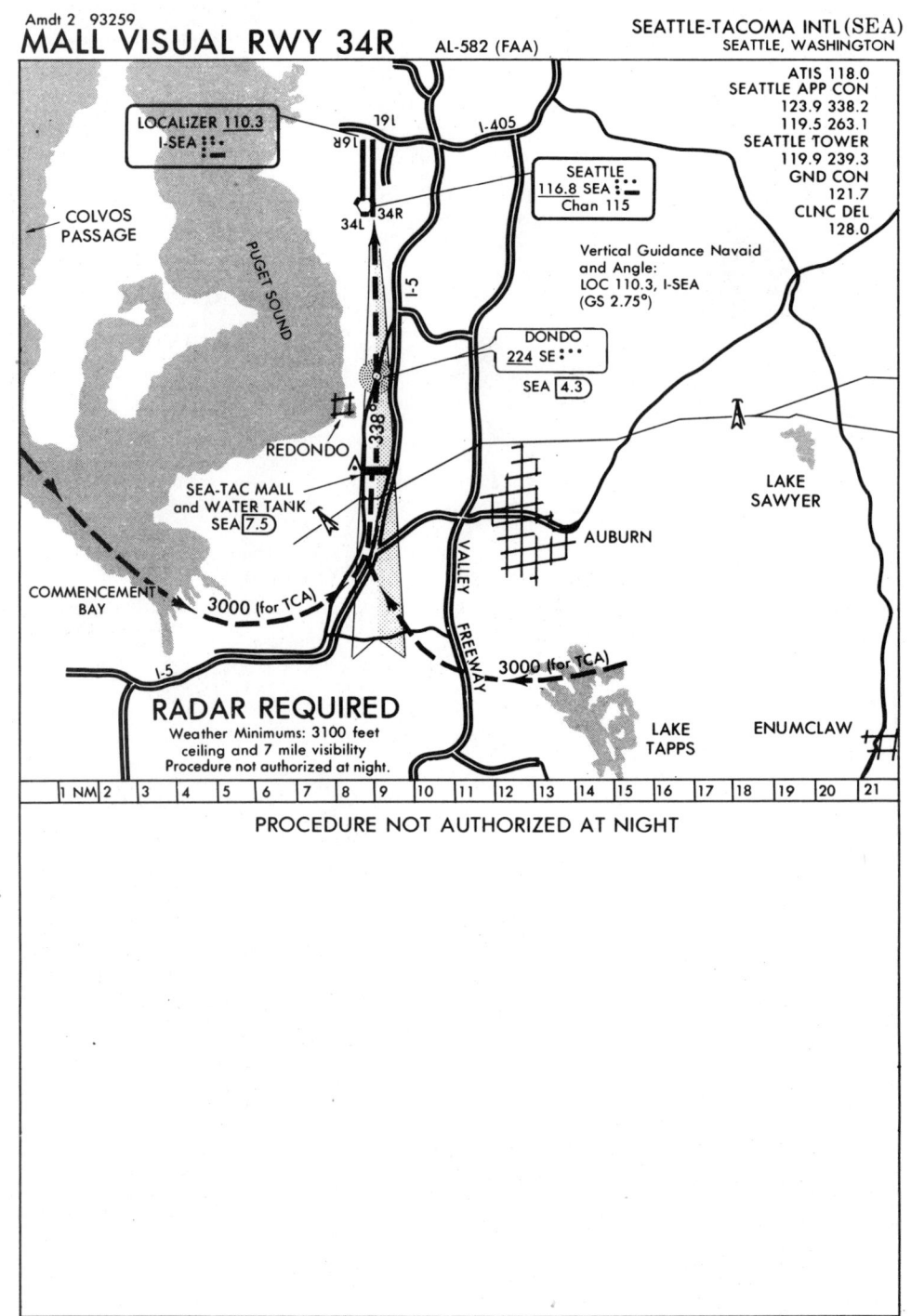

MALL VISUAL RWY 34R   AL-582 (FAA)

SEATTLE-TACOMA INTL (SEA)
SEATTLE, WASHINGTON

ATIS 118.0
SEATTLE APP CON
123.9 338.2
119.5 263.1
SEATTLE TOWER
119.9 239.3
GND CON
121.7
CLNC DEL
128.0

LOCALIZER 110.3
I-SEA

SEATTLE
116.8 SEA
Chan 115

Vertical Guidance Navaid and Angle:
LOC 110.3, I-SEA
(GS 2.75°)

DONDO
224 SE
SEA 4.3

COLVOS PASSAGE
PUGET SOUND
16R 34L
16L 34R
338°
I-405
I-5
REDONDO
SEA-TAC MALL and WATER TANK
SEA 7.5
COMMENCEMENT BAY
3000 (for TCA)
VALLEY FREEWAY
AUBURN
LAKE SAWYER
3000 (for TCA)
LAKE TAPPS
ENUMCLAW

RADAR REQUIRED
Weather Minimums: 3100 feet
ceiling and 7 mile visibility
Procedure not authorized at night.

| 1 NM | 2 | 3 | 4 | 5 | 6 | 7 | 8 | 9 | 10 | 11 | 12 | 13 | 14 | 15 | 16 | 17 | 18 | 19 | 20 | 21 |

PROCEDURE NOT AUTHORIZED AT NIGHT

MALL VISUAL RWY 34R
47°27'N–122°18'W

SEATTLE, WASHINGTON
SEATTLE-TACOMA INTL (SEA)

AIRPORT DIAGRAM

AL-582 (FAA)

SEATTLE-TACOMA INTL (SEA)
SEATTLE, WASHINGTON

93203

ATIS 118.0
SEATTLE TOWER
119.9 239.3
GND CON
121.7
CLNC DEL
128.0

FIELD ELEV 429
ELEV 426
NORTH APRON
ILS HOLD
FIRE STATION
NORTH SATELLITE RAMP
ELEV 400
ADMINISTRATION AND TERMINAL BUILDING
NWS CONTROL TOWER
SOUTH SATELLITE RAMP
HANGAR
U.S. CUSTOMS
ELEV 375
ILS HOLD
HANGARS
TANSIENT PARKING
TANKS
ELEV 359
ILS HOLD
WEST RAMP
SOUTH APRON
ELEV 343

JANUARY 1990
ANNUAL RATE OF CHANGE
0.1°W
VAR 19.7°E

160.6°
11,900 X 150
9425 X 150
0.7% UP
340.6°

RWY 16L-34R
  S100, T200, ST175,
  TT350, DDT825
RWY 16R-34L
  S100, T200, ST175,
  TT350, DDT800

Rwy 16L ldg 11410'

CAUTION: BE ALERT TO RUNWAY CROSSING CLEARANCES.
READBACK OF ALL RUNWAY HOLDING INSTRUCTIONS IS REQUIRED.

AIRPORT DIAGRAM

SEATTLE, WASHINGTON
SEATTLE-TACOMA INTL (SEA)

298 IFR Flights of "13MIKE"

APPENDIX C

Scenario Six
Approach Plates

Oceanside to Van Nuys

1. **TAKE-OFF MINS**

2. **OCEANSIDE MUNI (L32)**
   AIRPORT DIAGRAM (On VOR plate)

3. **ILS RWY 16R**
   VAN NUYS (VNY)

4. **VAN NUYS (VNY)**
   AIRPORT DIAGRAM

▽ TAKE-OFF MINS

94062

MODESTO, CA
MODESTO CITY-COUNTY AIRPORT-HARRY SHAM FIELD
TAKE-OFF MINIMUMS: **Rwys 10L, 28L,** 300-1 or std. with min. climb of 300' per NM to 300. **Rwy 10R,** 300-1 or std. with min. climb of 350' per NM to 300.
DEPARTURE PROCEDURE: **All Rwys** climb to 1000' on runway heading before proceeding on course.

MONTAGUE, CA
SISKIYOU COUNTY
TAKE-OFF MINIMUMS: **Rwy 17,** Categories A/B, 2400-2 or std. with min. climb of 350' per NM to 5500. Categories C/D, 4100-2 or std. with min. climb of 350' per NM to 7400. **Rwy 35,** 4000-2 or std. with min. climb of 300' per NM to 7000.
DEPARTURE PROCEDURE: **Rwy 17,** climb direct MOG NDB. Continue climb to 10,000 in MOG NDB holding pattern (hold N, RT, 172 inbound). **Rwy 35,** climb to 7000 via runway heading and 352° bearing from MOG NDB, then climbing right turn to 10,000 direct MOG NDB. **All aircraft** depart MOG NDB at or above MEA for route of flight.

MONTEREY, CA
MONTEREY PENINSULA
TAKE-OFF MINIMUMS: **Rwys 28L/R,** 600-2 or std. with a min. climb of 220' per NM to 900'. **Rwys 10L/R,** 1100-2 or std. with a min. climb of 360' per NM to 1100'.
DEPARTURE PROCEDURE: **Rwy 28L/R,** climbing right turn heading 330°. **Rwy 10L/R** climbing left turn heading 295°. **All aircraft** continue climb via the SNS R-260 to SNS VORTAC.

NAPA, CA
NAPA COUNTY
TAKE-OFF MINIMUMS: **Rwys 6,** 1200-2 or std. with min. climb of 290' per NM to 1500'. **Rwys 36L/R,** 1000-2 or std. with min. climb of 370' per NM to 1200.
DEPARTURE PROCEDURE: **Rwys 6, 18L/R,** turn right; **Rwys 24, 36L/R,** turn left; **all aircraft** climb direct SGD VORTAC. Aircraft departing SGD R-060 CW R-270 climb on course. All others continue climb via the SGD R-165 to 2000, then climbing right turn direct SGD VORTAC, climb on course.

NEEDLES, CA
NEEDLES
DEPARTURE PROCEDURE: **Rwys 2, 29,** turn right; **Rwy 20,** turn left. All aircraft climb direct EED VORTAC, then continue climb on curse. Departures on V12, J6, and J8 cross EED VORTAC at or above 2600.

OAKLAND, CA
METROPOLITAN OAKLAND INTL
DEPARTURE PROCEDURE: **Rwys 9R, 9L, 11, 15, 29,** turn right; **Rwy 33,** turn left. **Rwys 27L, 27R,** maintain runway heading; all aircraft climb to 4000 or above via V107 to COMMO Int. If not at 4000 at COMMO Int, Climb in holding pattern (Hold E, Right turns, 288 inbound) before proceeding on course.

OCEANSIDE, CA
OCEANSIDE MUNI
TAKE-OFF MINIMUMS: **Rwy 6,** 400-1 or std. with a min. climb of 320 per NM to 500. **Rwy 24,** 300-1 or std. with a min. climb of 670' per NM to 300.
DEPARTURE PROCEDURE: **Rwy 6,** climbing right turn; **Rwy 24,** climbing left turn; **All aircraft** climb via heading 235° to 1500, then climbing right turn direct OCN VORTAC.

ONTARIO, CA
ONTARIO INTL
TAKE-OFF MINIMUMS: **Rwys 8L/R,** Categories C and D 1000-2 or std. with min. climb of 220' per NM to 2200.
DEPARTURE PROCEDURE: **Rwys 8L/R,** climbing right turn. **Rwys 26L/R,** climbing left turn. **All aircraft** climb direct PDZ VORTAC. Aircraft departing PDZ R-091 CW R-140 and R-231 CW R-280 climb on course. All others continue climb in PDZ VORTAC holding pattern (NE, right turns, 210° inbound) to cross PDZ VORTAC at or above: R-281 CW R-090, 6700'; R-141 CW R-230, 4000'.

ORLAND, CA
HAIGH FIELD
DEPARTURE PROCEDURE: **Rwy 15,** climbing right turn to 3000 southbound aircraft heading 220°/ northbound aircraft heading 310° to intercept V87. **Rwy 33,** climbing left to 3000 northbound aircraft heading 310°/southbound aircraft heading 220° to intercept V87.

OROVILLE, CA
OROVILLE MUNI
TAKE-OFF MINIMUMS: **Rwy 1,** 900 and 1½ or std. with a min. climb of 300' per NM to 1000.
DEPARTURE PROCEDURE: **Rwys 1, 30,** turn left. **Rwys 12, 19,** turn right. Climb via MXW R-045 to intercept V-23 at or above 3000.

OXNARD, CA
OXNARD
DEPARTURE PROCEDURE: **Rwy 25,** climb via CMA R-249. **Rwy 07,** climbing left turn to intercept the CMA R-249. All aircraft continue climb to assigned altitude via SQUID Int, then RZS R-121 to RZS.

PALM SPRINGS, CA
PALM SPRINGS REGIONAL
TAKE-OFF MINIMUMS: **Rwys 31 L/R,** 3000-2 or std. with a min. climb of 360' per NM to 4000.
DEPARTURE PROCEDURE: **Rwys 13 L/R,** turn left heading 090° to intercept TRM R-304 to TRM VORTAC. **Rwys 31 L/R,** turn right direct PSP VORTAC, then via PSP R-124 and TRM R-304 to TRM VORTAC. Aircraft departing TRM R-300 CW R-160 climb on course. All others continue climb in TRM VORTAC holding pattern (E, right turns, 289° inbound) to cross TRM VORTAC at or above 7300.

SW-2

▽ TAKE-OFF MINS

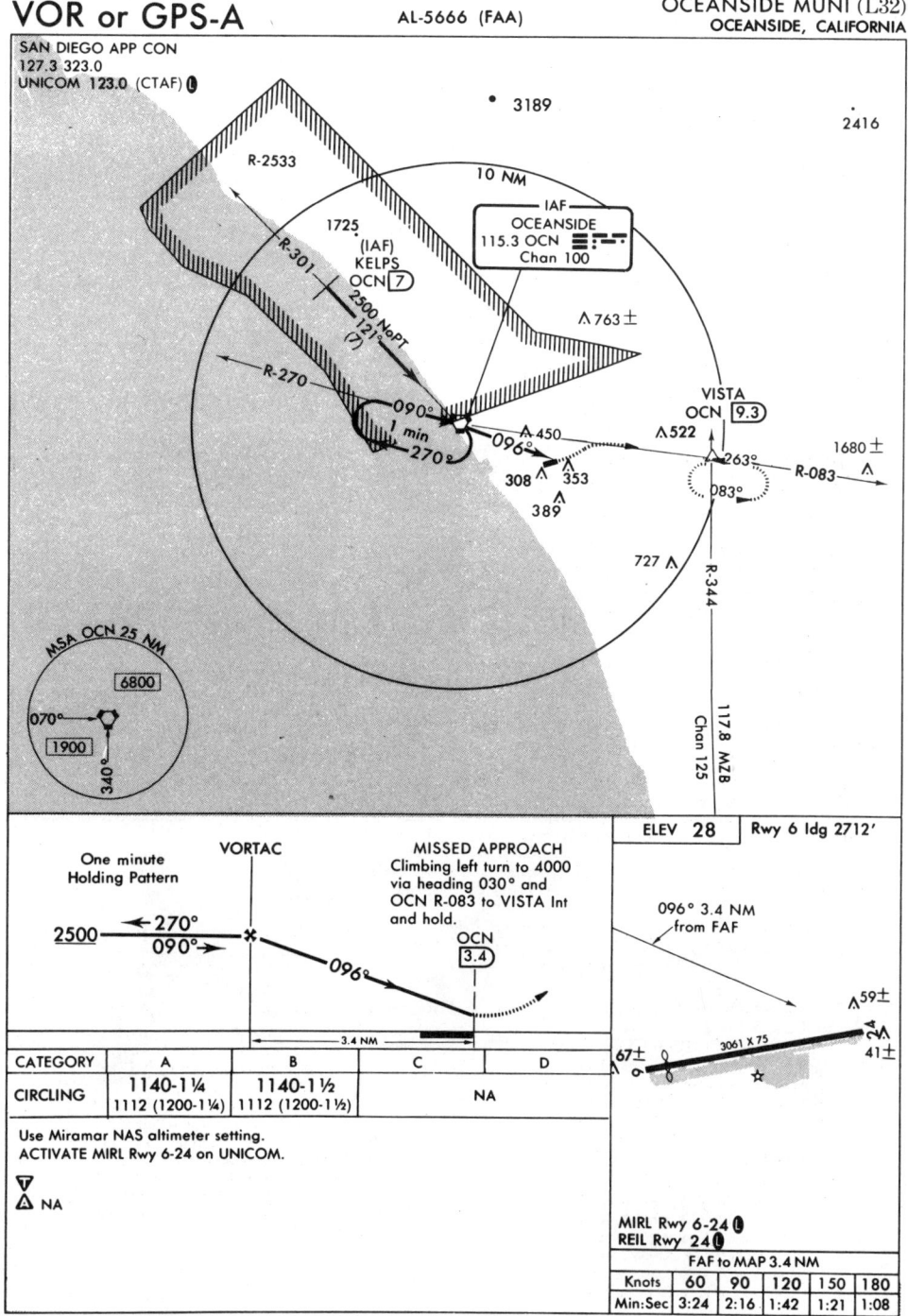

VOR or GPS-A

OCEANSIDE MUNI (L32)
OCEANSIDE, CALIFORNIA

Amdt 3 94118   AL-5666 (FAA)

SAN DIEGO APP CON
127.3   323.0
UNICOM 123.0 (CTAF) ⓛ

MISSED APPROACH
Climbing left turn to 4000 via heading 030° and OCN R-083 to VISTA Int and hold.

One minute Holding Pattern
2500 — 270° / 090°

CATEGORY	A	B	C	D
CIRCLING	1140-1¼ 1112 (1200-1¼)	1140-1½ 1112 (1200-1½)	NA	

Use Miramar NAS altimeter setting.
ACTIVATE MIRL Rwy 6-24 on UNICOM.

▽
△ NA

ELEV 28   Rwy 6 ldg 2712'

096° 3.4 NM from FAF

MIRL Rwy 6-24 ⓛ
REIL Rwy 24 ⓛ

FAF to MAP 3.4 NM

Knots	60	90	120	150	180
Min:Sec	3:24	2:16	1:42	1:21	1:08

VOR or GPS-A   33°13'N – 117°21'W   OCEANSIDE, CALIFORNIA
OCEANSIDE MUNI (L32)

Amdt 5 92233

ILS RWY 16R

AL-552 (FAA)

VAN NUYS (VNY)
VAN NUYS, CALIFORNIA

ATIS 118.45
BURBANK APP CON
120.4 360.6 (NORTH)
134.2 338.2 (WEST)
VAN NUYS TOWER *
119.3 (CTAF) 239.0
GND CON
121.7
CLNC DEL
126.6 239.0
UNICOM 122.95

MSA VNY 25 NM
185°: 6800 | 9100
095° — 275°
005°: 6000 | 4300

LOCALIZER 111.3
I-VNY

MISSED APPROACH: Climb to cross VNY 1.5 DME or FIM R-101 at or below 1750, then climbing left turn to 4000 via VNY R-101 to AMTRA Int and hold.

ELEV 799

161° 8.1 NM from FAF

TDZE 790

Procedure Turn NA

6000
GS 3.90°
TCH 55 *
*Displaced threshold

CATEGORY	A	B	C	D
S-ILS 16R	1040-¾ 250 (300-¾)		1090-¾ 300 (300-¾)	1140-1 350 (400-1)
APPROACH NOT AUTHORIZED WHEN GLIDE SLOPE NOT USED				
CIRCLING	1300-1 501 (600-1)		1340-1½ 541 (600-1½)	1360-2 561 (600-2)

When control zone not in effect, use Burbank altimeter setting and increase S-16R DH 10 feet and circling MDA Categories A, B, and C 20 feet. Inoperative table does not apply.

Rwy 16R ldg 6580'
Rwy 16L ldg 2580'
HIRL Rwy 16R-34L
MIRL Rwy 16L-34R
REIL Rwy 34R

FAF to MAP 8.1 NM

Knots	60	90	120	150	180
Min:Sec	8:06	5:24	4:03	3:14	2:42

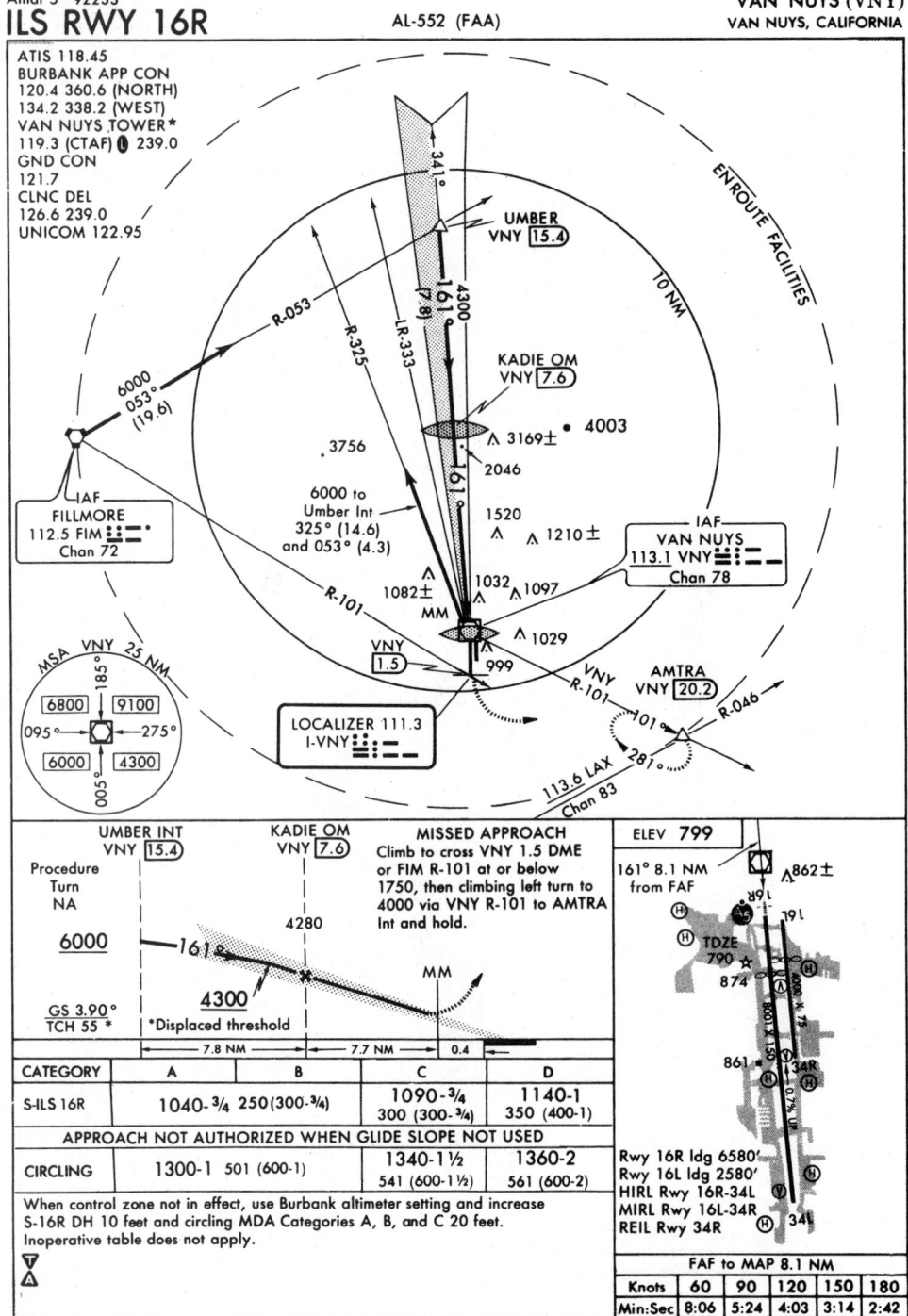

ILS RWY 16R

34°13'N – 118°29'W

VAN NUYS, CALIFORNIA
VAN NUYS (VNY)

383

AIRPORT DIAGRAM

AL-552 (FAA)

VAN NUYS (VNY)
VAN NUYS, CALIFORNIA

ATIS 118.45
VAN NUYS TOWER *
119.3 239.0
GND CON
121.7
CLNC DEL
126.6 239.0

FIELD ELEV 799

JANUARY 1990
ANNUAL RATE OF CHANGE
0.0°

VAR 14.0°E

RWY 16R-34L
S80, T110, ST139, TT175
RWY 16L-34R
S14

Rwy 16R ldg 6580'
Rwy 16L ldg 2580'

CAUTION: BE ALERT TO RUNWAY CROSSING CLEARANCES.
READBACK OF ALL RUNWAY HOLDING INSTRUCTIONS IS REQUIRED.

AIRPORT DIAGRAM

VAN NUYS, CALIFORNIA
VAN NUYS (VNY)

304 IFR Flights of "13MIKE"

APPENDIX C

Scenario Seven
Approach Plates

Watsonville to Oakland

1. **TAKE-OFF MINS**

2. **WATSONVILLE MUNI (WVI)**
   AIRPORT DIAGRAM (On VOR/DME - A plate)

3. **HADLY ONE ARRIVAL (BSR.HADLY1)**
   SAN FRANCISCO

4. **ILS RWY 27R**
   OAKLAND/METROPOLITAN OAKLAND INTL (OAK)

5. **OAKLAND/METROPOLITAN OAKLAND INTL (OAK)**
   AIRPORT DIAGRAM

TAKE-OFF MINS

WATSONVILLE, CA
WATSONVILLE MUNI
TAKE-OFF MINIMUMS: **Rwy 2,** 1000-2 CAT A/B, 1900-2 CAT C/D or std. with a min. climb of: CAT A/B 255' per NM to 1400, CAT C/D 265' per NM to 2400. **Rwy 26,** 300-2 or std. with a min. climb of 250' per NM to 800.
DEPARTURE PROCEDURE: **Rwy 2,8,20,** climbing right turn, **Rwy 26,** climbing left turn. **All aircraft** intercept the AY NDB bearing 212° to MOVER Int. Aircraft departing MOVER Int. 300° CW 100° climb on course. All other aircraft climb in MOVER Int. holding pattern (Hold NE, right turns, 212° inbound) to cross MOVER Int. at or above 1800' then climb on course.
NOTE: **Rwy 26,** 289' tower 0.8 NM from departure end of runway, 1200' right of centerline.

WILLOWS, CA
WILLOWS-GLENN COUNTY
DEPARTURE PROCEDURE: Climb direct to MXW VORTAC.

WOODLAND, CA
WATTS-WOODLAND
DEPARTURE PROCEDURE: Eastbound climb to 2000 via SAC R-296 to SAC VORTAC. Southbound or Westbound climb to 5000 via TZZ R-335 and SAC R-257 to RAGGS Int. Northbound climb to 5000 via ILA R-142 to ILA VORTAC.

TAKE-OFF MINS

Orig-A 93147

VOR/DME-A

AL-805 (FAA)

WATSONVILLE MUNI (WVI)
WATSONVILLE, CALIFORNIA

MONTEREY APP CON
127.15 387.0
UNICOM 122.8 (CTAF)

IAF
SALINAS
117.3 SNS
Chan 120

MSA SNS 25 NM
5100 — 130°
4200 — 280°
6100 — 040°

DYNER SNS 13
314°
1700 (5)

SNS 8 Arc
3200
SNS 8
R-314
R-293
R-264
R-011
3200 to SNS 8 DME 314° (8)

MISSED APPROACH
Climbing left turn to 4000 direct SNS VORTAC and hold.

SNS 18.6 — DYNER SNS 13 — SNS 8 3200
1700 — 314°
5.6 NM — 5 NM
Procedure Turn NA

CATEGORY	A	B	C	D
CIRCLING	1300-1¼ 1140 (1200-1¼)	1300-1½ 1140 (1200-1½)	1300-3 1140 (1200-3)	

Use Salinas altimeter setting.
Circling not authorized west of Rwy 2-20.

▽
△ NA

ELEV 160 Rwy 20 ldg 3911'

314° 5.6 NM from FAF

MIRL Rwy 2-20
REIL Rwy 2

Knots	60	90	120	150	180
Min:Sec					

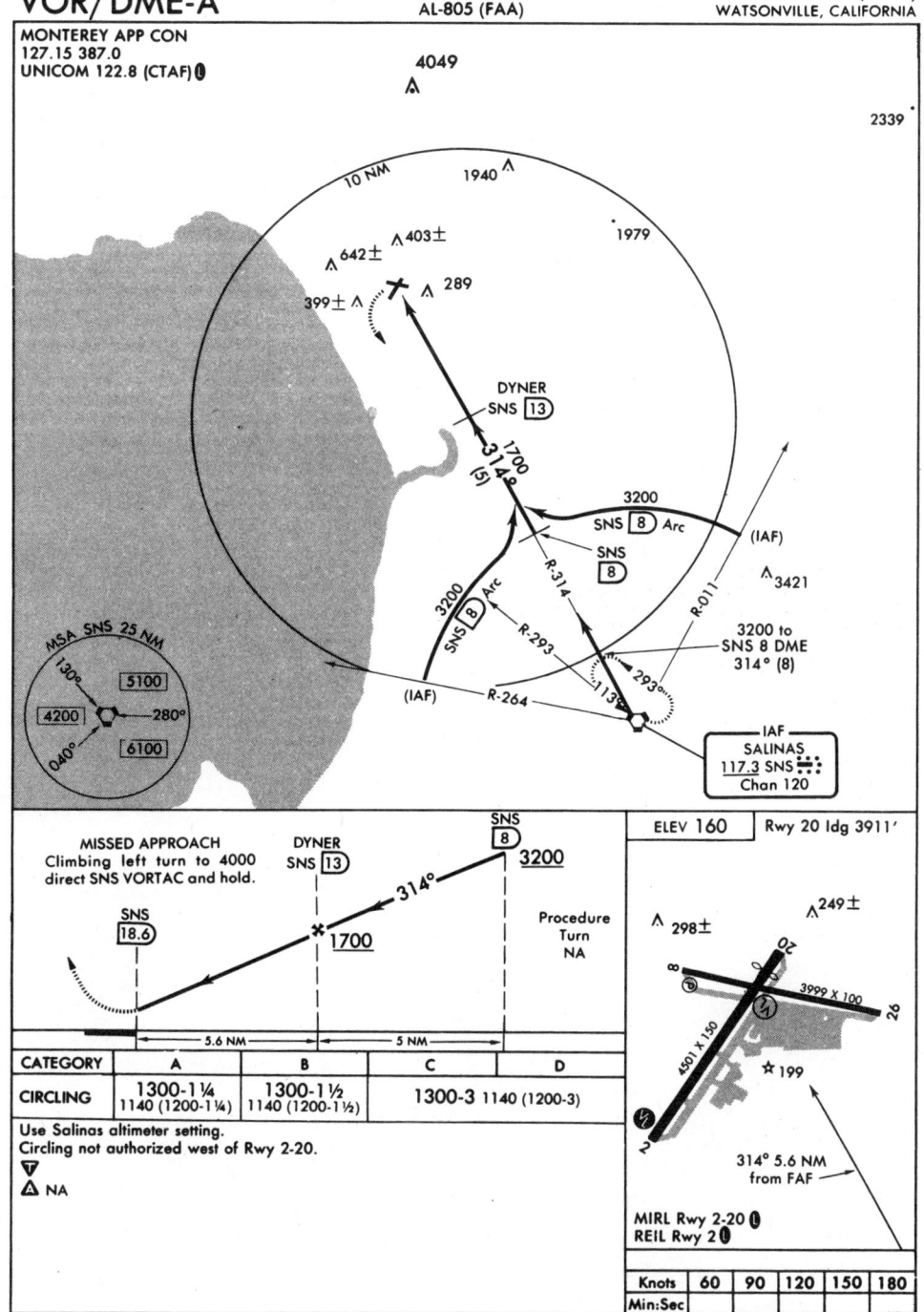

VOR/DME-A

36°56'N – 121°47'W

WATSONVILLE, CALIFORNIA
WATSONVILLE MUNI (WVI)

(BSR.HADLY1) 94118
HADLY ONE ARRIVAL

ST-375 (FAA)   SAN FRANCISCO, CALIFORNIA

BAY APP CON
133.95   317.6
SAN FRANCISCO INTL ATIS
113.7   118.85
METROPOLITAN OAKLAND ATIS
128.5

SAUSALITO
116.2 SAU   Chan 109
N37°51.32' W122°31.36'

LOCALIZER 108.9
I-SIA   Chan 26

POINT REYES
113.7 PYE   Chan 84

COMMO
N37°52.45'
W122°29.52'

BERKS
N37°51.79'
W122°12.60'

OAKLAND
116.8 OAK   Chan 115

METROPOLITAN OAKLAND INTL

SAN FRANCISCO INTL

SAN FRANCISCO
115.8 SFO   Chan 105

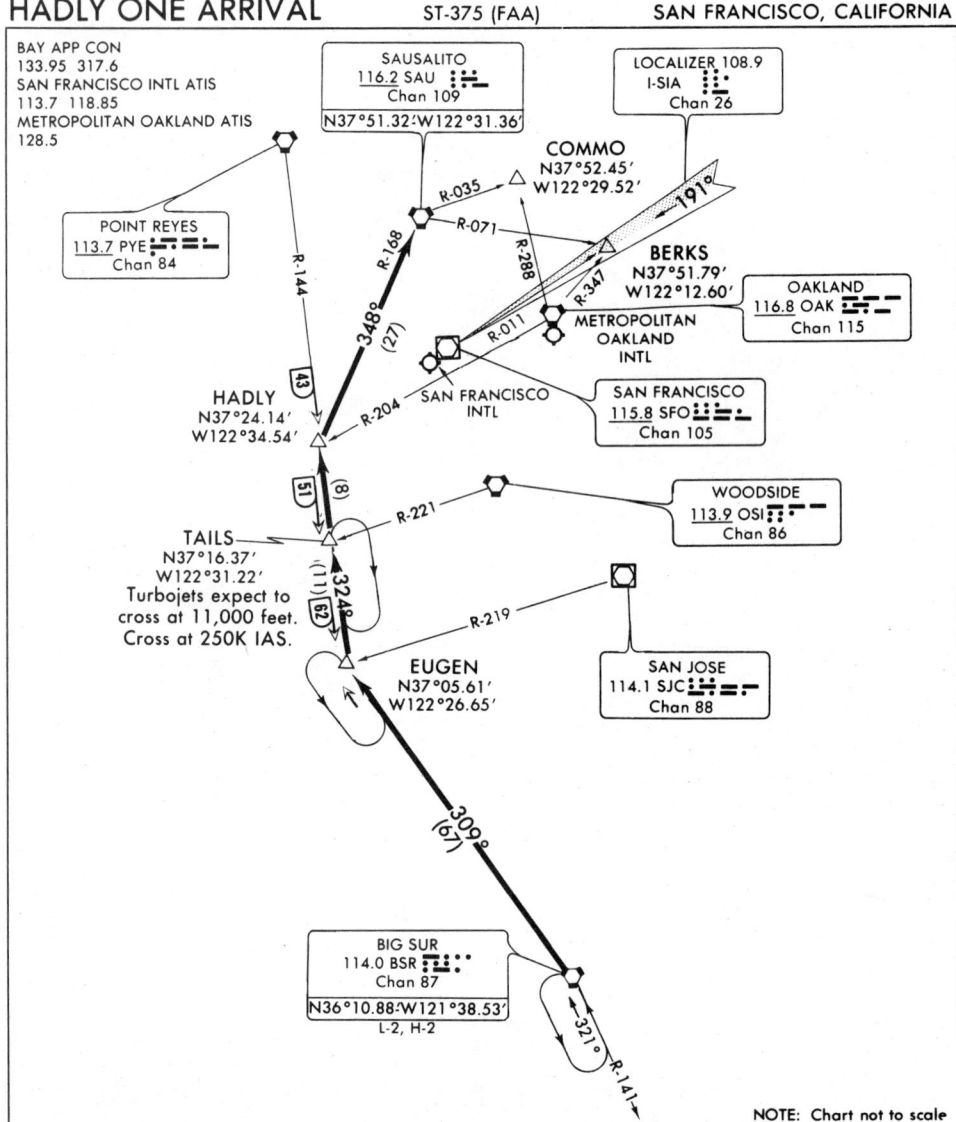

HADLY
N37°24.14'
W122°34.54'

WOODSIDE
113.9 OSI   Chan 86

TAILS
N37°16.37'
W122°31.22'
Turbojets expect to cross at 11,000 feet.
Cross at 250K IAS.

EUGEN
N37°05.61'
W122°26.65'

SAN JOSE
114.1 SJC   Chan 88

BIG SUR
114.0 BSR   Chan 87
N36°10.88' W121°38.53'
L-2, H-2

NOTE: Chart not to scale

From over BSR VORTAC via BSR R-309 to EUGEN FIX, then via PYE R-144 to HADLY FIX, then via direct SAU VORTAC. Expect vector to final approach course.

LOST COMMUNICATIONS
San Francisco Intl.: Depart SAU VORTAC via SAU R-071 to BERKS FIX.
Metropolitan Oakland Intl.: Depart SAU VORTAC via SAU R-035 to COMMO FIX.

HADLY ONE ARRIVAL
(BSR.HADLY1)

SAN FRANCISCO, CALIFORNIA

ILS RWY 27R

Amdt 31 93091

OAKLAND/METROPOLITAN OAKLAND INTL (OAK)
AL-294 (FAA)
OAKLAND, CALIFORNIA

ATIS 128.5
BAY APP CON 135.4 354.1
OAKLAND TOWER*
(Rwys 9-27, 15-33)
118.3 395.9
GND CON 121.9
OAKLAND TOWER
(Rwy 11-29)
127.2 256.9
GND CON 121.75
CLNC DEL 121.1

SAU 116.2 Chan 109
PEERE INT
LOCALIZER 109.9 I-OAK
LMM RORAY 341 AK
OAKLAND 116.8 OAK Chan 115
GROVE INT OAK 11.7
CASES OM OAK 5
HAYZE INT OAK 9
(IAF) SUNOL OAK 21

3500 to Grove Int 229° (0.7) and LOC (8.8)

MSA OAK 25 NM: 3700 / 4900

MISSED APPROACH
Climb to 500 then climbing right turn to 3000 via OAK R-313 to PEERE Int and hold.

Procedure Turn NA

* 3000 when authorized by ATC.

GS 2.90°
TCH 51

CATEGORY	A	B	C	D
S-ILS 27R	254-1 250 (300-1)			
S-LOC 27R	400-1 396 (400-1)			400-1¼ 396 (400-1¼)
CIRCLING	500-1 494 (500-1)	540-1 534 (600-1)	680-2 674 (700-2)	680-2¼ 674 (800-2¼)
SIDESTEP RWY 27L	420-1 415 (500-1)		420-1½ 415 (500-1½)	420-2 415 (500-2)

Inoperative table does not apply.
Air Carrier will not reduce landing visibility due to local conditions.
Autopilot coupled approaches below 350' not authorized.

ELEV 6
275° 4.2 NM from FAF
TDZE 9
TDZE 5

TDZ/CL Rwy 29
MIRL Rwy 15-33
HIRL Rwys 11-29, 9L-27R and 9R-27L

FAF to MAP 4.2 NM

Knots	60	90	120	150	180
Min:Sec	4:12	2:48	2:06	1:41	1:24

ILS RWY 27R
37°43'N-122°13'W
OAKLAND, CALIFORNIA
OAKLAND/METROPOLITAN OAKLAND INTL (OAK)

AIRPORT DIAGRAM

OAKLAND/METROPOLITAN OAKLAND INTL (OAK)
AL-294 (FAA)
OAKLAND, CALIFORNIA

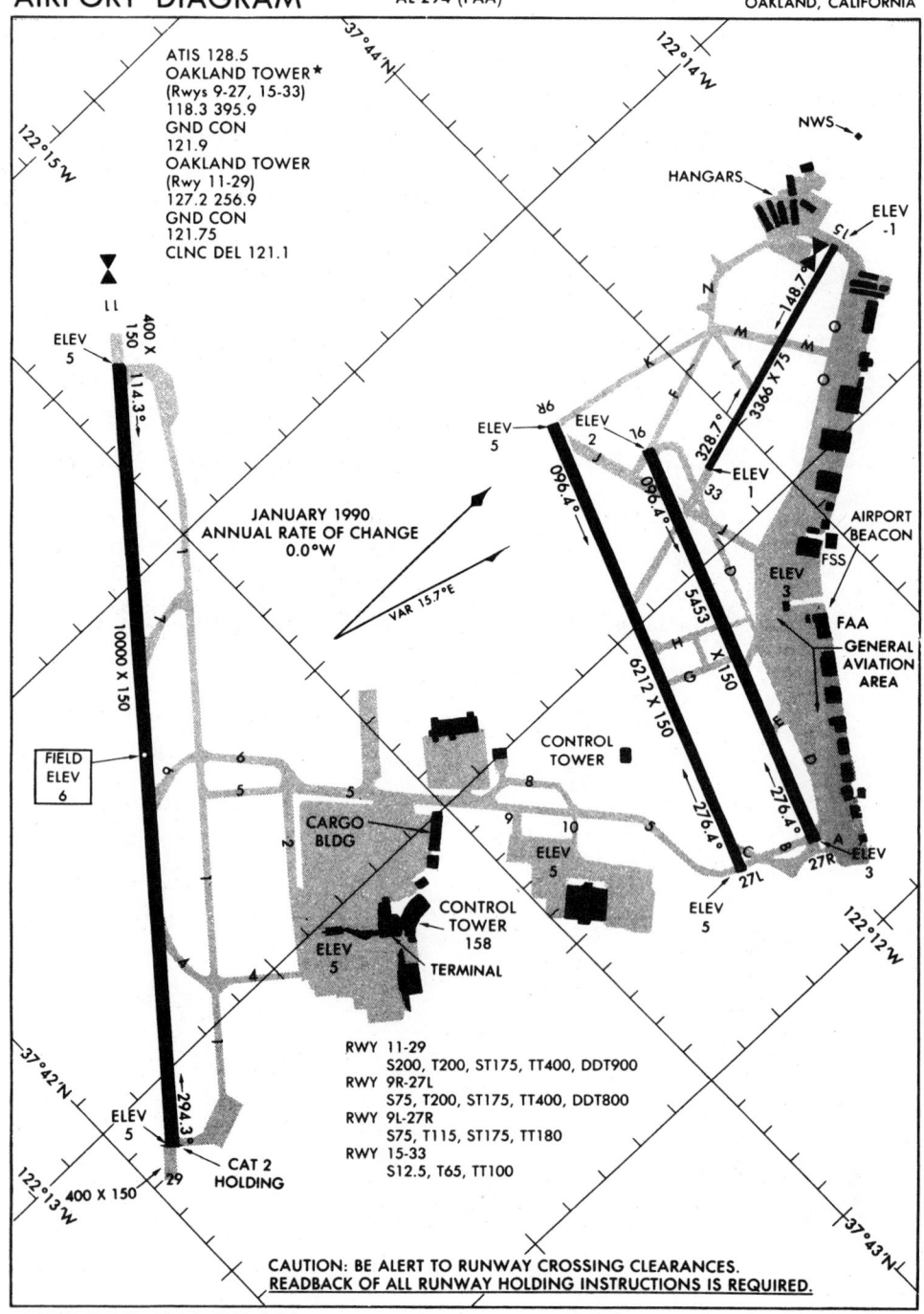

ATIS 128.5
OAKLAND TOWER *
(Rwys 9-27, 15-33)
118.3 395.9
GND CON
121.9
OAKLAND TOWER
(Rwy 11-29)
127.2 256.9
GND CON
121.75
CLNC DEL 121.1

JANUARY 1990
ANNUAL RATE OF CHANGE
0.0°W
VAR 15.7°E

FIELD ELEV 6

RWY 11-29
 S200, T200, ST175, TT400, DDT900
RWY 9R-27L
 S75, T200, ST175, TT400, DDT800
RWY 9L-27R
 S75, T115, ST175, TT180
RWY 15-33
 S12.5, T65, TT100

CAUTION: BE ALERT TO RUNWAY CROSSING CLEARANCES.
READBACK OF ALL RUNWAY HOLDING INSTRUCTIONS IS REQUIRED.

APPENDIX C

Scenario Eight
Approach Plates

Block Island to Marthas Vineyard

1. **BLOCK ISLAND STATE (BID)**
   AIRPORT DIAGRAM (On VOR/DME RWY 10 plate)

2. **ILS RWY 24**
   MARTHAS VINEYARD (MVY)

C8

Amdt 3A 94006

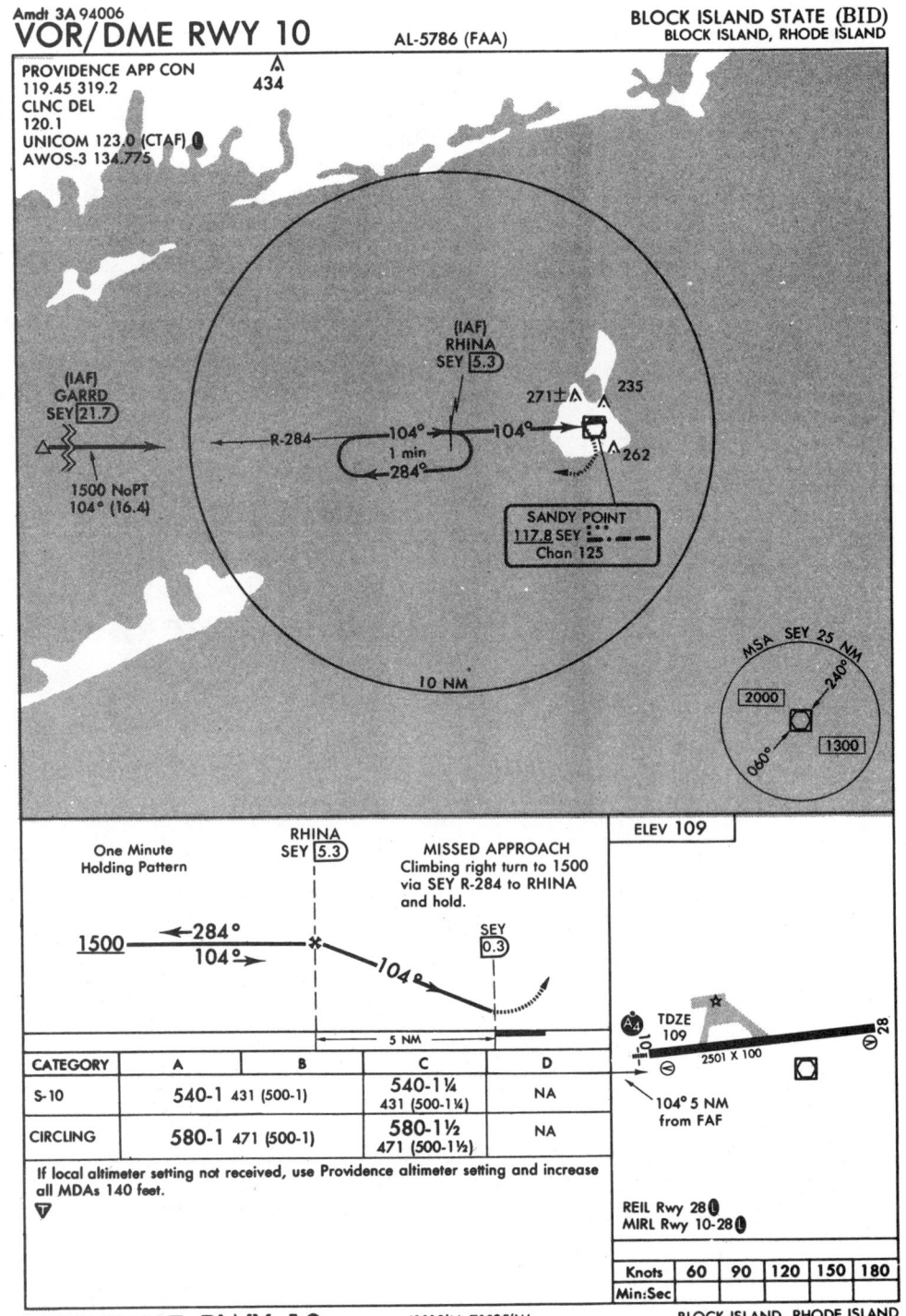

VOR/DME RWY 10

AL-5786 (FAA)

BLOCK ISLAND STATE (BID)
BLOCK ISLAND, RHODE ISLAND

PROVIDENCE APP CON
119.45 319.2
CLNC DEL
120.1
UNICOM 123.0 (CTAF)
AWOS-3 134.775

△ 434

(IAF) RHINA
SEY 5.3

(IAF) GARRD
SEY 21.7
1500 NoPT
104° (16.4)

R-284
104° → 104°
1 min
← 284°

271± △ △ 235
△ 262

SANDY POINT
117.8 SEY ·· ─ ·─
Chan 125

10 NM

MSA SEY 25 NM
2000 / 240° / 1300
060°

MISSED APPROACH
Climbing right turn to 1500 via SEY R-284 to RHINA and hold.

One Minute Holding Pattern

RHINA
SEY 5.3

SEY 0.3

1500
← 284°
104° →

104°

5 NM

ELEV 109

TDZE 109

2501 X 100

104° 5 NM from FAF

CATEGORY	A	B	C	D
S-10	540-1 431 (500-1)		540-1¼ 431 (500-1¼)	NA
CIRCLING	580-1 471 (500-1)		580-1½ 471 (500-1½)	NA

If local altimeter setting not received, use Providence altimeter setting and increase all MDAs 140 feet.

REIL Rwy 28
MIRL Rwy 10-28

Knots	60	90	120	150	180
Min:Sec					

VOR/DME RWY 10

41°10'N–71°35'W

BLOCK ISLAND, RHODE ISLAND
BLOCK ISLAND STATE (BID)

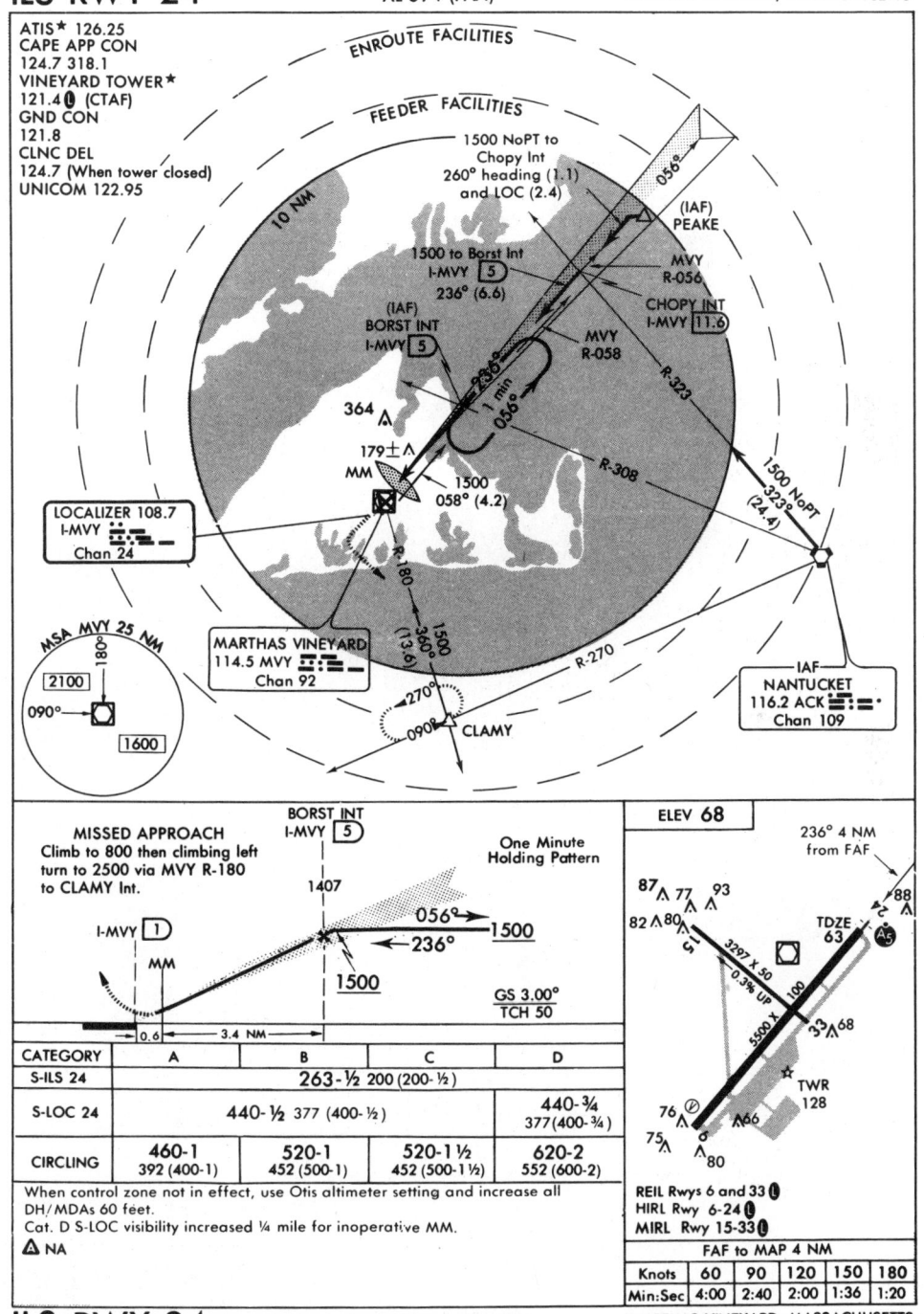

Amdt 8 94062
ILS RWY 24

AL-694 (FAA)

MARTHAS VINEYARD (MVY)
MARTHAS VINEYARD, MASSACHUSETTS

ATIS* 126.25
CAPE APP CON
124.7 318.1
VINEYARD TOWER*
121.4 (CTAF)
GND CON
121.8
CLNC DEL
124.7 (When tower closed)
UNICOM 122.95

ENROUTE FACILITIES
FEEDER FACILITIES

1500 NoPT to Chopy Int 260° heading (1.1) and LOC (2.4)

(IAF) PEAKE
MVY R-056
CHOPY INT I-MVY 11.6

1500 to Borst Int I-MVY 5 236° (6.6)

(IAF) BORST INT I-MVY 5

MVY R-058
MVY R-323

364 △
179± △
MM

1500 058° (4.2)

R-308

LOCALIZER 108.7
I-MVY
Chan 24

R-180
R-270

1500 NoPT 323° (24.4)

MARTHAS VINEYARD
114.5 MVY
Chan 92

1500 360° (13.6)

270°
090° CLAMY

IAF NANTUCKET
116.2 ACK
Chan 109

MSA MVY 25 NM
2100 / 1600
090° / 180°

MISSED APPROACH
Climb to 800 then climbing left turn to 2500 via MVY R-180 to CLAMY Int.

BORST INT
I-MVY 5

One Minute Holding Pattern

1407
056° 1500
236°
1500

I-MVY 1
MM
0.6 — 3.4 NM

GS 3.00°
TCH 50

ELEV 68

236° 4 NM from FAF

87△ 77△ 93△
82△ 80△
TDZE 63
88△

3297 X 50
0.3% UP
33△ 68△

5500 X 100

TWR 128

76△ 66△
75△ 80△

CATEGORY	A	B	C	D
S-ILS 24	263-½ 200 (200-½)			
S-LOC 24	440-½ 377 (400-½)			440-¾ 377 (400-¾)
CIRCLING	460-1 392 (400-1)	520-1 452 (500-1)	520-1½ 452 (500-1½)	620-2 552 (600-2)

When control zone not in effect, use Otis altimeter setting and increase all DH/MDAs 60 feet.
Cat. D S-LOC visibility increased ¼ mile for inoperative MM.
⚠ NA

REIL Rwys 6 and 33
HIRL Rwy 6-24
MIRL Rwy 15-33

FAF to MAP 4 NM					
Knots	60	90	120	150	180
Min:Sec	4:00	2:40	2:00	1:36	1:20

ILS RWY 24

41°24'N – 70°37'W

MARTHAS VINEYARD, MASSACHUSETTS
MARTHAS VINEYARD (MVY)

NOTES

NOTES

316 NOTES

NOTES

318 NOTES

Order Form

Upcoming Books

Airienteering with "13MIKE" .... $19.95 (Jan)

Now Available

Flights of "13MIKE" $19.95
IFR Flights of "13MIKE" $19.95

To Order Books

Quantity	Title	Unit Price	Total
_____	_____	_____	_____
_____	_____	_____	_____
_____	_____	_____	_____

"Quantity Discounts Available."   Subtotal _____
5% Sales Tax (Arizona only) _____
Shipping and Handling ($3.95) _____
TOTAL ORDER _____

How to Order

Credit card orders please call 1-800-3CALMIL. Monday - Friday 9 to 5 MST. To mail: Please remit a copy of the following form, with payment, to:

Calmil Publishing, 2224 Katahn, Prescott, AZ 86301-3976

Name:_____

Address:_____

City:_____State:_____Zip:_____

Visa/MC/AE#:_____Exp. date:_____

Signature:_____